Asians in Diaspora and Diasporas in Asia presents both a broad and deep exploration of Asian diaspora Christianity. It elegantly weaves together theological and practical perspectives on the many facets of this large, complex subject, including diaspora theology, current diaspora trends, social and justice issues affecting diaspora migrants, the economic power of the diaspora, and more. This book will surely open readers' eyes to the great opportunity God has given us through the diaspora peoples and help us all understand how the church can and should respond.

Rev. Dr. Patrick Fung, PhD
Global Ambassador,
OMF International, Singapore

Like the apostolic letter that was written to encourage "the exiles of the Dispersion in . . . Asia" (1 Peter 1:1) 2000 years ago, so also our colleagues have written from out of the Asian diasporas in and of the 2020s to illuminate us theologically and inspire us missiologically. Those interested in the exegetical, theological, sociological, and missiological aspects of migration, even within and beyond other continental regions, can learn from what is documented and presented here just as our friends have also learned from our apostolic predecessor.

Amos Yong, PhD
Professor of Theology and Mission,
Fuller Theological Seminary, California, USA

The flow of population, both within and beyond geo-political borders, represents both a global reality as well as a missional opportunity. With that flow, the mission field has indeed moved from out there to right here. Through this collection of papers, presented at the 2023 Global Diaspora Network Consultation, a thoroughly biblical, missiological, and practical examination provides an excellent in-depth study of the unprecedented global missional opportunities of reaching the diaspora for Christ on our very doorstep.

James Hudson Taylor IV, DMin
President,
China Evangelical Seminary, Taiwan

Asians in Diaspora and Diasporas in Asia explores the cultural transformation and revitalization of diaspora communities through holistic intervention and advocacy. With essays ranging from theological and missiological frameworks to immigration policy and legal assistance, this significant and timely compendium invites both collaborators and readers to engage prayerfully and responsibly in their mission work for the sake of evangelism.

Karen An-hwei Lee, PhD
Provost,
Wheaton College, Illinois, USA

This timely and insightful volume confronts the changing reality of how global migration has reshaped missions on a large scale, particularly in the Asian context. The book addresses the broad impact of migration and gives thoughtful attention to the diversity and uniqueness of various people groups and contexts across Asia. It is an invaluable resource for mission leaders, scholars, and practitioners seeking to understand and engage with the complex dynamics of the Asian diaspora today.

David Doong, PhD
General Secretary,
CCCOWE (Chinese Coordination Center of World Evangelization)

This is a valuable anthology of Christian reflections on migration and diaspora. With a particular focus on movements to and from Asia, the largest and most diverse continent in the world, the book strategically brings together scholars of the Bible, theology, and mission with grassroots practitioners working in churches, mission organisations, and faith-based NGOs. What a wonderful contribution to our continuing conversations about the mission of God amongst the people of God – on the move.

Alexander Chow, PhD
Senior Lecturer in Theology and World Christianity,
Co-Director, Centre for the Study of World Christianity, School of Divinity,
University of Edinburgh, UK

This groundbreaking book offers a comprehensive exploration of the complex and vibrant Asian diaspora, shedding light on the challenges and opportunities that come with migration and displacement. With contributions from leading scholars and practitioners, this volume provides a rich tapestry of perspectives and insights that will inform and inspire anyone interested in diaspora missions. As the world grapples with the complexities of migration, this book is a timely and invaluable resource for churches, mission organizations, and individuals seeking to understand and respond to the needs of migrants and diaspora communities.

Bishop Efraim M. Tendero
Global Ambassador,
World Evangelical Alliance

In the face of history's greatest global experience of migrations, here is a compendium that focuses on the diversity and complexity of diasporas from, and in, Asia. An invaluable resource for researchers, ministry leaders, and pastors.

Ivor Poobalan, PhD
Co-Chair, Theology Working Group of the Lausanne Movement
Principal, Colombo Theological Seminary, Sri Lanka

Asians in Diaspora and Diasporas in Asia

Langham
GLOBAL LIBRARY

Asians in Diaspora and Diasporas in Asia

Editors
Sam George, Bulus Galadima, and Jeanne Wu

© 2025 Sam George, Bulus Galadima, and Jeanne Wu

Published 2025 by Langham Global Library
An imprint of Langham Publishing
www.langhampublishing.org
Langham Publishing and its imprints are a ministry of Langham Partnership

Langham Partnership

PO Box 296, Carlisle, Cumbria, CA3 9WZ, UK

www.langham.org

ISBNs:
978-1-78641-038-2 Print
978-1-78641-138-9 ePub
978-1-78641-139-6 PDF

Sam George, Bulus Galadima, and Jeanne Wu hereby assert their moral right to be identified as the Author of the General Editor's part in the Work in accordance with sections 77 and 78 of the Copyright, Designs and Patents Act 1988.

All rights reserved. No part of this publication may be reproduced, stored in a retrieval system or transmitted, in any form or by any means, electronic, mechanical, photocopying, recording or otherwise, without the prior written permission of the publisher or the Copyright Licensing Agency.

Requests to reuse content from Langham Publishing are processed through PLSclear. Please visit www.plsclear.com to complete your request.

All Scripture quotations, unless otherwise indicated, are taken from the Holy Bible, New International Version®, NIV®. Copyright ©1973, 1978, 1984, 2011 by Biblica, Inc.™ Used by permission of Zondervan.

British Library Cataloguing-in-Publication Data
A catalogue record for this book is available from the British Library

ISBN: 978-1-78641-038-2

Cover & Book Design: projectluz.com

Langham Partnership actively supports theological dialogue and an author's right to publish but does not necessarily endorse the views and opinions set forth here or in works referenced within this publication, nor can we guarantee technical and grammatical correctness. Langham Partnership does not accept any responsibility or liability to persons or property as a consequence of the reading, use or interpretation of its published content.

Dedication

Rev. Dr. T. V. Thomas

An indefatigable champion for diasporas globally

Contents

Acknowledgments xiii

Introduction 1
Sam George

Section A

1. World Christianity and Global Diasporas: Coming, Staying, Going . . . 13
Kirsteen Kim

2. Global Chinese Diaspora and Recent Hong Kong Out-Migration to Canada. 27
Francis Tam

3. Remittances and Asian Diaspora: Globalization, Deglobalization, and the Future. 41
Prabhu Guptara

4. The State of the People on the Move: 2023 Update 55
Sam George and Bulus Galadima

Section B

5. Theology of Transnational Migrants as Kingdom Citizens 69
Tereso C. Casiño

6. Hospitality and *Imago Dei* in the Bible 83
Yoon Jong Yoo

7. Mission Through and Beyond the Chinese Diaspora in the Middle East: Two Case Studies. 97
Jeanne Wu

8. Migrant Mission Training in South Korea and Beyond 111
Hanna Hyun

9. Justice Issues among Labor Migrants in Asia. 125
Denison Jayasooria

10. Changes to Immigration Policy and Korean Immigration Society . . . 139
Kangmuk Ghil

11. Embracing Migrants and Refugees in Malaysia. 155
Ng Oi Leng

12 The Transnational Filipino Families: Pastoral and
    Missiological Issues 163
    Noel A. Pantoja

13 Love [Your City]: Diaspora Churches Start and Support
    City Movements 171
    Jacob Bloemberg

14 Asian Students Going Abroad and International Students in Asia 185
    Leiton Chinn and Lisa Espineli Chinn

15 Hybridity in Korean Missionary Kids: "Third Space" Pedagogy in
    International Schools 203
    Grace Eun-Sun Lee and Tessa Tubbs

16 Intentional Mission to Internal Migrants in India 213
    J. N. Manokaran

17 Holistic Mission with People Affected by Forced Migration and
    Human Trafficking 227
    Christa Foster Crawford

18 Climate Migration: Mission in the Face of Two Global Crises 243
    Jasmine Kwong and Sam George

Section C

19 A Diasporic Pastoral Letter: Background and Greetings of
    1 Peter 1:1–2 255
    Elizabeth Mburu

20 New Family of God: Rediscovering Diaspora Identity in
    1 Peter 1:3–2:10 265
    Narry F. Santos

21 Connecting with the World (1 Peter 2:11–4:11) 275
    Yoon Hee Kim

22 Power Structures within the Diaspora Community in 1 Peter 283
    Samson L. Uytanlet

    Conclusion 291
    Bulus Galadima

    Author Profiles 297

    Index 305

Acknowledgments

As we wrapped up the 2022 Lausanne Diaspora Consultation in Cape Town, South Africa, it was announced that the next consultation would be held in South Korea in August 2023. The decision to convene the next global consultation had been made the week before at the Global Diaspora Network executive team meeting, primarily on account of the forthcoming Fourth Lausanne Congress in Seoul, South Korea, in September 2024. In line with the consultation in Cape Town, it was decided that the theme for the next consultation would be "Asians in Diaspora and Diasporas in Asia." In the ensuing months, greater clarity emerged as we narrowed down a possible hotel venue on Jeju Island and identified various topics and potential speakers for the consultation.

We express our deepest gratitude to the executive committee of the Global Diaspora Network of the Lausanne Movement for organizing and convening this consultation. The committee includes Rev. Dr. T. V. Thomas (chair), Rev. Barnabas Moon (vice-chair), Rev. Art Medina (treasurer), Dr. Godfrey Harold, Dr. Hanna Hyun, Dr. Elizabeth Mburu, Dr. Paul Sydnor, and Rev. Joel Wright. The three editors serve on the executive committee of the Global Diaspora Network.

The Jeju Diaspora Consultation was held in association with two major local partners in South Korea, who were involved in hosting and convening this global event. First, the Korean World Mission Association (KWMA), which is one of the largest national mission networks in the world and has a long association with the Lausanne Movement and a growing interest in diaspora missions among its constituencies. Second, Torch Trinity Graduate University (TTGU), one of the leading evangelical seminaries in South Korea and Asia, which enjoys a close association with the Lausanne diaspora issue network and has hosted several conversations on the topic. We are deeply indebted to many professors and stakeholders from local Korean churches, mission agencies, and Asian mission networks who promoted this event. We gratefully acknowledge large and small donors who contributed to hosting this consultation. We sincerely thank the dedicated volunteers – including Grace Moon, Karen Medina, Jeong Gihwan, Raveen Burra, David Hanif, Jeong Hun

Heo, and others – who served sacrificially by helping with local transportation, reception, meals, and translations.

Undoubtedly the worship time, prayer, missionary passion, intellectual stimulation, and camaraderie were intense and profound, leaving a lasting impression on all attendees. We thank our audiovisual team and computer support team who helped to stream a virtual forum of the event live from the venue for ninety minutes each day. We thank the owner and directors of Shalom Hotel for offering the venue at a discounted rate during a peak tourist season and the hospitality team who attended to the needs of this global delegation. All participants were enriched by the hospitality, food, and fellowship of the Korean host team and volunteers from local churches. The local transportation team did an outstanding job, picking and dropping all delegates from the airport and transporting them to various sites for team-building activities. Hosting a global consultation involving several hundred delegates takes a great deal of behind-the-scenes work and many labored quietly to make such a gathering possible. We pray that God will richly bless them and make them a blessing to many more.

We express our sincere gratitude to Langham Publishing for trusting us with another book on diaspora while we were still working on our previous book project. Our special thanks to Luke Lewis, Mark Arnold, copyeditors, layout and cover designers, and those marketing these books across the majority world. We place on record our gratitude to Lausanne leaders like Dr. David Bennett, who serves as senior associate, and Tanya Van Horne, who serves as global director for Issue Networks, for their constant encouragement and support for the diasporas issue network.

Last but not least, we thank our families for their constant support and prayers for us. I (Sam) thank Mary, Daniel, and Joshua. I (Bulus) thank Rose, Atsen, Janna, Tim, Abi, Arum, Justine, Atu, Ezra, Josiah, Na'omi, Vitani, Azi, Motara, and Ayisa. I (Jeanne) thank Scott.

Introduction

Sam George

Asia is the largest and most populous continent in the world. Little wonder that Asia also sends out and hosts a significant share of migrants annually, as well as cumulatively over time. The Lausanne global consultation on diaspora missions held in Jeju Island, South Korea, in August 2023 generated a great deal of excitement and brought together an exceptional group of Christian leaders from all over the world. The theme of the consultation – "Asians in Diaspora and Diasporas in Asia" – was chosen in keeping with the previous Lausanne diaspora consultation held in South Africa, which had focused on the African diaspora.

The Jeju Diaspora Consultation aimed to convene church and mission leaders in Asia and global Asians, as well as other major people groups in Asia. This consultation deliberated on where Asians are going, who is coming to Asia, and how this will shape the mission of God in the twenty-first century. We wanted to bring together leading thinkers, mission champions, and ministry practitioners who are engaged in Asian diasporas and diaspora communities in Asia. Although we would have liked to have hosted a larger event, we were constrained by resources, timing, and expertise. Nevertheless, we successfully convened a consultation with broad representation, in-depth treatment of a range of topics, and a diverse mix of academics, policymakers, mission practitioners, ecclesial leaders, and laity from across Asia as well as from around the world.

This book is a compilation of papers presented at the Jeju diaspora consultation, which was designed as a working consultation where every participant actively contributed. Consequently, the chapters in this book emerged from extensive small group discussions following the presentation of each paper. Table groups compiled their critiques, along with inputs from their own contexts, and detailed feedback was given to the presenters. This collaborative process and the insights from multiple vantage points from well-informed and experienced participants greatly enriched these papers. After the consultation, the presenters were given three months to revise their papers, which were then edited according to the publisher's guidelines and published in this volume.

Having recently published a three-volume series on Asian Diaspora Christianity, which included forty chapters on various Asian diasporas from all over the world,[1] we were able to quickly identify subthemes and issues that were pertinent to the selected conference theme. While remaining firmly anchored in Asia and its diaspora, this volume also includes new voices from different regions of the world.

Significance of Jeju Island for a Diaspora Consultation

The choice of Jeju Island as the location for this consultation on migration and diaspora mission has great significance for South Korea and Asia in general. The history of this island is intricately tied to the theme of this consultation. This tiny island lies south of South Korea in the East China Sea, close to the southern islands of Japan and the city of Shanghai, China. Since 2000, Jeju Island has emerged as a major tourist destination and is often referred to as the Hawaii of South Korea. Due to its remarkable tourism infrastructure and growing popularity as a honeymoon and summer holiday destination, it is widely recognized across East Asia and Southeast Asia. With the provision of visa waivers to many countries, Jeju Island has become a popular conference venue. This was an important criterion for choosing the Island for the diaspora consultation as it ensured easy access without the hassle of obtaining a visa for South Korea.

In 2016, a group of people fleeing the civil war in Yemen came to Jeju Island as tourists and sought asylum on the island. These refugees took advantage of the visa waiver provision that South Korea had implemented to attract tourists at a time when a South Korean diplomat was the general secretary of the United Nations. As a signatory of the United Nations Refugee Convention of 1951, South Korea had a legal obligation to protect the rights of the displaced and was thus compelled to provide asylum for these desperate refugees. These Yemeni refugees had first gone to Malaysia, which allows a visa-free three-month stay and is the favored destination for many refugees from war-torn regions of Afghanistan, Bangladesh, and several Arab nations because of cultural similarities arising from their common Islamic religious traditions. However, when they could no longer stay in Malaysia, these refugees went to another visa-free state in the region. The commencement of a direct flight from Malaysia to Jeju Island by the budget airline Air Asia further increased the flow of these expelled refugees, and the significant presence of Middle Eastern and

---

1. See George, *Asian Diaspora Christianity*.

African refugees on this tiny island – which had previously only seen Koreans, Chinese, and Japanese people – soon erupted into a national crisis.[2]

This diaspora consultation was also significant because it was held at a time when South Korea's fertility rate had dropped to the lowest level in the world. South Korea is in the process of passing a major immigration reform law that will open up the nation for labor and skilled migration from around the world. This is expected to attract millions of people from the rest of Asia, particularly Southeast Asia, to work in its factories and sustain global exports of Samsung phones and Hyundai cars. A similar demographic decline can be seen in other rich Asia nations like Japan and Singapore. The year 2023 also marked a steady decline in China's population on account of the one-child policy of previous decades, allowing India to overtake China and become the most populous country on the planet. These demographic shifts will shape migratory flows in the coming years on account of changing labor needs, global supply-chain realignment, and recessionary pressures. The growing unemployment, nationalistic policies, political unrest, wars, and worsening climatic conditions in some parts of Asia are likely to accelerate the push factors for human out-migration in the coming decades.

As the most populous continent, a significant level of population movement is expected within and out of the region. The ongoing wars, economic instability, and political unrest in many parts of Asia will prompt more people to explore livelihood and living options in other parts of the world. The rise of Asia and fears of wars are accelerating the shift in capital and labor flows. While the advent of new technologies and the trend of remote work have democratized the global workforce, these developments have also marginalized many. To make matters worse, ecological catastrophes will disproportionately affect Asian nations in the form of natural disasters, such as tsunamis, coastal flooding, cyclones, and earthquakes.

Outline of the Book

This publication consists of three subsections. The first four chapters address macro and global issues related to Asian diaspora missions; the second section, which contains fourteen chapters, focuses on specific themes and regions

---

2. Murphy, "Hundreds of Yemenis," *Washington Post*, 22 June 2018, https://www.washingtonpost.com/world/asia_pacific/how-hundreds-of-yemenis-fleeing-the-worlds-worst-humanitarian-crisis-ended-up-on-a-resort-island-in-south-korea/2018/06/20/cf0b49fc-7381-11e8-805c-4b67019fcfe4_story.html.

related to diaspora missions in Asia and among Asians worldwide; and the third section, which contains four chapters, offers biblical reflections by Asian and African scholars on the book of 1 Peter, which was chosen for in-depth study during this consultation. These twenty-two chapters are bracketed by this introduction and a conclusion.

In Chapter 1, mission theologian Dr. Kirsteen Kim of Fuller Seminary situates the global diaspora missions within the framework of world Christianity by developing a theology of coming, staying, and going. She argues that as part of the global Christian community, both Christians on the move and those at home have complementary and overlapping roles to play in the mission of God.

In Chapter 2, Rev. Dr. Francis Tam takes a deep dive into the Chinese diaspora, with a particular focus on recent immigrants from Hong Kong to Canada. In the wake of the curb on civil liberties, political unrest, and economic uncertainties, there has been a large-scale exodus of capital and people from the former British colony to many Commonwealth nations. Pastor Tam provides findings from his field interviews – conducted in Cantonese – with ten Chinese pastors in Canada.

In Chapter 3, Professor Prabhu Guptara – a former Swiss banker who now lives in Cambridge, UK, and leads a new publishing venture – explores financial matters concerning the Asian diaspora. He discusses the growing remittances to Asian countries from their dispersed people worldwide and confronts the reality of deglobalization in the wake of rising nationalism and policies framed to curtail unmanageable rates of migration. He introduces the notion of "half-life" to remittance and discusses how the prospects of future remittance decline over time.

Chapter 4 is the annual report of Lausanne diaspora catalysts Dr. Sam George and Dr. Bulus Galadima. This chapter features the state of the migrants and diaspora communities in the world and gives the latest demographic data and sources for global migration while mapping major shifts and trends regarding the People on the Move. This chapter features four diaspora mission strategies and introduces three new focus areas for the issue network – namely, internal migration, human trafficking, and climate migration. This chapter briefly introduces the theological framework of God on the Move and the current new projects of the Global Diaspora Network – namely, Lausanne Occasional Paper No. 70 on the People on the Move and the GMove mobile app.

Section B of the book begins with two biblical and theological reflections – both by Asian scholars – that are particularly relevant for Asian diasporas. In Chapter 5, Filipino American theologian Dr. Terry Casiño develops a theology of kingdom citizenship for transnational migrants. He explores the processes of transnational identity formation and describes various hermeneutical approaches to understanding the plight of migrants besides ways in which they can be included in God's kingdom. Subsequently, in Chapter 6, Dr. Yoon Jong Yoo – a Korean Old Testament professor and dean of the Pierson School of Theology at Pyeongtaek University in South Korea – reflects on a theology of hospitality based upon the doctrine of *imago Dei*. Using contemporary exegetical work, he develops a migration theology based on Genesis 18 and 19 that is connected to the biblical tradition of hospitality. He argues that all people bear the image of God and could either be compassionate royal priests like Abraham or tyrants like the people of Sodom.

The next two chapters are written by two Asian women missiologists with extensive global experience in working with diverse diaspora communities. These women also serve on the executive team of the Global Diaspora Network. In Chapter 7, Taiwanese American Dr. Jeanne Wu explores missions through and beyond the Chinese diaspora in the Middle East. She explores the recent trend of short-term missions undertaken by Chinese churches in North America – aimed at serving the displaced and refugees in war-ravaged regions of the Middle East – and compares this with another mission movement involving the Chinese diaspora in the Gulf countries, which she links to the growing migration out of China prompted by the "One Belt, One Road" policy of 2013 and the new Regulation of Religious Affairs in 2018. She concludes that transnational Chinese leaders play a vital role as mission catalysts by linking Chinese Christians worldwide and encouraging them to expand their ministry beyond fellow Chinese to other socioreligious and political contexts. In Chapter 8, Korean missiologist Dr. Hanna Hyun assesses a mission training curriculum developed by the pioneering migrant ministry of WiThee Mission International. She begins with a brief history of migrant inflows into South Korea and the founding of a domestic cross-cultural mission among migrants when the country was focused on sending missionaries around the world. She then explores the distinctive approach of the Migrant Mission Training School (MMTS) and analyzes its content, pedagogy, teachers, students, and modes. Based on a field study she conducted among participants of the school, she offers several recommendations to revise and adapt the program for a more global audience, utilizing new technology platforms.

The next three chapters employ an unconventional lens in diaspora missions. Two of them are based in Malaysia and the other in South Korea, and the authors come from human rights, law, and medical backgrounds. Chapter 9 is about advocacy for labor migrants, Chapter 10 is about a politician framing new immigration laws for his native homeland, and chapter 11 is about holistic care for refugees.

Chapter 9 is authored by Datuk Professor Dr. Denison Jayasooria, of Sri Lankan ancestry and a Methodist minister turned policy advocate, who served as an adviser to the Malaysian government and representative to the United Nations and its Sustainable Development Goals. In this chapter, Professor Jayasooria reviews human rights violations and current practices of intervention to secure justice for labor migrants. He concludes by offering a set of recommendations for all Christian and faith-based organizations seeking the welfare of migrants arriving in their nations, along with practical intervention strategies.

In Chapter 10, Dr. Kangmuk Ghil, the current deputy director of the presidential committee of the Ministry of Justice of South Korea, who is involved in immigration policy changes for the country, provides a demographical analysis of South Korea, the low fertility crisis, and the need for skilled workers to sustain economic growth and social security for an aging society.

Chapter 11 is written by a former dental surgeon who is currently the executive director of a ministry with a vision to disciple nations at their doorstep. Dr. Ng Oi Leng makes a persuasive case for how Christians should embrace the refugees around them by providing holistic and integral care by meeting their felt needs and seeking community transformation.

The next two chapters are written by pastors who work with a wider network of church leaders in their cities and nations. These essays present the contexts of the Philippines and Vietnam. In Chapter 12, Bishop Dr. Noel Pantoja explores the role of a local church and the unique challenges posed by geographically dispersed families across many time zones. The reality of transnational families is pervasive when migrants are not able to take their immediate family members to foreign work locations and are forced to leave them with extended family members or to fend for themselves with the help of overseas remittances. Chapter 13 is written by Dr. Jacob Bloemberg, a Dutch American missionary who has lived and served in Vietnam for over two and a half decades and serves as lead pastor of an international church in Hanoi. Dr. Bloemberg shares the inspiring story of the "Love Your City" campaign and explores the missional role of international Christian communities as they work alongside national churches within the sociopolitical order to achieve a broader kingdom impact through collective efforts in training, resourcing, and networking Christians in our cities.

The next two chapters both focus on the next generation – Chapter 14 deals with international student ministry, focusing on Asian students and others who come to Asia for academic pursuits, while Chapter 15 explores hybridity among the children of missionaries in foreign lands. In Chapter 14, Leiton and Lisa Chinn, seasoned International Student Ministry (ISM) champions, point out that Asia sends out the greatest number of students to traditional destinations such as North America, Europe, and Oceania while also being home to new centers of education in places such as Singapore, Abu Dhabi, Qatar, Taiwan, the Philippines, Hong Kong, China, and India. Chapter 15, authored by two young scholars – Ms. Grace Eun-Sun Lee and Ms. Tessa Tubbs – introduces readers to the concept of hybridity among Korean missionary kids by exploring the pedagogy of international schooling. They argue that teachers at international schools help their students to embrace their hybrid identities in order to overcome identity struggles through third-space conversations and the practice of biblical hospitality.

The next three chapters are new areas of focus for the diaspora mission agenda – namely, internal migration, human trafficking, and climate migration. Written by leading experts in the field, who are firmly situated in Asia and widely involved in ministry in these contexts, these chapters broach topics that have not been dealt with until now in diaspora mission conversations. We hope that these insights will help the global church to deliberate on and embrace the challenges posed by such issues. While these essays emerge out of local and regional contexts, they are applicable widely across Asia as well as globally.

In Chapter 16, Indian urban missiologist Rev. Dr. J. N. Manoharan examines the massive migration taking place within India as people migrate within and across states at unprecedented levels, creating new challenges to existing sociocultural and religious institutions. He presents recent demographic data and an analysis of Indian internal migration and poses several missiological questions to expose the blind spots of the Indian church. Dr. Manoharan calls on local churches and pastors to be more responsive to migrants in their neighborhood and to recognize God-given opportunities as the mission fields relocate to their vicinity.

In Chapter 17, Dr. Christa Crawford – a Harvard-trained lawyer based in Thailand, who is extensively involved in global anti-trafficking efforts – addresses the issue of the "exploited diaspora" of sexual and gender-based violence victims who are forcibly sent across national borders. She presents biblical cases of trafficking, citing the stories of Joseph and Esther, to illustrate what holistic ministry might look like and what local churches at both ends of such migration can do to help bring an end to trafficking.

Finally, in this section, in Chapter 18, Ms. Jasmine Kwong – a Chinese Canadian now serving with a Christian environmental group in the Philippines – and Dr. Sam George address the emerging issue of climate migration. This is a new frontier in mission and migration studies as most Christians are ignorant of the impending tsunami of migrants who will soon crash on our shores. This chapter deals with climate change-induced migrations and considers reliable projections by climate advocates and researchers. It calls Christians to view creation care as an essential aspect of discipleship and stewardship and thus a fundamental gospel issue for all followers of Jesus Christ and not a concern applicable to only a few passionate about climate change.

The four chapters in the final section emerged out of the morning Bible expositions at the Jeju Diaspora Consultation. Four Bible scholars were invited to explore with the delegates the implications of the first Petrine epistle for diaspora ministries. This New Testament epistle of Peter is addressed to churches in Asia Minor – that is, modern-day Turkey – that are still considered part of Western Asia. The four Bible scholars were drawn from Kenya, Canada, South Korea, and the Philippines, with the latter three being of Asian origin and living in diasporic settings.

In Chapter 19, Kenyan Bible scholar and Global Diaspora Network (GDN) core team member Dr. Elizabeth Mburu provides a background of 1 Peter by presenting the world behind the text, the world of the text, and the world in front of the text. The Greek word for diaspora that appears in the introductory greetings of 1 Peter refers to recipients who were dispersed on account of Roman persecution and suffered greatly. This epistle calls its readers and all diasporic people to persevere, following the example of Jesus Christ, and to live in the light of their eternal hope.

In Chapter 20, Dr. Narry Santos focuses on 1 Peter 1:3–2:10 and unpacks the theme of diasporic identity and kinship bonds within the household of God. The apostle Peter urges his readers to rediscover their new identity as God's new family and to remain secure in their hope in God even though they may suffer briefly at the hands of a hostile world. He admonishes his diasporic readers, as holy people in a foreign land and as permanent exiles in this world, to live differently, loving one another deeply, and living with hope.

In Chapter 21, Dr. Yoon Hee Kim – an Old Testament scholar who, until recently, served as president of Torch Trinity Graduate University in Seoul and now leads the Faith and Work Institute Asia – discusses how Christians should relate to a hostile world. She argues that Christians must ensure that their conduct is honorable and beyond reproach and learn to live victoriously before an unbelieving world. Dr. Kim explores the various roles Christians play in diverse societal structures and emphasizes that our primary motivation in all these situations should be the fear of God.

Dr. Samson L. Uytanlet along with his wife Dr. Juliet Uytanlet, both of whom are Chinese Filipinos, recently published a new commentary on 1 Peter.[3] In Chapter 22, he develops his exposition using the lens of "sojourner" and links the exhortations found in the first four chapters of the epistle with Old Testament references to the Israelites. He then focuses on 1 Peter 5 and contrasts instructions given to elders and younger people in the community in the context of issues of power and abuse of power among Christians in diasporic settings.

References

George, Sam, ed. *Journeys of Asian Diaspora: Mapping Originations and Destinations.* Vol. 1 of *Asian Diaspora Christianity Series.* Minneapolis: Fortress, 2021.

———. *Interconnections of Asian Diaspora: Mapping the Linkages and Discontinuities.* Vol. 2 of *Asian Diaspora Christianity Series.* Minneapolis: Fortress, 2022.

———. *Reflections of Asian Diaspora: Mapping Theologies and Ministries.* Vol. 3 of *Asian Diaspora Christianity Series.* Minneapolis: Fortress, 2022.

Murphy, Brian. "How Hundreds of Yemenis Fleeing the World's Worst Humanitarian Crisis Ended Up on a Resort Island in South Korea." *Washington Post,* 22 June 2018. https://www.washingtonpost.com/world/asia_pacific/how-hundreds-of-yemenis-fleeing-the-worlds-humanitarian-crisis-ended-up-on-a-resort-island-in-south-korea/2018/06/20/cf0b49fc-7381-11e8-805c-4b67019fcfe4_story.html.

Uytanlet, Samson L., and Juliet L. Uytanlet. *Manual for Sojourners: A Study of Peter's Use of Scripture and Its Relevance Today.* Eugene: Wipf & Stock, 2023.

---

3. Uytanlet and Uytanlet, *Sojourners.*

Section A

1

World Christianity and Global Diasporas: Coming, Staying, Going

Kirsteen Kim

Introduction

"World Christianity and Global Diasporas" is the broad topic of this chapter, but let me begin by locating my approach in my own biography, which illustrates the subtitle "coming, staying, going." I grew up in England. So far as I can tell, my ancestors have lived there for centuries. I first migrated because of marriage. While doing missionary training at All Nations Christian College in England, I met Sebastian C. H. Kim, who had come there from South Korea. His family is similarly indigenous, and I moved to Korea to live with him and join them. After five years in Korea, we went to Fuller Theological Seminary in California, United States, for further study. Thereafter, we were sent as missionaries of the Presbyterian Church of Korea to teach at Union Biblical Seminary in Pune, India. After four years in India, now with two children born overseas, we reentered the UK as PhD students and missionaries to Britain. In 2017, after having lived and raised our family in England for twenty years, we moved internationally again. We came back to Fuller Seminary – this time, not as students but as faculty members.

I feel that my whole life has been a story of coming, staying, and going. But our mission work in theological education would not have been possible without Korean church members, who mostly stayed their whole lives in Korea and gave generously to support us. As we moved around the world, we also benefited from the network of the Korean diaspora – people who had gone and stayed and never come back but, instead, built diaspora communities in a new land.

I can see many permutations of coming, staying, and going. These words are interrelated. You have to come in order to stay. You have to stay before you can go. If I go, I may come to you. And so on. Your staying may support my going or be a home to receive someone else's coming. If everyone is going or everyone is coming, we have chaos. If everyone is staying and no one comes or goes, communities are isolated from one another. Coming, staying, and going are all needed to fulfill the mission of God, and all three activities make communities and make a world.

Mission as Migration versus Mission as Hospitality

My opening observation for this chapter is that missiological perspectives on migration tend to fall into two groups: on the one hand, there are those who celebrate migration as a means of spreading the gospel; on the other hand, there are those who view migration as suffering and regard mission as tending to its victims. The first group, which values coming and going, rejoices in the way that ever since Pentecost, migrants and travelers have been instrumental in carrying the good news so that Christianity is now a global faith. This group encourages contemporary Christian migrants and diasporas to see themselves as missionaries from everywhere to everywhere. The second group, which values staying, sees a humanitarian crisis as people are pushed into leaving their homes by traffickers, gangs, poverty, discrimination, conflict, natural disasters, and climate change. This view encourages churches to practice hospitality toward migrants and help them to resettle.

I will use insights from the study of world Christianity, including Christian migration and diasporas, as a frame to integrate these different perspectives of migration and settlement. I will propose a mission theology of coming, staying, and going. I aim to show that as part of the global Christian community, both Christians on the move and those who stay at home have complementary and overlapping roles to play in the mission of God.

Biblical Perspectives: Both Migration and Settlement

Let me begin with some biblical perspectives on coming, staying, and going that encompass both migration and settlement.

Migration

The Bible details a long history of the migration of the people of God. It has been said that "one can justifiably speak of the Bible as a collection of texts written by migrants to other migrants, often dealing with the issue of migration."[1] It has exile at the beginning – from Eden – and at the end – on the island of Patmos (Gen 3:23; Rev 1:9).[2] Migration is implied in God's command to "fill the earth" (Gen 1:28). Abraham, Isaac, and Jacob were nomadic. Moses and the people who had been enslaved in Egypt wandered until they reached the promised land. Then, many of the people of Israel and Judah were forcibly displaced by the imperial armies of Assyria and Babylon. Some later returned home, and others became part of a global Jewish diaspora.[3] The belief in being descended from a "wandering Aramean" (Deut 26:5) was integral to Israel's identity and shaped Jesus's self-understanding.[4]

According to the Gospels, Jesus sent his disciples to all nations (Matthew), to the whole creation (Mark), to the ends of the earth (Luke), and into the whole world (John). The catalyzing event of Pentecost reveals a key mechanism for this spread of the church – the Jewish diaspora. Diaspora settlements of Jews from modern Turkey south to Egypt and from Rome east to beyond Arabia are listed in Acts 2:9–11. Apostles like Paul went first to the synagogues – that is, they visited places where there was already a Jewish community, where they could find a place to stay and work to do. These diaspora communities acted as bases for regional work and provided networks for Christianity's spread. The diaspora communities provided hospitality for slaves (Philemon), sailors (Acts 27), traders (Lydia), itinerant workers (Priscilla and Aquila), and many apostles and missionaries who traversed the empire spreading the gospel.[5] Through such migrations, the early church expanded in multiple directions around the known world in Asia, Africa, and Europe.[6]

Settlement

However, although the Bible is full of references to migrants and itinerants, and even transnationals like the apostle Paul, much of Scripture is about set-

---

1. Strine, "Migration," 106.
2. Hanciles, *Beyond Christendom*, 140.
3. Crouch, *Israel and Judah*; Maoz, "Singing the Songs."
4. Senior, "Beloved Aliens."
5. Nguyen, "Migrants as Missionaries," 62.
6. Bantu, *Multitude of All Peoples*; Hanciles, *Migration*.

tled communities. Migration is not always commended in Scripture. Israel's recollection of hardship in Egypt is contrasted with the blessing of the promised land that they are going to settle in. While migration is redemptive in the case of Abraham, it is punitive in the case of Adam and Eve.[7] There are strong themes of rest, belonging, and land throughout Scripture.[8] The kingdom of God is where "they shall all sit under their own vines and under their own fig trees, and no one shall make them afraid" (Mic 4:4 NRSV). Although migration, diasporas, or globalization may be a source of blessing, this blessing is often born out of great suffering. Migration may be forced and involve abuse or exploitation. The role of migration in the contemporary spread of Christianity should not be celebrated without raising questions of justice for the migrants themselves and for unsupported hosts. Migrants are not only on the move but may also be longing for a stable home.

Diasporas may result from migration where communities have settled. Because they are staying, such communities are able to receive and support missionaries and other migrants. People on the move can welcome others on the move – as Abraham did at Mamre – but hospitality is more generally offered in the context of a settlement. Hospitality, centered on the home, was a means of transcending differences in the early church and also one of the marks of a Christian leader (see Rom 16:23; 1 Tim 3:2; 5:10; Titus 1:8). Hospitality met the needs of migrants – traveling missionaries, exiles, the poor, and the sick. Hospitality fostered family-like ties and reinforced a new identity because it was closely linked with worship, which also took place in the home.[9] The church – *ekklesia* – is literally a place where people are gathered together. The church "makes room" for the wanderer and stranger. The Eucharist, the Lord's Supper, is the central symbol of hospitality and of Christian table fellowship in the church as home. Such practices of hospitality have been developed as an approach to ministry to contemporary migrants.[10]

A World Christianity Perspective: The Interrelationship of Migration and Settlement

Given that both migration and settlement are characteristic of Scripture, we can bring the two groups together – those who rejoice in migration and those

---

7. Walls, "Mission and Migration," 20.
8. Gorringe, "Rethinking 'Migration.'"
9. See Groody, "Fruit of the Vine."
10. Pohl, *Making Room*; Yong, *Hospitality*; Kaemingk, *Christian Hospitality*.

who seek to mitigate its effects. Moreover, the study of world Christianity shows that, since Pentecost, the Christian faith has been globally widespread, locally rooted, and interconnected.[11] It also reveals that Christian diaspora communities and mission initiatives are closely related in the way the faith spreads. Christians may be people on the move but we are also welcoming people home. We may be both scattered (*diaspora*) and gathered (*ekklesia*). We are among the nations and also in Jerusalem, our heavenly home. Mission should not be equated with moving: mission in the way of Christ is also receiving migrants, bringing people home, offering hospitality, and making a just and peaceful homeland (see Matt 25:34–36).

In this section, I offer two case studies from world Christianity to illustrate my point about the interrelationship of migration and settlement. The first is from Korea and the second is from the US.

Korean Diaspora Communities and Mission

The Korean diaspora has been inseparable from Korean Christian growth and expansion.[12] In the late nineteenth century, living conditions in the Korean peninsula were dire due to shortages, injustices, and political instability. However, since the northern borders of Korea were porous, many families, and even whole church congregations, migrated northward into China, Russia, and Manchuria, where Koreans worked hard to develop uncultivated land and plant new villages. Other Koreans moved eastward to Japan to find work and opportunity in its growing economy. In the early twentieth century, when Japan annexed Korea, many Koreans were forcibly moved to work for the Japanese. After the liberation in 1945, not all returned. Meanwhile, in Russia, Stalin forcibly relocated Korean communities to different parts of the Soviet Union, where they remain today. In addition to the diasporas in northern Asia and Japan, in the mid-twentieth century, Koreans tried other ways to leave their occupied, impoverished, and war-ravished homeland. Some went to Hawaii, Mexico, and other parts of Latin America, and some were able to enter the US.

During the turbulent twentieth century, despite communication difficulties, the diaspora communities were connected to each other and supported Korea to resist and rebuild itself. Most Koreans who migrated were Christians or, if they had migrated to the West, had become Christians after their arrival. In most cases, Korean churches functioned as community centers to receive

---

11. Kim and Kim, *Christianity as a World Religion*.
12. For further details, see Kim and Kim, *History of Korean Christianity*.

new migrants and help them establish themselves in a new land.[13] The churches also disseminated news from the homeland, kept up the Korean language, and did what they could to promote Korea overseas. Although Korean churches had always aspired to be sending churches, it was not until they had grown significantly and the South Korean economy had expanded that the large-scale missionary movement from Korea began in the 1980s. Koreans also moved into Europe, South Asia, Southeast Asia, Africa, and the Middle East. Korean missionaries pioneered in new lands but they also had the advantage of a global Christian diaspora of several million to serve as bases for their work. From the 1980s, Koreans also began to move into Europe, southern Asia, and the Middle East, making the diaspora truly global. It is hard to imagine the scale and success of Korean Missions without the presence and support of this diaspora.

Mission Migration in and out of Los Angeles

Los Angeles, California, a global crossroads of migrating communities presents the second case study of immigration, emigration, transnationalism, and diasporas.[14] Many migrations in and out of Los Angeles during the last four hundred years have been mainly or partly motivated by religion. Four hundred years ago, Spain claimed, in the name of God, the land that was home to the Tongva – the indigenous people – and settled newcomers on it. In the eighteenth century, a chain of Spanish missions established along the Californian coast so forcefully resettled the native peoples into villages that today the Spanish have been accused of genocide.[15] In 1848, when Spain was forced to cede California to the US government, the new rulers regarded the Latino community as aliens even though some of them had been there since long before 1776. The indigenous peoples were treated as enemies within their own country and literally hunted down. Meanwhile, American Protestants of European descent, with a sense of "manifest destiny" or White supremacy, moved westward, hoping to convert Native Americans and re-evangelize this Catholic land.[16] Other migrants followed. Sustained by their faith, formerly enslaved African Americans came to California hoping to find a promised land

---

13. For examples, see Kim and Ma, *Korean Diaspora*.

14. Kim and Salvatierra, *Migration*.

15. Sandos, *Converting California*. For the treatment of native Americans in California, see Madley, *American Genocide*; and Sexton, "Borders and Barriers."

16. Hutchison, *Errand to the World*; Dochuk, *Bible Belt to Sunbelt*; Graber, *Gods of Indian Country*.

away from the harsh segregationist policies in the southern states, only to find themselves subjected to racism.[17] Since 1965, when racist laws excluding Asian migration were lifted, East Asians have established diasporas with churches that bear witness to the wider society.[18] More recent arrivals from Latin America, fleeing violence and poverty, stream across the southern border, which is only two hours from Los Angeles, bringing their Christian faith with them.[19]

As a result of these waves of migration, Los Angeles is one of the most ethnically diverse cities in the US.[20] Such a confluence of diverse migrating communities, each bringing a particular faith tradition, has spawned new religious movements and faith expressions. In the case of Los Angeles, the migrations have been largely Christian, encouraged by the religious freedom and culture of innovation of the so-called city of dreams.[21] For example, the global Pentecostal movement arguably originated in the 1906 revival meetings in Azusa Street in Los Angeles,[22] the International Church of the Foursquare Gospel was founded in Los Angeles in 1923 by Aimee Semple McPherson, and the Jesus Movement began in Los Angeles in the late 1960s. Such new religious movements expanded out of the city through emigrations, missionary movements, and mass communications. California's megachurches, like Saddleback Church, also expanded worldwide. Los Angeles, a hotbed of evangelism, became the base for many Christian nonprofits. In 1982, the *World Christian Encyclopedia*'s list of global evangelistic agencies revealed that a quarter of them were based in the Los Angeles area, including one of the largest – World Vision International.[23]

Despite all the excitement surrounding evangelism and world mission in "the city of angels," evangelicals in Los Angeles have not always been attentive to human dignity and humanitarian needs in their own city. For example, with respect to the Latino community, who now form a demographic majority in the Greater Los Angeles area, evangelistic efforts by White evangelicals aimed to Americanize them, as if their native culture was inferior. Little attempt was made to address the precarious legal status of many of these people, making

---

17. Gates and Yacovone, *African Americans*.
18. Kim, "Making Their Mark."
19. On Latin America, see Romero, "Mexican Americans"; Martínez, "Missiological Reflections."
20. Greater Los Angeles comprises the city and five surrounding counties. For details of the people groups, see Hannaman, et al. *Ethno LA*.
21. Flory, "City of Dreams," 33; Dochuk, "Errands in the Wilderness."
22. Robeck, *Azusa Street*; Anderson, *Spreading Fires*.
23. Barrett, *World Christian Encyclopedia*, 914.

the whole community feel as if they were "in-between"– neither foreigners nor citizens.[24] Furthermore, evangelical Christians, for the most part, mostly turned a blind eye to the discrimination against Latinos in education and public services, ignoring the fact that they were forced to live in segregated areas.[25] However, through the growth and witness of the largely Pentecostal "Brown Church"[26] and the rise of "integral mission," as pioneered by Latin American evangelical leaders, evangelical churches and organizations based in California, such as Matthew 25, are working for justice for Latinos who are settled and wish to claim citizenship, as well as for migrants who face harassment at the border or within the immigration system.

A Mission Theology of Migration and Settlement

Both those who celebrate migration as a means of spreading the gospel and those who view migration as suffering and support its victims are participating in the mission of God. Within a world Christianity perspective, the kingdom of God needs people who are coming and going, and also those who are staying. As I have demonstrated above, the Bible affirms both states – moving and settling. Two theological themes show that a theology of "coming, staying, going" reflects the nature of God: the incarnation and the Trinity.

Incarnation: Coming, Staying, Going

Christian faith is centered on the God who came and stayed with us or who "moved into the neighborhood" (John 1:14 MSG). The Word incarnate, Jesus Christ, was sent by the Father into the world out of love for us (John 3:16), and Jesus told his disciples that he was sending them as the Father had sent him (John 20:21). So, we go because Jesus went. Not only did Jesus migrate from heaven, but he was also part of migrations on earth. At the time of his birth, his parents were displaced to Bethlehem. Due to Herod's terror, the family became refugees in Egypt and later relocated to Nazareth. As an adult, Jesus had an itinerant ministry in Galilee and journeyed to Jerusalem. To be a migrant is to be imitating Christ.[27]

---

24. Martínez, "Missiological Reflections."
25. Romero, "Mexican Americans."
26. Romero, *Brown Church*, 11.
27. Phan, "Migration in the Patristic Era," 58.

Jesus's migration from heaven – his incarnation – was not an illusion but a flesh-and-blood reality. But the story does not end with Jesus on earth. In both John's Gospel and in the famous hymn in Philippians 2:5–11, we see a parabolic or U-shaped movement.[28] According to John, the Word came down from heaven and dwelled among us. Then, through his crucifixion, Jesus was "lifted up" and glorified with the Father. In Philippians, Paul says that Jesus came down from heaven and was made human, became obedient to the point of death, and then God exalted him to heaven. Jesus's trajectory is to come, stay, and then go or return. As Jesus's disciples, we also both stay and return or abide and go. Just as Jesus abides in the Father, we abide in Christ as we participate in God's mission in the world (John 15:5), and we are raised with him (Rom 6:4).[29]

Trinity: Staying, Coming, Going

The mission of God or the *missio Dei* is often described as a Trinitarian theology of mission. Much *missio Dei* theology describes God as missionary or missional, as if God is sent as we are. However, that is only partly true. From the very beginning, in creation – according to Genesis 1:1 and 1:2 – the Father sent both the Word and the Spirit, who work together in creation and recreation. The Word and the Spirit are the "two hands of the Father," according to the second-century theologian Irenaeus. But God the Father is not sent; the Father is the Sender, but the Father stays. In John's Gospel especially, we read about God the Father as the home to which Jesus expects to return (John 13:3) and where his disciples can expect to find a place to stay (John 14:2). As the pioneer Indian theologian Keshub Chunder Sen wrote, the Trinity is "the Still God [the Father], the Journeying God [the Son], and the Returning God [the Spirit]."[30] Going forth or procession is the essence of the triune God – but only if we consider the movement of each person in relation to the others.

In both the incarnation and the Trinity, coming and going – movement or mobility – are seen as integral to the Christian faith. However, dwelling and staying are also enshrined in doctrine. The mission of disciples is to come when called, stay when there is an invitation, and go when they are sent. The staying may be short or long. On the one hand, if there is no welcome, we are to move on (Luke 10:10–11). But, on the other hand, according to church tradition,

---

28. Harris, *Mission in the Gospels*.
29. See Gorman, *Abide and Go*.
30. Scott, *Keshub Chunder Sen*, 228.

many of the first apostles, evangelists, and church fathers, who were the missionaries of the early church, stayed in one place long enough to become associated with it. Thomas stayed in India, Mark in Egypt, and John in Asia Minor.

Conclusion

In conclusion, from a world Christianity and diaspora perspective, the dichotomy between mission as migration versus mission as hospitality cannot be sustained. Successful world mission movements depend on the synergy between relatively settled communities who can offer hospitality to migrants and missionaries who are on the move. From a mission theological perspective, too, coming, staying, and going are intertwined in our understanding of God and the human community. Both the scattered church and the gathered church are part of God's mission. Whether we are staying in our family's homeland or an adopted land, or coming and going as missionaries and transnationals, we are part of world Christianity. Belonging to one whole Christian church throughout God's world, although with different callings and with varied gifts, we all belong in God's economy of salvation. Whether we are coming, staying, or going, we are all potentially participants in God's mission.

We do not have to view migration as either a wholly good thing or an unmitigated disaster. This is the way the world is and has been, at least since biblical times. However, migrants suffer because today's globalized world encourages mobility in the service of global capitalism but national governments struggle to receive people in humane ways. As world Christianity, as the church everywhere and for all, we can, together, do a lot to challenge this injustice and help migrants who are suffering. First, we can normalize migration as a common human experience. We are all in some sense aliens, exiles, or pilgrims on a journey. Second, we can appreciate, from historical examples, how God uses coming, staying, and going to grow the church. Third, we can embrace the challenge posed by migrant churches to the settled churches and to missions. Fourth, we can promote coming, staying, and going as characteristic of God as the Trinity and Christ with us. Finally, we can diversify our responses to migration beyond evangelism and church growth on the one hand and hospitality on the other. For example, we can draw on biblical teachings on justice for all migrants and the flourishing of all people in order to inspire the moral treatment of migrants, transnationals, and settled but marginalized groups in our own societies. We can affirm both the human right to mobility and the rights of citizens, and work toward justice for both groups. And whether we come, stay, or go, we can look to the biblical teaching on neighbors to discern what our relationships with others who are moving relative to us should look like, and what responsibilities we have toward others.[31] Just think what we could do to spread the gospel and help suffering migrants if we do it together as the world Christian community!

References

Anderson, Allan H. *Spreading Fires: The Missionary Nature of Early Pentecostalism.* London: SCM, 2007.

Bantu, Vince L. *A Multitude of All Peoples: Engaging Ancient Christianity's Global Identity.* Downers Grove: IVP Academic, 2020.

Barrett, David B., ed. *World Christian Encyclopedia.* London: Oxford University Press, 1982.

Crouch, Carly L. *Israel and Judah Redefined: Migration, Trauma, and Empire in the Sixth Century BCE.* Cambridge: Cambridge University Press, 2021.

Dochuk, Darren. *From Bible Belt to Sunbelt: Plain-Folk Religion, Grassroots Politics, and the Rise of Evangelical Conservatism.* New York: Norton, 2011.

Flory, Ricahrd. "City of Dreams: Los Angeles as a Cradle for Religion Activism, Innovation and Diversity" in *Migration, Transnationalism and Faith in Missiological Perspective: Los Angeles as a Global Crossroads,* eds. Kirsteen Kim and Alexia Salvatierra. Lanham: Lexington Books, 2022.

Gates, Henry Louis, Jr., and Donald Yacovone. *The African Americans: Many Rivers to Cross.* Carlsbad: Hay House, 2013.

Gorman, Michael J. *Abide and Go: Missional Theosis in the Gospel of John.* Eugene: Cascade Books, 2018.

Gorringe, Timothy. "Rethinking 'Migration' and 'Mission.'" In *Mission and Migration,* edited by Stephen Spencer, 129–40. Sheffield: Cliff College Publishing, 2008.

Graber, Jennifer. *The Gods of Indian Country: Religion and the Struggle for the American West.* New York: Oxford University Press, 2018.

Groody, Daniel G. "Fruit of the Vine and Work of Human Hands: Immigration and the Eucharist." In *A Promised Land, a Perilous Journey: Theological Perspectives on Migration,* edited by Daniel G. Groody and Gioacchino Campese, 299–315. Notre Dame: University of Notre Dame Press, 2008.

Haniciles, Jehu J. *Beyond Christendom: Globalization, African Migration, and the Transformation of the West.* Maryknoll: Orbis Books, 2008.

———. *Migration and the Making of Global Christianity.* Grand Rapids: Eerdmans, 2021.

---

31. I am indebted in this paragraph to Sánchez M., "Theological Approaches to Migration," 177–94.

Hannaman, Jerome, Gerry Gutierrez, Donald Gene Overstreet, and Kallie Jo Ho, *Ethno LA: Reaching the Nations, Tongues, and People of the Greater Los Angeles Metro Area*. Los Angeles: Tree of Life Publishing, 2017.

Harris, R. Geoffrey, *Mission in the Gospels*. Eugene: Wipf & Stock, 2014.

Hutchison, William R. *Errand to the World: American Protestant Thought and Foreign Missions*. Chicago: University of Chicago Press, 1987.

Kaemingk, Matthew. *Christian Hospitality and Muslim Immigration in an Age of Fear*. Grand Rapids: Eerdmans, 2018.

Kim, Kirsteen, and Alexia Salvatierra, eds. *Migration, Transnationalism, and Faith in Missiological Perspective: Los Angeles as a Global Crossroads*. Lanham: Lexington, 2022.

Kim, Rebecca Y. "Making Their Mark: Asian Americans and the Californian 'Christian' Landscape." In *Migration, Transnationalism, and Faith in Missiological Perspective: Los Angeles as a Global Crossroads*, edited by Kirsteen Kim and Alexia Salvatierra, 93–112. Lanham: Lexington, 2022.

Kim, S. Hun, and Wonsuk Ma, eds. *Korean Diaspora and Christian Mission*. Oxford: Regnum, 2011.

Kim, Sebastian, and Kirsteen Kim. *Christianity as a World Religion*. London: Bloomsbury, 2016.

———. *A History of Korean Christianity*. Cambridge: Cambridge University Press, 2015.

Madley, Benjamin. *An American Genocide: The United States and the California Indian Catastrophe, 1846–1873*. New Haven: Yale University Press, 2017.

Maoz, Daniel. "Singing the Songs of the Lord in a Strange Land: Forced Exile versus Chosen Exile in Early Jewish History." In *Strangers in This World: Multireligious Reflections on Immigration*, edited by Hussam S. Timani, Allen G. Jorgenson, and Alexander Y. Hwang, 81–92. Minneapolis: Fortress, 2015.

Martínez, Juan F. "Missiological Reflections on the 'In-Betweenness' of Latino Protestantism." In *Migration, Transnationalism, and Faith in Missiological Perspective: Los Angeles as a Global Crossroads*, edited by Kirsteen Kim and Alexia Salvatierra, 79–92. Lanham: Lexington, 2022.

Nguyen, vanThanh. "Migrants as Missionaries: The Case of Priscilla and Aquila." In *God's People on the Move: Biblical and Global Perspectives on Migration and Mission*, edited by vanThanh Nguyen and John M. Prior, 62–75. Eugene: Pickwick, 2014.

Phan, Peter C. "Migration in Patristic Era: History and Theology" in *A Promised Land, A Perilous Journey*, eds. Daniel G. Groody and Gioacchina Campese, 35–61. Notre Dame: University of Notre Dame, 2008.

Pohl, Christine D. *Making Room. Recovering Hospitality as a Christian Tradition*. Grand Rapids: Eerdmans, 1999.

Robeck, Cecil M. *The Azusa Street Mission and Revival: The Birth of the Global Pentecostal Movement*. Nashville: Thomas Nelson, 2006.

Romero, Robert Chao. *Brown Church: Five Centuries of Latina/o Social Justice, Theology, and Identity*. Downers Grove: IVP Academic, 2020.

———. "Mexican Americans and the Southern Errand." In *Migration, Transnationalism, and Faith in Missiological Perspective: Los Angeles as a Global Crossroads*, edited by Kirsteen Kim and Alexia Salvatierra, 67–78. Lanham: Lexington, 2022.

Sánchez M., Leopoldo A. "Theological Approaches to Migration: Their Impact on Missional Thinking and Action." In *Migration, Transnationalism, and Faith in Missiological Perspective: Los Angeles as a Global Crossroads*, edited by Kirsteen Kim and Alexia Salvatierra, 177–94. Lanham: Lexington, 2022.

Sandos, James A. *Converting California: Indians and Franciscans in the Missions*. New Haven: Yale University Press, 2008.

Scott, David C., ed. *Keshub Chunder Sen*. Bangalore: CLS, 1979.

Senior, Donald. "'Beloved Aliens and Exiles': New Testament Perspectives on Migration." In *A Promised Land, a Perilous Journey: Theological Perspectives on Migration*, edited by Daniel G. Groody and Gioacchino Campese, 20–34. Notre Dame: University of Notre Dame Press, 2008.

Sexton, Jason S. "Borders and Barriers: Citizenship in California." In *Migration, Transnationalism, and Faith in Missiological Perspective: Los Angeles as a Global Crossroads*, edited by Kirsteen Kim and Alexia Salvatierra, 131–50. Lanham: Lexington, 2022.

Strine, C. A. "Migration, Dual Identity and Integration: A Christian Approach to Embracing Others Across Enduring Lines of Difference." In *Christian Citizenship in the Middle East: Divided Allegiance or Dual Belonging?*, edited by Mohammed Girma and Cristian Romocea, 103–20. London: Jessica Kingsley, 2017.

Walls, Andrew F. "Mission and Migration: The Diaspora Factor in Christian History." In *Global Diasporas and Mission*, edited by Chandler H. Im and Amos Yong, 19–37. Oxford: Regnum Books, 2014.

Yong, Amos. *Hospitality and the Other: Pentecost, Christian Practices, and the Neighbor*. Maryknoll: Orbis Books, 2008.

2

Global Chinese Diaspora and Recent Hong Kong Out-Migration to Canada

Francis Tam

Introduction

The Chinese diaspora is a significant global phenomenon, with a large number of Chinese individuals living outside China. Recently, there has been an increase in Hong Kong residents moving to the United Kingdom, Canada, and Australia due to political unrest and the erosion of civil liberties. This chapter explores how Chinese churches in Canada adapt and grow by applying diaspora missiology, specifically in welcoming Hong Kong migrants.

Diaspora Missiology

Diaspora missiology is an interdisciplinary approach that combines Christian mission study with diaspora studies and highlights the need to understand the cultural, social, and religious contexts of diaspora communities to create effective strategies for Christian mission. This chapter examines how Hong Kong out-migration affects the growth and development of Chinese churches in Canada. It uses diaspora missiology as a framework to understand and address the challenges and opportunities that arise from migration and the dispersal of individuals across the world.[1] This approach focuses on how people moving

---

1. Wan, *Diaspora Missiology*.

across geographical, cultural, and religious boundaries shape the mission and ministry of the church.

In diaspora missiology, the concept of gathering the scattered refers to the process of bringing together individuals from a specific cultural or ethnic group who have been dispersed and relocated due to migration, displacement, or persecution.[2] In order to accomplish this, mission workers and churches work to locate and connect with these dispersed groups, building relationships, providing practical assistance, and creating inclusive church communities that honor the cultural and linguistic diversity of the scattered group.

The main objective of gathering the scattered is to establish a feeling of belonging and togetherness for displaced people, as well as to provide opportunities for encountering the gospel and nurturing their faith. To achieve this objective, it is necessary to adopt a sensitive and intentional approach that takes into consideration the unique cultural, linguistic, and social dynamics of each scattered group. Studies have shown that religious establishments such as churches are vital in helping immigrants assimilate into their new communities. Such institutions provide a strong sense of belonging, social support, and spiritual guidance, all of which are essential for migrants adapting to unfamiliar surroundings.[3]

Diaspora missiology acknowledges migration and displacement challenges, including identity, integration, and cultural adaptation. Guided by diaspora missiology, Chinese churches can address these challenges by offering practical support, spiritual guidance, and a sense of belonging to help migrants navigate their new lives in Canada. Furthermore, they can play a pivotal role in preserving and nurturing the cultural and religious identity of Hong Kong migrants by providing culturally relevant ministry opportunities and fostering spaces for dialogue and cultural exchange. Migration can lead to greater religious diversity and innovation within host societies as migrants bring their unique cultural and religious practices.[4] This can result in the creation of new religious institutions as well as the adaptation of existing institutions to better serve the needs of diverse migrant populations. Canadian Chinese churches can benefit from diaspora mission insights and perspectives in relation to Hong Kong's out-migration. This approach offers many opportunities for the spreading of the gospel, forming new relational networks, and growth of the

---

2. Tira and Yamamori, *Scattered and Gathered*.
3. Ebaugh and Chafetz, *Religion and the New Immigrants*, 91.
4. Levitt, *God Needs No Passport*, 17.

church. By engaging with Hong Kong migrants, these churches can establish inclusive communities and expand their local and global ministry.

Diaspora missiology promotes diversity and inclusion, recognizing the richness brought by people from various cultures, languages, and backgrounds to the body of Christ. Chinese churches can create inclusive and welcoming environments that celebrate the contributions and perspectives of Hong Kong migrants, thereby cultivating a vibrant faith community. This view is consistent with studies indicating that migration can contribute to church growth as migrants seek religious communities for support and belonging, particularly those from countries with a strong Christian tradition – for example, Hong Kong.[5] Furthermore, diaspora missions leverage the movement of people across borders as an opportunity for sharing the gospel and addressing social issues. Although it is a sensitive matter, Canadian Chinese churches can work with Hong Kong migrants to raise awareness about the sociopolitical situation in China by advocating for human rights, religious freedom, and social justice both locally and globally.

In summary, diaspora missiology offers a valuable framework for Chinese churches in Canada to understand and respond to the impact of Hong Kong out-migration. By embracing the opportunities and addressing the challenges presented by this dynamic, these churches can effectively support Hong Kong migrants, foster a diverse and inclusive faith community, and engage in transformative mission work.

Global Chinese Diaspora

The global Chinese diaspora has its roots in ancient times but has gained momentum since the mid-nineteenth century due to factors such as political instability, economic hardships, and population pressures. In particular, the Chinese Exclusion Act in the United States limited Chinese immigration, resulting in the formation of Chinatowns and the isolation of Chinese communities in North America. The establishment of the People's Republic of China in 1949 and events like the Tiananmen Square incident of 1989, and the return of Hong Kong to China in 1997 further fueled the dispersion of Chinese people around the world.[6]

---

5. Yang and Ebaugh, "Transformations," 280.
6. Li, "Rise and Fall," 9–32.

As of 2022, it is estimated that there are about fifty million Chinese people residing in 180 countries of the world today.[7] This figure represents the number of Chinese people who reside outside the Chinese mainland, Hong Kong, Macau, and Taiwan, excluding tourists, visitors, and short-term residents. If the current rate of population growth in different regions continues, the overseas Chinese population is estimated to reach fifty-two million by 2030 and fifty-nine million by 2040.[8] The Chinese diaspora is characterized by its diversity, with variations in language, culture, and identity among different communities.[9] Chinese immigrants and their descendants have made substantial contributions to the global economy, playing key roles in various industries. In addition, Chinese cuisine, music, and literature have enriched the world's cultural heritage.

Economic factors have played a vital role in shaping the global Chinese diaspora.[10] Chinese migrants have been motivated by the prospect of better economic opportunities and improved living standards. They have excelled as entrepreneurs and business owners, establishing successful enterprises in their host countries. Extensive networks of Chinese businesses and traders have facilitated the exchange of goods, services, and capital across borders. Remittances from overseas Chinese people have also provided significant income and investment for their home communities in China.

Understanding the complexities of the global Chinese diaspora requires a consideration of generational perspectives. First-generation migrants face challenges – such as language barriers, cultural differences, and discrimination – in adapting to new environments. In contrast, second- and third-generation migrants often have a more integrated cultural identity and are better able to balance their Chinese heritage with influences of their host country. The generational differences undoubtedly impact family dynamics, resulting in intergenerational conflicts and affects how cultural values and traditions are transmitted to the future generations. The Chinese diaspora in Canada is one of the country's largest and most established communities, boasting a rich history and culture. Many Chinese Canadians have a Christian background, rooted either in Protestant or Catholic traditions.

However, connecting and nurturing the Chinese Christian community in Canada poses challenges due to their dispersion across cities, language barri-

---

7. Overseas Chinese Affairs, "Annual Report 2022."
8. See Tan, *Routledge Handbook*, 4.
9. Poston and Wong, "Chinese Diaspora," 348.
10. Yu, "Empirical Study," 185.

ers, cultural differences, and the need for greater understanding and support from non-Chinese congregants, especially during the early years of immigration. To address these challenges, local churches in Canada have developed strategies to embrace the "gathering of the scattered" Chinese diaspora. These include offering services in Cantonese and Mandarin, providing language classes, hosting cultural events, and establishing Chinese-language congregations or ministries within larger churches. Collaborations with churches in Hong Kong and Taiwan have also been established to support and provide guidance to Chinese Christians in Canada.

In summary, the global Chinese diaspora has a rich and diverse history, with varying cultural, linguistic, and generational factors contributing to its complexity. By understanding these complexities and addressing the unique challenges faced by Chinese Christians in Canada, local churches can effectively "gather the scatter" and provide a supportive and inclusive environment for the Chinese Christian community. This approach fosters a sense of belonging and connection while preserving and nurturing the cultural and spiritual heritage of the Chinese diaspora in their new home.

Recent Hong Kong Out-Migration

Hong Kong, once a British colony, has played a crucial role in the global Chinese diaspora due to its favorable location and economic opportunities. However, recent sociopolitical developments have led to a decline in civil liberties, political unrest, and economic uncertainty in Hong Kong. The National Security Law (NSL) enacted by the Chinese central government in 2020 has significantly impacted the sociopolitical climate in Hong Kong and driven out-migration from the region. The broad definitions of offenses and concerns over the erosion of civil liberties and autonomy have prompted many residents to consider leaving the country. Economic stagnation and limited job opportunities have also contributed to out-migration from Hong Kong to Canada. Canada's history of welcoming immigrants, its strong rule of law, and its respect for civil liberties make it an attractive destination for Hong Kongers seeking a better quality of life and political freedom.

The deterioration of church development in Hong Kong is another sociopolitical factor driving out-migration. The increasing influence of the Chinese government, particularly after the implementation of the NSL, has raised concerns about potential religious freedom restrictions. The broad scope and ambiguous provisions of the law have created fear and uncertainty within the Christian community. Challenges to church autonomy and conflicts arising from political alignment have further hindered church development. Threats, harassment, and the declining number of experienced church leaders contribute to the demoralization of the Christian community in Hong Kong, prompting some residents to consider migration to a more supportive religious environment such as Canada.

In 2023, the Alliance Bible Seminary hosted the "Shaping the Future of Hong Kong Churches Conference." The conference report, which is based on focus group research, addresses various challenges faced by Hong Kong churches in the context of immigration trends, the pandemic, and political changes. This study involved pastors from churches of different sizes, discussing issues like service personnel shortages, congregation loss, and economic impacts. This report highlights approaches to mission redefinition, church leadership, and adapting ministry models in response to societal changes in order to provide guidance for churches navigating these complex times.[11]

In summary, the recent surge in Hong Kong's out-migration to Canada can be attributed to a combination of factors, including the implementation of the National Security Law, economic stagnation, limited job opportunities, and the deterioration of church development. These factors have prompted many Hong Kong residents to seek better economic opportunities, political freedom, and a more supportive religious environment. The impact of this out-migration on the development of Chinese churches in Canada highlights the need for churches to adapt their strategies and services to cater to the evolving needs of the growing Hong Kong diaspora.

Pastoral Interviews

The trend of out-migration from Hong Kong has implications for the broader Chinese diaspora. Countries like Canada are seeing an influx of immigrants from Hong Kong, which could bring new opportunities for cultural exchange, collaboration, and the growth of local Chinese churches. However, tensions and challenges may arise if established Chinese churches feel threatened by the arrival of new immigrants.

I grew up in Hong Kong and arrived in Canada as a university student in the mid-1970s. As a Canadian Chinese minister who has experienced the diaspora firsthand, I am interested in exploring the unique situation of Hong Kong emigrants. I used qualitative research methods to explore the impacts of

---

11. 劉思銘。〈塑造香港教會前景會議焦點小組研究報告〉。建道神學院。香港，[Shaping the Future of Hong Kong Churches], 2023.

Hong Kong's out-migration on Chinese churches in Canada. Data was gathered through a literature review and interviews with practicing pastors from Chinese evangelical churches across Canada.

Between April to May 2023, ten successful semi-structured interviews were conducted with anonymous evangelical pastors who served as key informants and ministry stakeholders. These interviews were conducted in Cantonese, and each interview consisted of eight preformatted questions as well as an open-ended question to encourage discussion.

Interview Questions	Answers
#1. Do you agree that "the influx of Hong Kong migrants presents an opportunity for Chinese churches in Canada to engage in evangelism and outreach within their local communities, leading to church growth and expansion"?	YES 100%
#2. Do you agree that "Chinese churches in Canada can help Hong Kong migrants maintain their cultural and religious identity while adapting to their new environment, ultimately contributing to better integration and cooperation between bi-literate trilingual congregations"?	YES 80%
#3. Do you agree that "the unique perspectives and experiences of Hong Kong migrants can contribute to the emergence of new leaders who can effectively serve the growing congregations, resulting in a more vibrant and diverse church leadership"?	YES 100%
#4. Do you agree that "the increased population of Hong Kong migrants may lead to a rise in both human capital and financial contributions, enhancing the local church's capacity to engage in mission work both locally and globally"?	YES 60%
#5. Do you agree that "the presence of Hong Kong migrants in Canadian churches can foster stronger links, facilitating the sharing of resources, ideas, and support, which can contribute to the overall growth and development of Chinese churches worldwide"?	YES 70%
#6. Do you agree that "the cultural, linguistic, and contextual differences between Hong Kong and Canada may require Chinese churches in Canada to adjust their ministries and approaches to effectively serve the needs of Hong Kong migrants"?	YES 100%

#7. Do you agree that "Hong Kong migrants who join Chinese churches in Canada face questions of identity and integration, and need help to navigate these issues"?	YES 90%
#8. Do you agree that "Chinese churches across Canada can serve as platforms for raising awareness about the sociopolitical situation in Hong Kong, advocating for human rights, and promoting social justice, etc."?	YES 40%
#9. Open Discussion: thoughts and ideas you may have regarding this topic.	

Findings
Evangelism and Church Growth

100 percent of the pastors have a positive view that migration helps in church growth and evangelism. As Hong Kong migrants seek spiritual guidance and a sense of community in their new home, they are more likely to join Chinese churches that offer culturally relevant worship services, programs, and support. Chinese churches in Canada are well-positioned to connect with Hong Kong migrants due to their shared cultural and linguistic background. This commonality facilitates effective communication, fosters trust, and enables churches to share the gospel and more effectively address the spiritual needs of migrants.

Cultural Mediation

Most of the pastors interviewed (80 percent) agreed that Chinese churches can provide a familiar spiritual environment for Hong Kong migrants. They can offer worship services, Bible studies, and religious activities that cater to the cultural and linguistic preferences of the migrants, as well as community centers for Hong Kong migrants where programs and activities are organized to facilitate connections among the members.

Cultivating Leadership

All pastors agreed that Hong Kong migrants bring a range of diverse experiences, skills, and talents to their new communities. This diversity of backgrounds can enrich the leadership of local churches because individuals with different expertise and perspectives can contribute to decision-making and problem-solving processes. The varied skill sets and experiences of Hong Kong migrants can provide fresh insights and innovative approaches to church leadership.

Resource Mobilization

Of the pastors interviewed, 60 percent believed that the increased population of Hong Kong migrants may lead to a rise in human capital and financial contributions, which can strengthen the local church's capacity to engage in mission work, both locally and globally. However, 40 percent of interviewees were not so optimistic.

Transnational Connections

The majority of pastors interviewed (70 percent) believed that the presence of Hong Kong migrants in Canadian churches has the potential to foster stronger links and facilitate the sharing of resources, ideas, and support, ultimately contributing to the overall growth and development of Chinese churches worldwide.

Challenges and Adaptation

All pastors interviewed recognized that they have many challenges with new immigrants. The findings suggest that the cultural, linguistic, and contextual differences between Hong Kong and Canada necessitate adjustments in the ministries and approaches of Chinese churches in Canada if they are to effectively meet the needs of Hong Kong migrants. Hong Kong migrants may face challenges related to integration and adaptation to their new environment. Chinese churches in Canada can play a vital role in assisting migrants to navigate these challenges. This assistance can include practical support – such as helping them find housing and employment – as well as spiritual guidance and facilitating community connections to promote a sense of belonging and support during the integration process.

Identity and Integration

The findings suggest that most pastors (90 percent) agreed that Hong Kong migrants who join Chinese churches in Canada encounter questions of identity and integration and require assistance to navigate these issues effectively. Chinese churches in Canada can play a crucial role in supporting migrants in finding a balance between their cultural heritage and the process of integration.

Advocacy and Social Justice

Many pastors interviewed for this study (60 percent) did not favor the idea of Chinese churches serving as platforms for raising awareness about the sociopolitical situation in Hong Kong. The findings suggest that several factors contribute to these reservations. Chinese communities encompass diverse opinions on political and social issues. Some Chinese churches in Canada may choose not to discuss certain topics in order to maintain unity and avoid exacerbating internal divisions within their congregations, and they may prioritize their religious mission and activities over sociopolitical advocacy. Churches in Canada, including Chinese churches, must operate within the country's legal framework. Legal considerations and compliance may influence the decision of Chinese churches to refrain from openly discussing sensitive sociopolitical issues.

Moreover, some Chinese churches may practice self-censorship to avoid attracting attention or backlash from authorities in China or Canada. Chinese churches in Canada may face pressures from the Chinese government, which has been known to exert control over religious organizations within and even, to some extent, beyond its borders. Fear of potential retaliation or adverse consequences for their members or affiliated organizations can impact the willingness of churches to engage in sociopolitical advocacy.

Further Reflections

When considering the topic of Hong Kong migrants in Canada and the role of Chinese churches, several additional points deserve consideration and discussion. First, Chinese churches in Canada have the opportunity to promote cultural exchange. By organizing cultural events and activities, these churches can facilitate mutual understanding and appreciation among Hong Kong migrants and the broader Canadian community. This would involve fostering an understanding of different traditions, values, and perspectives.

Second, Chinese churches can develop new youth ministry programs to address the unique challenges faced by the younger generation of Cantonese-speaking Hong Kong migrants. These programs can provide counseling, guidance, opportunities for personal growth, and cultural and linguistic assistance.

They can also offer emotional and spiritual support and promote social integration. Educational and career counseling can also help young migrants achieve their goals and adapt to their new environment in Canada.

Third, Chinese churches could consider providing emotional health support services to help Hong Kong migrants cope with the challenges they face. Adapting to a new environment, dealing with the loss of their previous life, and navigating the ongoing sociopolitical situation in Hong Kong can significantly impact their mental health. Prayer, counseling, and support groups are examples of services that could be offered.

Moreover, it may be beneficial for Chinese churches to partner with secular organizations that share similar goals related to social justice, human rights, and migrant integration. Such partnerships could lead to more comprehensive support services, advocacy efforts, and a broader reach within the community. Given the increasing importance of digital communication, Chinese churches should consider developing a strong online presence. This would involve using social media, live-streaming services, and other digital platforms to engage with their congregation and the broader public. Through these channels, they can share information, resources, and updates related to their work with Hong Kong migrants.

In some cases, it may be appropriate to establish new Hong Kong-focused churches that cater to the unique cultural and linguistic needs of Hong Kong migrants. While this phenomenon is observed in larger cities with significant numbers of Hong Kong immigrants, smaller cities may face challenges due to the relatively low percentage of newcomers compared to the existing congregation.

Mentoring groups within Chinese churches can significantly assist Hong Kong migrants as they adapt to life in Canada. These groups can provide emotional and spiritual support, cultural and linguistic assistance, and promote social integration. Mentors can offer valuable guidance while encouraging church and community involvement, helping migrants to maintain their religious identity and navigate potential faith-related challenges.

It is important to recognize that recent Hong Kong out-migration differs from previous waves of migration due to political tensions, diversity of migrant demographics, and expanded destination options for migrants. This rapid exodus places greater pressure on both migrants and receiving countries. Unlike earlier out-migration waves, where a "brain drain" was followed by eventual reconnection, the deep-rooted political and social divisions associated with the current wave may lead to a more permanent loss of talent and resources, impacting Hong Kong's future stability.

Finally, the recent out-migration from Hong Kong to Canada impacts theological schools by increasing the demand for Cantonese theological education and greater diversity in student body. Schools may need to expand course offerings relevant to Hong Kong migrants and incorporate their language preferences in their course offerings. Collaboration and exchange between theological institutions in Canada and Hong Kong may also be encouraged, enhancing the quality of theological education and fostering a stronger global network of Chinese churches and theological schools.

Summary of Interview Findings

The table below highlights responses from the ten pastors, with additional annotations of "strong (+)" or "weak (-)" for deeper insight into each pastor's perspective. This summary offers a glimpse into the diverse experiences within the Chinese church community in Canada, especially amid Hong Kong's out-migration. The use of these annotations provides a nuanced view of the pastors' responses, revealing more than just affirmative or negative responses. This approach enables a more detailed analysis that uncovers in-depth insights. The findings reveal the need for ongoing dialogue, learning, and adaptation among church leaders in a multicultural context, contributing significantly to understanding how Chinese churches in Canada are adapting to the challenges and opportunities of the recent Hong Kong out-migration.

Pastor	Q#1	Q#2	Q#3	Q#4	Q#5	Q#6	Q#7	Q#8
A	YES-	YES	YES+	YES	YES	YES	YES	YES
B	YES	NO	YES	YES-	YES	YES+	YES	NO
C	YES	YES-	YES	NO	YES	YES	YES	YES
D	YES	YES	YES-	YES	YES+	YES	YES	YES
E	YES+	YES	YES-	NO	YES	YES-	YES	NO
F	YES	YES	YES-	NO	NO	YES	YES	NO
G	YES+	YES	YES	YES-	YES+	YES	YES	YES
H	YES	YES-	YES	YES	YES	YES-	YES	NO
I	YES	NO-	YES	NO-	NO	YES+	NO	NO-
J	YES	YES-	YES	YES-	NO	YES	YES	NO
Summary	YES 100%	YES 80%	YES 100%	YES 60%	YES 70%	YES 100%	YES 90%	YES 40%

Conclusion

The recent out-migration of Hong Kong residents to Canada has presented challenges and opportunities for Chinese churches in the country. By utilizing diaspora missiology as a framework, this paper has demonstrated some ways in which these churches may have adapted to the unique needs of this growing population. As the global Chinese diaspora continues to evolve, it is crucial that Chinese churches remain adaptable and responsive to the changing needs of their congregations so that they may foster a sense of belonging and cultural identity among new migrants.

In conclusion, this study underscores the importance of understanding the complexities of Hong Kong's out-migration to Canada and its implications for the landscape of the Chinese church. By acknowledging these challenges and seizing these opportunities, Chinese churches in Canada can effectively support Hong Kong migrants, foster a vibrant faith community, and contribute to the continued growth and development of the global Chinese diaspora.

References

"Christian Witness to the Chinese." Lausanne Occasional Paper No. 6. *Lausanne Movement*, 1980. https://lausanne.org/occasional-paper/lop-6.

"Diasporas and International Students: The New People Next Door." Lausanne Occasional Paper No. 55. *Lausanne Movement*, 2004. https://lausanne.org/occasional-paper/diasporas-and-international-students-the-new-people-next-door-lop-55.

Ebaugh, H. R., and J. S. Chafetz, eds. *Religion and the New Immigrants: Continuities and Adaptations in Immigrant Congregations*. Walnut Creek: AltaMira, 2000.

Goodkind, Daniel. *The Chinese Diaspora: Historical Legacies and Contemporary Trends*. Washington, DC: US Census, 2019.

Levitt, P. *God Needs No Passport: Immigrants and the Changing American Religious Landscape*. New York: New Press, 2007.

Li, Peter S. "The Rise and Fall of Chinese Immigration to Canada: Newcomers from Hong Kong Special Administrative Region of China and Mainland China, 1980–2000." *International Migration* 43, no. 3 (August 2005), 9–34.

Overseas Chinese Affairs. "2022 Statistical Yearbook." Taiwan. https://www.ocac.gov.tw/OCAC/Pages/VDetail.aspx?nodeid=30&pid=313.

Poston, D. L., and J. H. Wong. "The Chinese Diaspora: The Current Distribution of the Overseas Chinese Population." *Chinese Journal of Sociology* 2, no. 3 (2016): 348–73.

Tan, Chee-Beng, ed. *Routledge Handbook of the Chinese Diaspora*. New York: Routledge, 2013.

Taylor, William D., ed. *Global Missiology for the 21st Century: The Iguassu Dialogue*. Grand Rapids: Baker Academic, 2000.

Tira, Sadiri Joy, and Enoch Wan, eds. *Missions in Action in the 21st Century*. Ontario: Filipino Intrenational Network and Institute of Diaspora Studies – Western Seminary, 2012.

Tira, Sadiri Joy, and Juliet Lee Uytanlet, eds. *A Hybrid World: Diaspora, Hybridity, and Missio Dei*. Littleton: William Carey Library, 2020.

Tira, Sadiri Joy, and Tetsunao Yamamori, eds. *Scattered and Gathered: A Global Compendium of Diaspora Missiology*. Carlisle: Langham Global Library, 2020.

Wan, Enoch, ed. *Diaspora Missiology: Theory, Methodology and Practice*. Portland: Institute of Diaspora Studies, 2011.

Yang, F., and H. R. Ebaugh. "Transformations in New Immigrant Religions and Their Global Implications." *American Sociological Review* 66, no. 2 (2001): 269–88.

Yu, L. "An Empirical Study of Recent Mainland Chinese Migration to Vancouver." *Journal of the Canadian Historical Association* 19, no. 2 (2008): 180–96.

劉思銘。〈塑造香港教會前景會議焦點小組研究報告〉。建道神學院。香港，[Shaping the Future of Hong Kong Churches], 2023.

3

Remittances and Asian Diaspora: Globalization, Deglobalization, and the Future

Prabhu Guptara

Many were thrilled, though others were perhaps stunned or astounded, to learn that total remittance flows to India between 1 April 2021 and 31 March 2022 were the highest received by India in a single year, according to figures released by India's Ministry of Finance.[1] But were these figures correct? Was US$90 billion the highest ever remittances by the Indian diaspora? Or was the correct figure 11 percent more than that – US$100 billion – as estimated by the World Bank last year?[2]

In view of this and other discrepancies, a caveat is in order: calculating remittances is an inexact art, just as calculating the number of migrants is an inexact art – both rely not only on the thoroughness and reliability of the records used but also on the definitions and criteria used.[3] While the broad direction may be clear, the details of such "facts and figures" are hard to verify. Facts and figures must be treated with caution, even skepticism, keeping in mind the adage "There are lies, there are damned lies, and then there are statistics."

---

1. Rahman, "India Received $90bn."
2. India West, "Unprecedented."
3. For instance, is someone born in the US to Indian parents a "migrant"? How about someone whose parents came from India two generations ago? What if one of the parents or grandparents is a White American? Or a Black American of slave ancestry going back to the eighteenth century? What if you are the grandchild of a second-generation Indian migrant to the Caribbean and a Spanish-background second-generation American from Latin America?

Interpretations of facts by commentators must also be treated with caution. For instance, a review of the literature suggests that there is evidence for two contrasting views. The first view suggests that remittances remain stable despite fluctuations in economic activity, which is beneficial to families and countries of origin.[4] The second perspective suggests that remittances are susceptible to economic fluctuations, which has significant effects on migrant flows and the welfare of families and countries of origin. Another aspect about which caution must be exercised is the future projections of current trends and the associated views and interpretations. Some comments in this chapter, especially in the final section, may fall into this category. Let us now turn to the available data, for which the primary source is the World Bank – rather than governments of individual countries – because of its objective nature and reliance on a large number of information sources.

Remittances to Asia: Why Focus on India?

Regionally, Asia receives the highest amounts of remittances, with India heading the global list over the last fifteen years. Clearly, Asian countries exhibit significant cultural, social, economic, and political divergence, which is impossible to describe in a short paper such as this. Therefore, this paper will focus primarily on India, making occasional references to other Asian countries when required.

Table 1: Remittances to Asian Countries

Rank	Country	Remittance Inflow (USD)
1	India	111 billion
3	China	53 billion
4	Philippines	38 billion
6	Pakistan	30 Billion
8	Bangladesh	21 Billion
10	Vietnam	19 Billion

---

4. Ratha, "Workers' Remittances."

Remittances to India: A Historical View

For a broader and historical perspective on the subject, let us take 1990 as the base year, when remittances to India stood at US$2.4 billion. Remittances then went up more or less steadily to US$10.3 billion by 1997. However, they declined to US$9.5 billion in 1998, increased again to US$21 billion by 2003, declining yet again to US$18.8 in 2004, then rose to US$70.4 billion by 2014, dropped by nearly 10 percent to US$62 billion by 2016, and have since resumed their upward climb. The purpose of this narrative is to show that when we consider trends over thirty years, we find that there are periods of stagnation, and reversal, as well as growth. The evidence also suggests that remittances have not resumed at all in some countries and, in some cases, remittances have remained stuck near zero for long periods. Why is this?

Remittances: An Analysis

Clearly, remittances depend on the ability to remit, which involves at least three fundamental elements: first, having surplus money after meeting one's requirements so that some money could be remitted; second, values and relationships that motivate a person to remit money; and third, the practical means to remit money. The third aspect is easily explored since most countries now have numerous channels through which money can be sent – this includes both financial institutions and hawala-type arrangements.[5] Since there is extensive discussion of these channels in the literature, the matter need not be addressed here. There is also sufficient discussion regarding the cost of transferring money, both in scholarly literature and in the popular media.[6] Therefore, a more useful contribution to the topic can be made by focusing on the second element mentioned above – values and relationships that motivate one to send money – as there has not been much discussion about this aspect. We should acknowledge, that there is undoubtedly at least some degree of affection or love between the people sending remittances and the people receiving them. However, in recent years, there has been a huge flow of money (nearly $159

---

5. A popular and informal means of transferring money, based on mutual individual trust and honor between the parties. It is outside and parallel to formal financial and remittance systems.

6. In December 2022, the global average remittances fee was 7.14 percent. Banks were by far the most expensive method to remit money, with the average fees being 10.8 percent. Money transfer operators charged 6.2 percent on average, while post offices charged the lowest fee of 5.5 percent. Although there are legal ways to pay lower fees by using channels that claim to charge minimal or near-zero amounts, such methods may pose higher risks for the sender, the recipient, or both.

million between 2001 and 2019 from seven Hindu charitable organizations in the US) into India that is motivated by a "spirituality of hate."[7]

The key factor behind remittances is the balance between income and expenditures. This can lead to savings as well as remittances. There is a limit to earnings at any given time, while migrants do have flexibility regarding expenditures. Perhaps that is most dramatically illustrated by reference to an experience from my own family history. During her final year of nursing training, my mother discovered that her parents and family had lost their small plot of land because my grandfather was cheated by a business partner who absconded. She remitted nearly all of her scholarship money to support her parents and siblings while she lived on three cups of black tea a day. Her family survived on her remittances. She graduated and secured a job that enabled her to continue supporting her family until each family member became financially independent.

In contrast, if relatives "back home" are not in a desperate situation, migrants are more likely to be inclined to invest their savings into their own lives and futures. In other words, migrants face the delicate and difficult task of balancing what they contribute to mitigating survival challenges "back home" and their own survival challenges in the country where they live as migrants. To summarize our discussion of the "values and relationships" factor that influences remittances, we may say that the key elements include the values of individual migrants, the individual migrant's closeness to people "back home," and the individual migrant's family conditions "back home." Since the best financial future for any individual or family is likely to be in one of the more economically developed countries, it is worth exploring how this factor influences remittances.

Where Do Remittances Come From?

Since there are approximately 3.9 million people of Indian origin living in the UAE and 4.4 million in the USA (2022 figures) and given that GDP per capita in the UAE is US$45,320 but US$76,622 in the USA, we should expect more remittances from the USA than from the UAE. The data shows that 23.4 percent of remittances came from the USA, 6.8 percent from the UK, 5.7 percent from Singapore, and 28.6 percent from what could be called an "Arab bloc"

---

7. Macher, "Hindu Nationalist Influence," 3. http://www.sacw.net/article14915.html. The "spirituality of hate" refers to the use of foreign funding by radical Hindu nationalists to persecute Christians and other religious minorities in India.

for purposes of this discussion: that is, 18 percent from the UAE, 5.1 percent from Saudi Arabia, 2.4 percent from Kuwait, 1.6 percent from Oman, and 1.5 percent from Qatar. Considering that the average educational and professional background of Indian-origin people in the UAE seems quite different from those in the USA, is it not surprising that 28.6 percent of remittances came from that Arab bloc? Is that wholly a matter of values and relationships as mentioned earlier? Or, despite the educational, professional, and openness-related matters referred to above, do brute numbers trump everything else? Interestingly, the Arab bloc has some 10.5 million people of Indian origin.[8]

What Are Remittances Used For?

The most extensive research on this topic seems to have been undertaken by Professor Prema Kurien (2008), who did ethnographic fieldwork on remittances in three village communities in Kerala, India. She concluded that how recipients spend the remittances received varies significantly "according to community cohesiveness and the cultural-religious background of villages."[9] In the Muslim village, remittances were distributed to the widest circle of people within the community to support caste-specific religious activities. In the Hindu village, migrant households spent large sums of money on caste-based life-cycle rituals that involved lavish gift-giving and entertaining. In the Syrian Christian community, the gains of migration were largely confined to the immediate family, for factors influencing upward mobility, such as education and dowries.[10]

Another important finding of Professor Kurien's research is that large-scale migration to the Middle East by relatively poor migrants, and their subsequent rapid enrichment, has resulted in a reconstruction of the ethnic identities of the three communities. Kurien found that in earlier times, it was the Syrian Christians who were instrumental in founding the first banks and joint stock companies in the state. As a high-status minority community, the Syrian Christians had a strong sense of ethnic identity and exclusiveness, which fostered a sense of mutual obligation. Over time, however, the Syrian Christians, who had been a devout, hardworking, and frugal farming community, turned to occupations in the tertiary sector, adopted a more luxurious lifestyle living,

---

8. The figures in this paragraph are from the 2021 report of the Reserve Bank of India on remittances, which was the latest available at the time this paper was written.
9. Kurien, "Socio-Cultural Perspective."
10. Rahman and Fee, "Understanding Remittances," 33–51.

and began to display a greater degree of individualism. All this brought about changes in their community identity. Their economic prosperity changed their earlier Puritan-like ethic to one that tended to be more complacently religious, viewing their economic success as a sign of divine favor. With the deepening of the nuclearization process, the ties between extended family members – which had traditionally been very strong – were weakened.[11]

On the other hand, Justin Sunny examined eight Kerala Migration Surveys (1998–2018), looking for interconnections among remittance receipts, household-level investment, and changing emigration patterns in Kerala.[12] This analysis revealed that remittances improved household per capita incomes and changed spending patterns, with a larger share of monthly income being allocated for the consumption of durable goods other than food. Remittances also enabled households to save and invest in assets such as land and buildings as well as in human capital through increased spending on education and health. Households that spent relatively more on education[13] and health reported a relatively higher share of skilled emigration to the Global North or Oceania regions,[14] as opposed to the traditional low-skilled emigration to the Gulf.[15]

K. C. Zachariah argues that despite the small size and declining proportion of the Syrian Christian community, their socioeconomic position transformed

---

11. Kurien, "Socio-Cultural Perspective."

12. Sunny, Parida, and Azurudeen, "Remittances," 5–29.

13. The distribution of emigrants by level of education shows that the share of emigrants with "up to secondary level of education" has been declining since 1998 – approximately 70 percent in 1998 to approximately 37 percent in 2018. In contrast, the share of emigrants with higher secondary or graduate-level education increased during this period, rising from 16 percent to 60 percent. This significant increase in educational attainment has been an outcome of Kerala's human capital investments over the years, as well as cultural movements led by figures such as Sree Narayana Guru, Vakkom Abdul Kader Maulavi, and Mahakavi Simon.

14. The share of emigration to Europe and the United States increased from 2.3 percent in 1998 to 7.2 percent in 2018. In addition, emigration to all other countries – including Oceania and the African subcontinent – increased from approximately 1 percent in 1998 to approximately 3.5 percent in 2018. These changing patterns in the destinations of migrants reflect the upward mobility of Kerala emigrants from low-skilled labor to "white-collar jobs" and professional work.

15. The changing pattern of emigration is also reflected in the employment status of emigrants. While the share of emigrants engaged in casual labor – including low-skilled technicians, drafters, salespersons, masons, plumbers, carpenters, waiters, cooks, and other helpers – has been declining since 1998, the share of emigrants in regular jobs – including government employees and private professionals such as doctors, engineers, scientists, professors, lecturers, teachers, accountants, lawyers, architects, and designers – has been increasing. The percentage of emigrants engaged in casual labor has decreased from about 44 in 1998 to around 12 in 2018. On the other hand, the percentage of emigrants working as nurses increased from 3 in 1998 to 9 in 2018. Similarly, the percentage of emigrants engaged in high-paid occupations increased from 40 in 1998 to 52 in 2018.

significantly between the end of the nineteenth century and the end of the twentieth century. At the end of the nineteenth century, they were a backward community. The 1881 Cochin State Census Report says that about 42 percent of adult men in the community were laborers, 32 percent were cultivators, and 18 percent were traders. Only about 0.33 percent of Syrian Christian men were in government service, with less than 0.50 percent of Syrian Christian men employed in the major professions of the time. The 1891 Census Report for Travancore describes the Syrian Christian community of the time as poor, with churches in dilapidated conditions and priests receiving no regular salaries.

By the end of the twentieth century, however, Christians had reached the top of the socioeconomic ladder in Kerala, having forged ahead of Kerala's Hindu and Muslim communities in terms of demographic transition, education, land ownership, housing, and ownership of consumer durables.[16] "The key driver behind the success of the Syrian Christian community has been their educational achievements."[17] The impressive transformational prosperity of Kerala Christians, and what Kurien referred to as "a reconstruction of ethnic identity" is an appropriate point at which to turn to some broader reflections.

Relationship between State Capture, Migration, Globalization, and Remittances

Global remittances have risen dramatically along with the growing number of migrants. Therefore, it is worth reflecting on the fact that migration represents, on one hand, the impact of state capture by elites or cliques – with the consequent pressures on groups of people who feel compelled to leave their own homeland – and, on the other hand, the impact of globalization, which has created unprecedented possibilities and opportunities for migration.[18]

Globalization and migration have not merely generated money. The societies from which migrants remit money may not all be as open as the USA, but they are generally much more open than the migrants' countries of origin – for example, India. This openness – even in countries that are far less open than North America, the UK, Australia, or New Zealand – provides greater opportunities for people of Indian origin to excel and advance in every profession and industry. This has consequences for the level of integration of migrants in

---

16. Zachariah, "Syrian Christians of Kerala."

17. Samuel, "Kerala Christian Diaspora," 41–43.

18. The "pull" and "push" factors that lead to migration and how those factors impact different ethnic groups are well portrayed in Kurien "Impact of International Migration," 110.

society, leading to migrants being either isolated, accommodated, integrated, assertive, or, following the rise of ideologies of hate, "integrated-assertive."[19]

Despite the openness and opportunities in the largest economies of the world, wealth concentration has accelerated over the last several decades, with 1 percent of the world population currently owning more than half of the world's wealth.[20] At the same time, in developed countries, the middle class – as well as the biblical values based on which the middle classes emerged[21] – have been squeezed, resulting in a decline in philanthropy as a percentage of GDP over the past few decades.[22]

Country-to-country aid has also declined, leaving foreign direct investment (FDI) and remittances as the two key reasons for hope that are celebrated by commentators who favor liberal or humane values. But the top four countries in terms of charitable giving by individuals as a percentage of GDP are still the United States of America, New Zealand, Canada, and the United Kingdom. Of these, the USA is head and shoulders above its nearest competitors.[23] Since drawing attention to such facts is psychologically fraught for some people and politically contentious for others, people tend to ignore such facts. Instead, they focus on less politically charged topics such as remittances and FDI, especially remittances which are easier to portray positively.

The World Bank estimates that about US$630 billion was sent in remittances to low- and middle-income countries in 2022, which is about the same as FDI in those countries. In 2022, remittances accounted for over 15 percent of

---

19. These terms are used in the following way in this paper: (1) isolated: in ghettos or bubbles but looked down upon by the host society; (2) accommodated: more or less in their ghettos or bubbles but also more or less accepted as being a part of the overall community or set of communities; (3) integrated: able to retain their individual sense of identity as a part of "their own bubble or ghetto" but, equally, accepted as being a valuable and valued contributor and participant in the country in which they are guests, settlers, or citizens; (4) assertive: as in the slogan "black is beautiful," standing up for the values represented by their own identity; (5) integrated-assertive: integrated economically and personally but also seeking to convert the values of the host community to their own specific and usually narrow values and working to convert other countries, including their own countries of origin, to the values represented by their own narrow identity.

20. Oxfam, "Richest 1%," https://www.oxfam.org/en/press-releases/richest-1-bag-nearly-twice-much-wealth-rest-world-put-together-over-past-two-years.

21. Holland, *Dominion*; Mangalwadi, *Book That Made*.

22. In the USA, the GDP per capita in 1960 was US$3,007 (I have not been able to find earlier figures), whereas the GDP per capita in 2022 was US$76,266 – this is an increase of around 25.5 times. Meanwhile, total philanthropy in the USA grew from US$333 per capita to US$1,204 in 2022 – that is, only about 4 times. Philanthropy Roundtable, "Statistics," www.philanthropyroundtable.org/almanac/statistics-on-u-s-generosity.

23. *Gross Domestic Philanthropy*, 3.

the GDP of twenty-five receiving countries. In the most extreme case, Tonga's remittances accounted for 49.9 percent of its GDP. While the misfortunes or mismanagement of the economies of such countries is discouraging, it is heartening to consider that such mismanagement is at least partially alleviated by remittances. On that note – which might be regarded as either good or bad depending on one's point of view – it is appropriate to turn to broader questions.

The Future of Remittances and Migration

It is undeniable that the wave of remittances and migration seen over the last several decades are the fruits of the post-WWII wave of globalization, particular since the 1980s. However, it is worth considering whether the beginning of the end of that era of globalization and the emergence of the new wave of Slowbalization[24] – though the more objective and elegant term is "deglobalization"[25] – did not formally begin with the introduction of the American Recovery and Reinvestment Act of 2009 and the Patriot Act of 2001 by the Obama and Bush administrations. These Acts were part of a massive stimulus package designed to favor US-produced goods over others. The "Buy American" provision of these Acts applied to public buildings and public works projects funded by the new stimulus package, compelling these projects to buy iron, steel, and other goods manufactured exclusively in the USA. Since then, the USA has moved more and more in the direction of protectionism and higher subsidies for its own industries, in a pale imitation of what China has been doing for decades, and both China and the USA have influenced many of their allies to follow this path of deglobalization.[26] The EU's subsidies are well-known, as are those of the UK, China, and India – although, in the case of the latter two, these subsidies involve the additional complication of cronyism.

Furthermore, China has been the production engine of globalization over the last few decades, but the major consumer has been the US. How can there be a return to a world of free-spending US consumers when a significant

---

24. CAF, "Gross Domestic Philanthropy," 3.
25. Gong et al., "Globalisation in Reverse?," 167.
26. The latest straw in the wind is: Kelly, "Japan Aligns," https://www.reuters.com/technology/space/japan-aligns-with-us-chip-curbs-china-some-tokyo-feel-uneasy-2023-07-24/.

proportion of US consumers are now bankrupt, unemployed, or earning low wages?[27]

Given current global trends, the uncomfortable truth is that not only are Foreign Direct Investment, Official Development Assistance, and philanthropy likely to continue shrinking in real terms per capita, but the number of migrants is also likely to decrease since ChatGPT and newer generations of artificial intelligence enable greater productivity with fewer people. In fact, we can foresee a future where near-infinite production of all goods and services is possible with the employment of near-zero numbers of people.[28]

Therefore, the quantum of remittances is also likely to shrink, possibly as early as within the next year or two, or perhaps some years later, and while a forecaster may rightly predict that this will happen, only a very foolish forecaster would attempt to pinpoint a precise date! To understand why remittances are likely to decrease, we must recognize at least three different dimensions. Most money is remitted by first-generation migrants. With the second generation, there may already be a substantial decline,[29] and remittances are likely to begin to fade with the third generation of migrants. While there is limited longitudinal research on this subject, it would be both interesting and useful to explore to what extent the continuation of remittances depends on the closeness of the third generation's relationships with their relatives in the country of origin, as well as with how connected the third generation is with other people from "back home" in comparison with the level of their integration with wider American society. Taking the example of Malayalam speakers from Kerala, South India, in the USA, the more the third generation knows

---

27. Around 17.75 million Americans were unemployed in June 2020, resulting in an unemployment rate of 11.1 percent on a seasonally adjusted basis. U.S. Bureau of Labor Statistics, https://www.bls.gov/opub/reports/minimum-wage/2022/. Almost half of all working Americans are in low-wage jobs. Picchi, "Almost Half," www.cbsnews.com/news/minimum-wage-2019-almost-half-of-all-americans-work-in-low-wage-jobs. Only a third of US consumers have zero debt. www.statista.com/statistics/944954/personal-debt-source-usa. The top 10 percent of households own 76 percent of all wealth in the US, while the bottom 50 percent of households own just 1 percent of all wealth, and 10 percent of Americans have negative net wealth. Kent and Ricketts, "Wealth Inequality," www.stlouisfed.org/open-vault/2020/december/has-wealth-inequality-changed-over-time-key-statistics.

28. Elon Musk is among the many experts who, in March 2023, urged a halt to AI training. Vallance, "Elon Musk." https://bbc.co.uk/news/technology-65110030.

29. Kurien, "Religion," 81–104; Kurien also reports that "following complaints from the second generation and some of their parents that the church should support projects in North America, the diocese initiated a mission to fishing communities in Mexico and a Native American mission in 2002" – clear evidence of diffusion of interest beyond India on the part of the second generation, which would inevitably impact remittances "back home." Kurien, "Impact of International Migration.

their own language and socializes with other Malayalam speakers, the more likely they are to continue remitting money to relatives and community service projects in India; but the more thoroughly integrated that generation is with non-Malayali American society – through marriage, friendships, work colleagues, relationships with neighbors, sports, hobbies and other interests – the less likely they are to continue remitting money back home.

Simultaneously, as people from even the first and second generations lose close relatives "back home" through death, the motivation to remit money grows weaker. In addition, when people "back home" are doing better economically, the less the need and motivation to remit money back home.

Do Remittances Also Have a "Half-Life"?

The concept of half-life may be useful in thinking about the future of remittances. What is half-life? In physics, it is the time required for half the nuclei in a sample of a specific isotopic species to undergo radioactive decay; in relation to pharmaceutical drugs, it is the time required for half the quantity of a drug or other substance deposited in a living organism to be metabolized or eliminated by normal biological processes; in the case of physiology, it is the time required for the radioactivity of material taken in by a living organism to be reduced to half its initial value by a combination of biological elimination processes and radioactive decay. Similarly, could we say that the half-life of remittances is one generation?

In a like manner, we can reasonably argue that remittances grow only because the number of first-generation migrants is still growing. The second and subsequent generations of immigrants who were born and raised in foreign lands do not sent remittances like their parents or Indian forebearers. In that case, the key question is this: Will the number of migrants itself continue to grow? I doubt this, partly because the world appears to be entering an age of deglobalization and partly because the latest generation of technologies makes it possible to produce almost infinite quantities of any product or service with hardly any humans needing to be employed.[30] Therefore, I fear that migration

---

30. That is one reason why more than one thousand technology leaders and researchers, including Elon Musk, recently urged artificial intelligence labs to pause development of the most advanced systems, warning in an open letter that AI tools present "profound risks to society and humanity." https://www.nytimes.com/2023/03/29/technology/ai-artificial-intelligence-musk-risks.html.

will decline rapidly and remittances will come to a grinding halt within, say, one-and-a-half generations after that.[31]

Conclusion

Many nonprofits and ministries are heavily dependent on remittances. This paper is part of a one-man campaign, spanning several decades, aimed at raising awareness about the impacts of deglobalization and highlighting how deglobalization fuels spiritualities of hatred, which make it increasingly difficult to remit money into receiving countries for constructive purposes, whereas money that supports crony-based regimes is allowed to flow in freely. Therefore, individuals and organizations in receiving countries might find it profitable to discuss the following questions: (1) What is the core of the organization's purpose or mission? (2) What activities lie outside that core and, therefore, should be discontinued as soon as practical so that money thus saved can be redirected to purposes that have some likelihood of safeguarding the organization's future? (3) Should an inventory of all assets – human, financial, and institutional – be conducted in order to rethink organizational strategy and undertake a program of action that could better fit the organization for a world of deglobalization and radically new technology? (4) During the period when remittances are still possible, should money allocated to materially unproductive activities be redirected to materially productive activities so that the nonprofits stand a reasonable chance of being supported from within the receiving countries themselves, rather than depending on continuing remittances?

While deglobalization will undoubtedly have many negative consequences, positively, it will expose the hollowness and inadequacy of many current trends in politics, economics, technology, and society. Depending on the choices made by global and national elites, there could be significant opportunities for genuine development and growth. In order to survive and flourish in the radically different future that lies ahead, organizations and individuals must be prepared to identify and engage in a necessary process of struggle.

---

31. It would be easy to get the contrary impression from the United Nations "Global Compact for Safe, Orderly and Regular Migration," which commits signatory Member States to "making migration work for all." However, there is a foreseeable risk that it could soon turn into an anti-migration forum. https://undocs.org/A/RES/73/195.

References

CAF, *Gross Domestic Philanthropy: An International Analysis of GDP, Tax and Giving.* West Malling: Charities Aid Foundation, 2016. https://www.cafonline.org/about-us/publications/2016-publications/gross-domestic-philanthropy.

Gong, Huiwen, Robert Hassink, Christopher Foster, Martin Hess, and Harry Garretsen. "Globalisation in Reverse? Reconfiguring the Geographies of Value Chains and Production Networks." *Cambridge Journal of Regions, Economy and Society* 15, no. 2 (July 2022): 165–81. https://academic.oup.com/cjres/article/15/2/165/6591934.

Holland, Tom. *Dominion: The Making of the Western Mind.* New York: Basic Books, 2019.

India West. "Unprecedented: Indian Diaspora Sends Home Record $100 Billion in 2022." *India West*, 5 December 2022. https://indiawest.com/unprecedented-indian-diaspora-sends-home-record-100-billion-in-2022/.

Jones, Claire. "Was Hyperglobalisation an Anomaly?" *Financial Times*, 17 November 2020. https://www.ft.com/content/a89f5911-5cba-4d62-8746-5213303a92ec.

Kelly, Tim, Karen Freifeld, and Kantaro Sugiyama. "As Japan Aligns with U.S. Chip Curbs on China, Some in Tokyo Feel Uneasy." *Reuters*, 24 July 2023. https://www.reuters.com/technology/space/japan-aligns-with-us-chip-curbs-china-some-tokyo-feel-uneasy-2023-07-24/.

Kent, Ana Hernández, and Lowell R. Ricketts. "Has Wealth Inequality in America Changed Over Time? Here Are Key Statistics." *Federal Reserve Bank of St. Louis*, 2 December 2020. https://www.stlouisfed.org/open-vault/2020/december/has-wealth-inequality-changed-over-time-key-statistics.

Kurien, Prema. "The Impact of International Migration on Home Churches: The Mar Thoma Syrian Christian Church in India." *Journal for the Scientific Study of Religion* 53, no. 1 (2014): 109–29.

———. "Religion, Social Incorporation, and Civic Engagement: Second-Generation Indian American Christians." *Review of Religious Research* 55 (2014): 81–104.

———. "A Socio-Cultural Perspective on Migration and Economic Development: Middle Eastern Migration from Kerala, India." Geneva: International Organization for Migration, 2008. https://www.ssrc.org/publications/a-socio-cultural-perspective-on-migration-and-economic-development-middle-eastern-migration-from-kerala-india/.

Macher, Jasa. "Hindu Nationalist Influence in the United States, 2014–2021: The Infrastructure of Hindutva Mobilizing." *South Asia Citizens Web*, May 2022. http://www.sacw.net/article14915.html.

Mangalwadi, Vishal. *The Book that Made Your World.* Nashville: Thomas Nelson, 2012.

Philanthropy Roundtable. "Statistics on U. S. Generosity." www.philanthropyroundtable.org/almanac/statistics-on-u-s-generosity.

Picchi, Aimee. "Almost Half of All Americans Work in Low-Wage Jobs." *MONEYWATCH*, 2 December 2019. https://www.cbsnews.com/news/minimum-wage-2019-almost-half-of-all-americans-work-in-low-wage-jobs/.

Rahman, Fareed. "India Received $90bn in Remittances in 2022, with UAE as Second-Biggest Source." *The National*, 18 July 2023. https://www.thenationalnews.com/business/money/2023/07/18/india-received-90bn-in-remittances-in-2022-with-uae-as-second-biggest-source/.

Rahman, Md Mizanur, and Lian Kwen Fee. "Understanding Remittances: Theoretical and Methodological Issues." In *Migrant Remittances in South Asia: Social, Economic and Political Implications*, edited by Md Mizanur Rahman, Tan Tai Yong, and A. K. M. Ahsan Ullah, 33–51. Basingstoke: Palgrave Macmillan, 2014.

Ratha, Dilip. "Workers' Remittances: An Important and Stable Source of External Development Finance." In *Global Development Finance*. Washington DC: World Bank, 2003. https://documents1.worldbank.org/curated/en/698051468128113998/310436360_20050014094932/additional/multi0page.pdf.

Samuel, Cherian. "Kerala Christian Diaspora: A Stocktaking." *FOCUS*, April 2023 Volume 11, Issue 2:41–43; https://issuu.com/diasporafocus/docs/focus_april_-_2023.

Sunny, Justin, Jajati K. Parida, and Mohammed Azurudeen. "Remittances, Investment and New Emigration Trends in Kerala." *Review of Development and Change* 25, no. 1 (2020): 5–29.

Thériault, Annie. "Richest 1% Bag Nearly Twice as Much." *Oxfam International*, 16 January 2023. https://www.oxfam.org/en/press-releases/richest-1-bag-nearly-twice-much-wealth-rest-world-put-together-over-past-two-years.

Vallance, Chris. "Elon Musk among Experts Urging a Halt to AI Training." *BBC*, 30 March 2023. https://www.bbc.com/news/technology-65110030.

Zachariah, K. C. "The Syrian Christians of Kerala: Demographic and Socioeconomic Transition in the Twentieth Century." Working Paper no. 322. Thiruvananthapuram: Centre for Development Studies, 2001. http://14.139.171.199:8080/xmlui/handle/123456789/219.

4

The State of the People on the Move: 2023 Update

Sam George and Bulus Galadima

We all are either migrants or offspring of migrants, regardless of how settled we think or feel. Migration is the common thread that runs through the human tale.[1]

Introduction

As Catalysts for Diasporas of the Lausanne Movement, one of our responsibilities is to keep track of information related to migration, refugees, and diasporas that is pertinent to the global church. This has steadily permeated into the ethos of the Global Diaspora Network (GDN), and we receive and circulate numerous emails related to the latest reports and reflections on global migration, diaspora communities, refugees and associated topics. These updates include news clippings, journal articles, book reviews, and doctoral dissertations on missions and theology about migrants, diasporas, refugees, etc. every week from all parts of the globe.

In recent years, with human migration becoming a global reality, there has been a surge of interest in the area of migration and an overwhelming amount of information on migration worldwide. Since diaspora studies is a multidisciplinary field, there has been a steady surge in interest from diverse perspectives. Although many of these studies lack theological and missiological reflections, they have provided fodder for deeper ruminations and the

---

1. See Miller, *Migrants: A Story of us all*; and Manning, *Migration in World History*.

development of practical understandings and missional implications. This annual report aims to distill these reports and developments to discern their implications for Christianity worldwide and consider how the global church can respond in effective witness to Christ among migrants and diaspora communities worldwide.

The aim of this report is to highlight key developments over the last year that have significant relevance to our constituencies – namely, churches, mission agencies, seminaries, and Christians at large. These latest figures and trends on global migration were distilled from various reports and a wide range of literature that is pertinent to mission studies and engagement with migrants and diaspora communities. This information was synthesized in consultation with our team and other key voices, including thought leaders, missiologists, and theologians who are interested in diaspora missions from diverse perspectives and locations. In keeping with the theme of the consultation this year on "Asians in Diaspora and Diasporas in Asia," this chapter derived from the presentation we made at the consultation which highlighted many themes related to Asia.

Annual Update on Migration and Diaspora Missions

In this chapter, we highlight three major global trends related to migration and diaspora peoples that are relevant to the fields of mission studies and missiology. We have organized these trends along the three current focus areas of the GDN diaspora agenda: economic migrants, international students, and refugees.

One of the significant demographic developments since our last report is that India became the most populous nation in the world, overtaking China for the first time. According to the United Nations Population Division, the population of India reached 1.426 billion in April 2023 and is projected to continue growing for several decades, while the population of China has begun to decline.[2] Changes in fertility rates and the aging of the population have enormous implications for migration out of and into a country. India's population surge, with a bulge of teen and young adult population with no viable educational or vocational avenues, is likely to lead to a record level of out-migration over the next decade. Other noteworthy trends include the population declines in Japan, Singapore, and South Korea, which are resulting in significant changes in the social and immigration policies of these nations.

---

2. United Nations, "India Overtakes China."

According to the latest World Migration Report of the United Nations, there were 281 million international migrants in 2022, which amounts to 3.6 percent of the world population, which represents about one in every thirty persons worldwide[3] and is an increase from previous years. In 2020, international migrants were 270 million, which represents 3.5 percent of the world population. In comparison, in 2010, there were only 220 million international migrants, about 3.2 percent of the global population, and in the year 2000, the figure was 173 million. In 2022, India was the largest migrant-sending country in the world, with 18 million migrants. Following India were Mexico with 11 million, Russia with 10.8 million, and China with 10 million migrants. The United States remained the largest migrant destination country in the world over the last fifty years and had 51 million international migrants as of 2022. The next most prominent destinations were Germany, with nearly 16 million international migrants, Saudi Arabia with 13 million, Russia with 12 million, and the United Kingdom with 9 million migrants. India was the leading recipient of remittances in 2022, receiving US$111.2 billion, while China was in second place with US$51 billion. While both India and China have retained these positions over the last ten years, India's remittance inflows surged ahead, China's declined after the COVID-19 pandemic. Other nations among the top five recipients are Mexico with US$42.9 billion, the Philippines with US$34.9 billion, and Egypt with US$29.6 billion. The next five nations in the list are Pakistan, France, Bangladesh, Germany, and Nigeria.[4]

The forcibly displaced population – which includes refugees, asylum seekers, and internally displaced people (IDP) – crossed the 100-million mark for the first time, reaching 108.4 million at the end of 2022, with 35 million of these being refugees. The recent wars in Ukraine and Gaza have forced a record number of people to seek shelter abroad. The wars and political instability in Syria and Venezuela have displaced several million people to other countries. The ongoing Ukraine-Russia war has scattered 6.2 million people globally, with another 5.1 million being internally displaced as of July 2023.[5] Asian hotspots include Myanmar and Afghanistan, while South Sudan has the highest number of displaced people in Africa. In 2022, the top hosting nations for those forcibly displaced were Turkey, Iran, Colombia, Germany, and Pakistan. Over the last two decades, there has been a sharp decline in

---

3. All figures in this section are taken from https://worldmigrationreport.iom.int/ or reports of the World Bank and other international agencies tracking global migration.
4. MPI, "Global Remittances Guide."
5. UNHCR, Ukraine Emergency report.

refugee settlements in the United States, while there has been an increase in Canada and some EU nations.

The third major focus area for the GDN diaspora agenda is international students, a segment that continues to exhibit robust growth and vitality after a recent decline during the COVID years due to widespread travel restrictions and the closure of foreign consulate offices offering visas to prospective students. In addition to traditional destinations like the United States, the United Kingdom, Canada, Germany, and Australia, there are emerging destinations for international students – for example, China, India, the United Arab Emirates, Qatar, and Singapore. Furthermore, several American universities such as Yale, Georgetown, Texas A&M, and Northwestern have established regional campuses in Asian nations such as Singapore, Qatar, and the UAE, allowing students to study closer to their homes in a culture closer to their own, at lower costs. Another observation is that in recent years, more Anglophone African countries have sent students to China than to the US and the UK combined, primarily because of scholarships and the prospect of jobs with Chinese companies working in Africa. While most traditional student ministry organizations across Asia remain oblivious to the need for international student ministries in their nations, some have begun to explore such possibilities.

The 2023 Open Doors report on international students noted that the United States remains the top destination in the world, hosting over a million students, with over half (52 percent) of them coming from China and India.[6] Similarly, the number of international students studying in Australia totaled 746,080 in September 2023, with nearly half of this number coming from China and India alone.[7] The United Kingdom attracted nearly 680,000 international students in the academic year 2021–2022, representing a significant growth of over 12 percent from the previous year. The top two countries sending international students were China (152,000) and India (127,000), while the top African nation was Nigeria (44,000), and the United States was the fourth-largest sender, with nearly 23,000 students enrolled in UK higher education institutions.[8] There are major shifts taking place in higher education that have great significance for academic diasporas. These include the introduction of online teaching, new learners, Artificial Intelligence, the knowledge explosion, pedagogical transformation, and new economic models. More people are likely to pursue education in diverse modes and in different places over longer

---

6. Institute of International Education, Open Doors, 2023.
7. International Students in Australia.
8. International Students in the UK.

periods of time than is currently possible. These developments are bound to disrupt higher education in significant ways in the coming years and change international student ministries in momentous ways.

Four Diaspora Mission Strategies

As shown above, this upward surge in human migration of every kind from and to every region of the world is a grave concern in some circles but also presents many opportunities in Christian missions. Christian responses in the wake of the growing diaspora phenomenon could be divided into the following four areas: (1) humanitarian assistance and advocacy; (2) evangelism, ministry among immigrants, and community building; (3) discipleship and mission training; and (4) ethical considerations and challenges.

First, the global church is ideally placed to welcome new immigrants and those who have sought shelter from troubles in their native lands. Christians are often compassionate and eager to offer assistance to marginalized or less-resourced communities "out there" in the world, but they may not be as aware or as enthusiastic to do the same in their own neighborhoods. This attitude arises from the notion of mission as something "out there in the world," which overlooks mission in their immediate neighborhoods. A first step to remedy this would be to meet and learn more about their new neighbors in migrant-receiving nations, particularly who they are, where they are coming from, and the conditions of their migration. Not all migrants are refugees or illegal migrants; some are highly educated professionals. Not everyone needs English as Second Language (ESL) classes or is seeking handouts since some may have completed advanced degrees in English and even have higher household incomes than Christians of the host nation. Migrant mission not only involves providing practical help but also advocating on behalf of immigrant communities to change existing laws and other provisions for newcomers, and there are several good examples of this in Uganda, South Korea, Malaysia, and the United States.

Second, most Christians perceive missions as sending or supporting missionaries in foreign lands or working among people of other faiths and cultures, and they fail to recognize doing missions among those same people who have now come to live among them. When the world is here in our own front or backyards, it offers amazing opportunities to mobilize and equip every member of the church to engage in cross-cultural missions without the need to travel to remote parts of the world or to obtain visas. The mission here is different from the mission out there as it is no longer limited to a few select professionals who are highly trained full-time workers with long-term commitments. This new world mission in our town, city, or state would require building cultural competency among our church members and seeking to understand more about the people who are coming to live in geographical proximity to our churches. Often, the uprooted people are more open to receiving the gospel in foreign lands than in their native places among their own people. Since it takes the whole church to reach the whole world, everyone in our churches needs to be equipped to proclaim and demonstrate the gospel to the world that has come to live next door to us, instead of limiting mission work to a few professionals who may reach fewer people in the far corners of the globe.

Third, since most of the immigrants are Christians or convert to Christianity after moving to the host country, it is common to see a proliferation of immigrant churches. These churches tend to be homogeneous, ethnocentric, language-based fellowships, which may or may not have official ties with churches in their ancestral homelands or with churches in the host countries. Most of these churches remain isolated in their respective silos, unaware of the presence of local Christians or other immigrant Christians in their host countries. These immigrants in these churches often experience a fresh or renewed commitment to their faith after moving to a foreign land because migration is a theologizing experience and culturalized religiosity acts as a powerful glue in community building when living among strangers in an alien culture. However, as their children assimilate into the dominant culture, these immigrants struggle with anxiety and fear because of the influence of friends and popular culture. The generational divide and the transition of church culture and leadership remain major challenges confronting immigrant churches. Thus, diaspora churches require a deeper understanding of the nature and purpose of discipleship and mission within their faith, an understanding that extends beyond their own communities and denominations so that they can become global Christians with a global kingdom mindset, nurturing healthy relationships with other Christians in their new land, their ancestral homeland, and elsewhere.

Fourth, geographical and cultural displacement creates many ethical dilemmas for both immigrants and host nations. The barriers of language, culture, and prejudice pose many problems for diaspora communities. Ignorance of legal pathways and necessary documentation requirements often prove challenging for vulnerable populations. Immigrants may feel torn between adhering to the laws of their host nation and maintaining their own moral beliefs and values, especially with regard to food habits, gender roles, family practices, and dress codes. In the workplace, they often face exploitation in the form of unfair wages, unsafe conditions, and discrimination. While some immigrants comply with legal provisions, others find them overwhelming or seek loopholes to bypass them. When they receive unfair treatment, many immigrants are reluctant to report this or to seek help because they fear repercussions or deportation. In addition, familial obligations to support elderly parents and relatives back home may conflict with their integration into the host society, resulting in feelings of isolation. Christians in host nations can play a vital role in helping immigrants navigate these ethical, social, and moral dilemmas.

Three New Focus Areas

In preparation for the Lausanne Congress 2024, the GDN has been in regular conversation with several mission strategists and scholars around the world whose area of expertise is diaspora communities. Many listening calls were conducted with church and mission leaders from every region of the world. A series of virtual meetings was held with mission educators from various Christian institutions and seminaries worldwide to discuss the diaspora mission agenda. Both these activities highlighted numerous issues pertinent to diaspora mission and underscored the great need for resources and training in this area.

When the diaspora mission agenda was first framed in Lausanne circles in 2010, it focused particularly on two groups: economic migrants and international students. Since then, both these groups have grown phenomenally in number and importance, receiving increased attention from mission communities worldwide. In response to a global refugee crisis in the middle of the last decade, refugee mission was added to this list of focus areas. We conducted research, developed resources, established or supported existing ministry networks, consulted with churches and mission agencies, coached field workers, trained leaders, and served in an advisory capacity to catalyze these issues broadly across the world in all three focus areas.

At the Korea Diaspora Consultation held on Jeju Island in August 2023, we launched three new focus areas in the diaspora agenda for the global church: Internal Migration, Human Trafficking, and Climate Migration. For each of these areas, we invited leading advocates and experts stationed in Asia to present papers, which are now included in this volume. These new focus areas intersect on many points, with all migration and diaspora communities, offering many lessons that can cross-pollinate and mutually enrich each other. All three issues are found in Scripture and are growing realities in the world today.

Over the last decade and a half, whenever migration was discussed in mission circles, the focus was primarily on international migrants; the movement of people within a geopolitical entity was generally overlooked as it does not involve international border crossings. However, internal migration has grown significantly over the last few decades and is vital to the study of migration globally. Most international migrants were first internal migrants, relocating from their places of birth and upbringing to the nearest town or city, which served as a launching pad for their subsequent overseas relocation. Thus, urbanization and city-making can be viewed as outcomes of internal migration, and lessons from diaspora missions can easily be applied to such realities, especially in highly populous nations with massive internal migration – for example, China, India, Nigeria, and Brazil. There are many similarities between internal and international migrations, which enjoy a symbiotic relationship.

The second new focus area is human trafficking, which is the forced displacement of individuals or groups of people – against their will or without their knowledge – by human smugglers for purposes such as prostitution, bonded labor or slavery, and domestic servitude. Some minors are sold by their parents, while others are lured by prospects of lucrative employment or marriage, and still others are tricked into the trafficking network for organ sale or to serve as child soldiers. Although some nations have strict laws against human trafficking, these laws are often difficult to enforce and, therefore, these crimes continue unabated and have reached record levels in recent times. Those trafficked abroad or to another part of the country seldom have in their possession their passports or identity documents and are not aware of their basic rights in these new places. Without knowledge of the language and without any friends or acquaintances, they become victims of perpetual abuse and bondage.

The third new focus area is climate migration, an emerging issue that does not appear in traditional diaspora mission conversations but is of critical importance for the church. As climate change realities become more evident and frequent around the world, these are likely to spark an unprecedented level of out-migration from regions that have become uninhabitable as a result of natural disasters and ecological crises. At this year's diaspora consultation, we partnered with the Lausanne Issue Network on Creation Care to research and present a paper on the emerging issue of climate migration.

Two New Projects

The GDN has been working on two new projects: official Lausanne position papers and a mobile app. At the Seoul Incheon Congress of the Lausanne Movement, we released two new Lausanne Occasional Papers (LOPs).[9] LOPs are missiological position papers on specific issues, built upon the larger framework of *The Lausanne Covenant* and Lausanne Congress statements that are relevant to all regions of the world. The previous LOP that related to the diaspora issue network of Lausanne was titled "The New People Next Door" (LOP #55), and it emerged from a meeting of the Lausanne Forum held in Pattaya, Thailand, in 2004 that was catalytic to the inclusion of diaspora missions in the Lausanne Congress in Cape Town in 2010.[10]

To generate the new LOP on diaspora missions, we consulted with previous Lausanne leaders and others who have served in this field. We reviewed all previous statements, literature, and other publications developed by Lausanne's diaspora team. Following the general guidelines for LOPs provided by the Lausanne content team, we engaged in several rounds of discussions to arrive at the broad structure of the new position paper. Our preliminary draft was circulated among the GDN executive team members and their feedback was incorporated into this position paper. Subsequently, during the annual GDN retreat before the diaspora consultation in South Korea, the team – in smaller groups – deliberated in detail and offered responses on the paper. A draft version was then sent to several mission scholars and practitioners for their comments and was also introduced at a few seminaries in Asia, Africa, and the US. An attempt was made to translate this version of the LOP into other languages to gauge its applicability in different contexts and languages. Finally, this paper, designated LOP #70, was launched in November 2023 by posting it on the Lausanne website.

Another exciting new project of the GDN this year has been the development of a mobile app called GMove. This app was officially launched at the South Korea consultation on Jeju Island and is now available worldwide to download as a mobile application for those who work with migrants and diaspora peoples. GMove is a free mobile app, available on both Android and Apple platforms, designed as a dedicated and secure online community to connect people working in the diaspora space. It was developed by Afrosoft IT Solutions – a mobile software company based in Kampala, Uganda and aims to disseminate relevant information and create an online community similar to popular social media platforms. Membership is free and linked to Google or other online accounts, allowing users to choose regional, linguistic, or thematic interest groups. They can post news items and reports related to

---

9. Lausanne Movement, "People on the Move" and "Forcibly Displaced People."
10. Lausanne Movement, "Diasporas and International Students."

global migration and diaspora ministries, access various resources, and view videos related to this topic. This app offers personal connectivity, broadcasts of upcoming events, and also shares new resources in the field of diaspora missions. We hope and pray that GMove will serve as an additional conduit for effective connection and collaboration on diaspora missions globally.

God on the Move

Finally, the annual update included a short review on *Motus Dei* (meaning, "God on the Move") – a theological and missiological framework for mission in the age of migration. God is not static, stoic, or stagnant but a moving being. Such a framing of these foundational doctrines of God, humanity, sin and salvation, missions, and other core doctrines have been developing over the last few years and have been globally disseminated through recent publications.[11] Any static conception of divinity makes God no more than an idol who is confined to space and time. Since we are created in the image of God, we are created to move. "I move, therefore I am" (*moveo ergo sum*). Migrants and diaspora communities are people on the move and they see the divine being as a God who is on the move. Movability is a characteristic of human beings since we are created "in the likeness of God," just like human rationality, relationality, dignity, identity, solidarity, freedom, worth, and other dominant interpretations of the image of God found in classical theological texts. The God of the Bible is not a tribal deity confined by geography, culture, or people, for God cannot be parochial and territorial by nature. Moreover, the Bible itself is diasporic literature, framed within stories of various forms of displacements. All key characters in the Bible were migrants or descendants of migrants.

The incarnation is divine displacement, where a God comes to pitch his tent among humanity to save them from their alienation, expulsion, and distanciation. Such a view of incarnation seeks to understand salvation in relational and motile terms as a transformative experience of moving from the kingdom of darkness into the kingdom of light to be adopted into the family of God. Soteriology cannot only be conceived as acquittal, expiation, justification, atonement, and redemption from sin and death – as commonly done in Western theological writings – but must also be viewed in relational, religious, and motion terms such as reversal of estrangement, alienation, ostracization, and contamination using ideations like brought near, reconciliation, purification, and restoration.

---

11. George, "God on the Move," 95–122.

Furthermore, this dynamic conceptualization of divinity gives nuanced meaning to the church as a gathered community that is to be scattered for the mission of God in the world. It reclaims Trinitarian foundations and reinforces relationality at the core of missiology, where discipleship is viewed relationally, emphasizing life-on-life learning and transformation to become more like the Master, for whom being matters more than doing. It breathes fresh wind into pneumatology and brings deeper vibrancy to Spirit-filled living. It creates a global framework for an "ends of the Earth" missiology where every place is both a mission field and a mission force and all communities of Jesus-followers are called to be discipled into a global movement. Such ecclesiology and missiology are intertwined as a dynamic scattering and gathering of the people of God, ushering in the kingdom of God in the world. This framework views eschatology as a final move, for the pilgrim people of God have no abiding city on earth but are "looking forward to the city with foundations, whose architect and builder is God" (Heb 11:10).

These conceptualizations need further development, and people on the move are ideally positioned to engage in such diaspora hermeneutical activities and the development of theological and missiological resources – not only for people on the move but also to help all people of God everywhere to be on mission with God in the world.

References

Australian Department of Education. International Students by State and Territory, https://www.education.gov.au/international-education-data-and-research/international-student-numbers-country-state-and-territory.

George, Sam. "God on the Move." In *Reflections of Asian Diaspora: Mapping Theologies and Ministries*, edited by Sam George, 95–122. Vol. 3 of *Asian Diaspora Christianity Series*. Minneapolis: Fortress, 2023.

———. "*Motus Dei* (The Move of God): A Theology and Missiology for a Moving World." *Pharos Journal of Theology* 102 (2021): 1–12.

Institute of International Education. "Report on International Educational Exchange." *Open Doors*, 2023. https://opendoorsdata.org/annual-release/international-students/#fast-facts.

International Student Statistics in the UK 2023, https://www.studying-in-uk.org/international-student-statistics-in-uk/.

Lausanne Movement. "Diasporas and International Students: The New People Next Door." Lausanne Occasional Paper No. 55, 2004. https://lausanne.org/occasional-paper/diasporas-and-international-students-the-new-people-next-door-lop-55.

Lausanne Movement. "People on the Move." Lausanne Occasional Paper No. 70, 2023. https://lausanne.org/occasional-paper/lausanne-occasional-paper-people-on-the-move.

Lausanne Movement. "Forcibly Displaced People." Lausanne Occasional Paper No. 78, 2024. https://lausanne.org/occasional-paper/forcibly-displaced-people.

Manning, Patrick, *Migration in World History*, 3rd edition. New York: Routledge, 2020.

Miller, Sam. *Migrants: The Story of Us All*. London: Abacus Books, 2023.

MPI. "Global Remittances Guide," Migration Policy Institute, https://www.migrationpolicy.org/programs/data-hub/global-remittances-guide.

United Nations. "India Overtakes China as the World's Most Populous Nation." *UN-DESA*, 24 April 2023. https://www.un.org/development/desa/dpad/publication/un-desa-policy-brief-no-153-india-overtakes-china-as-the-worlds-most-populous-country/.

UNHCR. Ukraine Emergency Report 2024, https://www.unrefugees.org/emergencies/ukraine.

Section B

5

Theology of Transnational Migrants as Kingdom Citizens

Tereso C. Casiño

The Bible is replete with narratives of transnational migration, beginning with Adam's descendants, through the generations of the patriarchs, the periods of the exile and return, and all the way to New Testament times. A theology of transnational migrants as kingdom citizens is rooted in biblical narratives. Transnational migrants hold "flexible citizenship" as they straddle both their adopted country and their homeland.[1] Consequently, people in this position may hold dual or multiple identities, depending on the number of countries they live in, the nature of their work, the circumstances they face, and the diversity of their environments. While adopting a new identity in their adopted country, they retain significant elements of the heritage of their land of birth.

This chapter outlines the processes leading to transnational identity formation and explores various interpretive frameworks for understanding the condition and plight of transnational migrants. It also considers pathways for inclusion of transnational migrants in the kingdom of God. The chapter concludes with a discussion of some implications for various disciplines that are affected by the realities of transnational migration.

---

1. Ong, *Flexible Citizenship*, 4.

Identity Formation of Transnational Migrants

In the process of identity formation, transnational migrants must navigate the complexities of citizenship and national identity. Crossing borders offers both challenges and opportunities – people either hold on to their heritage or surrender it for the sake of a new one. Wrestling with this reality is not easy, and transnational migrants must contend with the modification of their identity. Since ethnic identity is tied to a particular nation, an additional identity is developed through systematized processes that involve a plethora of linguistic nuances and descriptions. The construction of transnational identity is evidently a product of significant progressions and processes.

Flexible citizenship involves specific processes and multilayered understanding of culture. We see this in the lives of transnational migrants in the Bible – for example, the nomadic patriarchs like Abraham, Isaac, and Jacob, as well as others in the New Testament whose destiny and future were shaped by various circumstances and events. Among the many migrants in the Old Testament, Joseph the dreamer stands out. He went through specific processes that facilitated his dual identity – Hebrew by birth and Egyptian by tragic circumstances. Their thought patterns and behaviors underwent significant changes as they crossed geographic lines, settled into new spaces, learned new thought patterns and customs of other cultures, and strove to maintain boundaries.

Some degree of hybridity exists in transnational realities. Steven Chang observes that "it is now common to think that all civilizations and peoples reflect some degree of hybridity, and none can legitimately claim racial purity. Any claim of homogeneity must be viewed with suspicion because the mixing of races and cultures cannot be avoided in society."[2] In other words, the formation of transnational identity is a paradox with complex elements.[3] Hybridity highlights the often-complicated processes that transnationals must grapple with.

The first aspect is the reality of "transnationalization." As migrants move from their homeland to another place, they go through a process of maintaining transnational ties and practices that include a variety of exchanges in goods, services, capital, and ideas. Border crossing facilitates these exchanges as people move, either as a planned step or randomly, depending on events and circumstances. Some movements are favorable – for instance, for economic, trade, or educational purposes – while others are unfavorable – as in the case

---

2. Chang, "Hybridity," 37.
3. See Faist, Fauser, and Reisenauer, *Transnational Migration*, 2.

of human trafficking, smuggling, and adverse circumstances caused by wars, conflicts, persecution, or climate change.

The second element involves the creation of "transnational spatial spaces." As people migrate, they establish and develop social formations that result from their interactions with host people, which may include kinship groups, circuits and communities. However, people do not have to physically move or leave their homelands to *adopt and practice* a transnational mindset or lifestyle. They can also create transnational spatial spaces by interacting with relatives or friends who live in other countries. With advanced technology and social media platforms available today, these "stayers" can get a taste of what it means to live transnationally without leaving home and stay connected to migrants through networks of social relations. Peggy Levitt explains,

> One does not have to move to engage in transnational practices. Because people who stay behind are connected to migrants' social networks, they are exposed to a constant flow of economic and social remittances (or ideas, practices, and identities that migrants import) on a regular basis. Even individuals who have barely left their home villages adopt values and beliefs from afar and belong to organizations that operate transnationally.[4]

The third process is "transnationality." As people migrate, they establish connectivity with the host population. To survive and thrive, transnational migrants strive to build connections, spaces, and bridges across "national, ethnic, racial, and linguistic boundaries."[5] Connectivity is indispensable to avoid a vacuum in transnational identity formation and to lessen the impact of trauma and grief in border crossings. The degree of connectivity varies, depending on the extent to which migrants retain their heritage and assimilate sociocultural elements from other agents of the host society.[6]

A common practice among transnational migrants is to hold dual or multiple identities. This type of existence defies the extreme aspect of globalization that might prevent the retention of the original local identity. Transnationalism overcomes the danger of globalization, which Ji-Hoon Jamie Kim rightly iden-

---

4. Levitt, "Transnational Migrants," https://www.migrationpolicy.org/article/transnational-migrants-when-home-means-more-one-country/.

5. You, "Introduction," 2.

6. This also concerns seafarers who move across oceans and seas but do not necessarily live temporarily or permanently on shore outside of their homelands. For an extensive treatment, see Otto, who laments that "the majority of churches worldwide have never heard about churches on the oceans." Otto, *Church on the Oceans*, 103.

tifies as "homogenization." Kim explains, "Instead of celebrating our diversity, there is a tendency to downplay the differences and celebrate our unity."[7] In the New Testament, the apostle Paul is a good example of someone who held a dual identity. Despite his Jewish heritage, Paul was born in Tarsus, with exceptional proficiency in Greek on account of Hellenization, and asserted his Roman citizenship. Paul's focus was not on having two ethnicities but about maintaining a dual identity that allowed him to live in both worlds without disparaging either of these identities. Another example would be the Greek-speaking Jewish diaspora who maintained a dual transnational identity as Jews but lived in predominantly non-Jewish communities. These transnational Christians with Hellenistic Jewish origins contributed to the expansion of the early church (Acts 8:4–8; 11:19–21).[8]

Transnationalism is, therefore, intrinsic to the experience of migrants. In the life of Joseph the dreamer, he demonstrated that he was fully Hebrew and fully Egyptian. His dual identity was not a matter of preference but cultural and political convenience in a positive sense. Joseph was called a Hebrew when accused by Potiphar's wife (Gen 39:17) and was so Egyptianized as a governor that his brothers could not recognize him (Gen 42:8). Joseph retained his ethnic heritage while also benefiting from his adopted country. Dual identity worked to Joseph's advantage although, as Levitt notes, there are some unanswered questions regarding transnational existence:

> Are transnational practices primarily economic, or are other aspects of life also enacted across borders? How does their impact vary by type and level of social activity? Are transnational migrants only those who regularly engage in cross-border activities, or do those who remain behind also become embedded in the transnational social fields created by migration? What forms do different transnational communities assume? And, finally, what are the consequences of these arrangements for sending and receiving country life?[9]

---

7. Kim, "Transnational Identity Formation," 73.
8. See Santos, "Diaspora," 6.
9. Levitt, *Transnational Villagers*, 6.

Realities in Transnational Identity

As transnational migrants seek, adopt, and embrace a new identity in their places of settlements, they must grapple with various issues. Rogers Brubaker finds three core elements among the diaspora community that also apply to transnational migrants: dispersion in space (including those still within national borders), homeland orientation, and boundary maintenance.[10] Most migrants find it beneficial to adopt a transnational identity to help them face challenges such as racial attacks, discrimination, and inequality.[11]

The first generation faces its own challenges, typically in relation to linguistic, social, cultural, economic, and political adjustments. If they move to a place where the language is foreign, they may struggle to learn the local language as they interact with the host community. Even simple activities such as reading street signs and understanding directions can be stressful. Other challenges include selecting good and affordable schools for their children, finding a job, participating in civic activities, and dealing with culture shock.

The realities faced by the 1.5 and 2.0 generations could be different, although they bear some resemblance to the struggles of the first generation. The 1.5 generation lives in two worlds – the land of their birth and that of their adopted society. This generation may be described as "straddling transnational migrants," who contend with two intersecting worlds – their birthplace and their adopted society. Existential realities vary depending on the age at which migrants relocate. If they move as infants or toddlers, they may be raised closer to native cultures. However, if they move as teenagers or young adults, they face a new set of challenges as they must navigate life between two worlds or even multiple worlds. It is not uncommon for many of the younger generation to wrestle with the realities of transnational identity through bloodline, ethnic heritage, or generational association.[12] Because many of these younger people have not even visited the birthplace of their migrant parents, they find it difficult to establish ties with family members abroad despite the availability of current social media platforms. As a result, intimate social bonding with relatives living overseas is stressful.

Therefore, it seems easier for first-generation transnational migrants to maintain a strong link with their heritage than for the second and third-generations. In the case of the second generation, their identity often happens

---

10. Brubaker, "Diaspora," 5–7.

11. Kim, "Transnational Identity Formation," 74.

12. Levitt, "Transnational Migrants," https://www.migrationpolicy.org/article/transnational-migrants-when-home-means-more-one-country/.

by "extension" (by default) because of their parents. Although their attachment to an idealized homeland may be strong for the first generation it fades over time. Although still ingrained in their psyche, this longing may turn foggy as first-generation migrants experience memory lapses due to age and have to deal with pressing needs and demands of life away from their homeland. It is not clear for how long they can maintain this "boundary identity."[13]

Transnational migrants face several legitimate challenges. The first issue relates to *loyalty*. Can a transnational migrant be equally devoted to both their homeland and the new settlement? For example, can someone simultaneously be 100 percent Filipino and 100 percent American? What degree of identification should a person embrace to be considered a true transnational – for instance, should it be 50 percent original heritage and 50 percent naturalized identity? Do naturalization and oath-taking ceremonies bridge the gap between two worlds or multiple worlds? Will transnationals fight for their adopted county as fervently as they would for their land of birth?

The second issue relates to *civic duty*. Immigrants are expected to be responsible participants in their host society. Corporate citizenship is crucial for the active participation of people who hold dual or multiple identities. If transnational migrants are naturalized away from home and have pledged allegiance to their newly adopted nation, would they fulfill their duties as legal citizens of two contesting societies?

The third issue concerns *patriotism*. If a mainland Chinese immigrates to Canada, can such a person claim equal love for both countries at the same time, given the different political ideologies and ethical norms in these societies? In a hypothetical scenario such as war, which country would transnational immigrants defend? Would they stop patronizing Chinese products and support all-North American businesses? How would they effectively, efficiently, and realistically navigate between two competing ideologies? All these questions have significant implications for Christian migrants who wrestle with their residential and ecclesiastical identity.[14]

Hermeneutical Variables of Transnational Migrants

Quantifying transnational migrants remains a challenge because migrants may be core, marginal, or dormant members of a migratory community.[15] Her-

---

13. Cohen, *Global Diasporas*, 185–86.
14. Werntz, "Addressing Migration," 317.
15. These categories are applied to the diasporas, with fuller treatment, in Sheffer, *Diaspora Politics*, 100.

meneutical approaches used to identify and interpret the migrant experiences are wide-ranging. For one thing, the "socio-economic-anthropological hermeneutic" situates transnational migrants in terms of cross-border exchanges in family ties, goods, communication, ideas, transactions, relationships, and structured processes and events. There is a discernible link between the homeland and the settlement, which demands "that ethnic boundaries affirm a self-ascribed identity in both the migrant's society of settlement and society of origin simultaneously."[16] However, it is difficult to determine how many migrants actively hold on to their core transnational identity over time.

Another factor to consider in transnational migration is the "political hermeneutic." This is crucial because people with transnational identities are expected to abide by local, regional, or national policies and regulations. Every country has laws – even though these laws may not be uniform or parallel – that govern the movements of people. Some laws governing migration and diasporic actions are favorable, while others may be draconian – although effective in some sense, at least from the perspective of host governments. What applies to one nation may not be applicable to others. Circumstances regarding migration and refugee conditions could vary from one country to another, but the underlying realities are similar and identifiable. Each country crafts, implements, and evaluates policies according to its political climate.

Then there is a "theological hermeneutic" that views transnational migration through the lens of creation, specifically the concept of *imago Dei* (meaning, "image of God"). This theological hermeneutic is crucial for understanding humanity because it affirms that God created men and women in his own image and that every individual is precious to God. Therefore, people on the move should be afforded equal respect and dignity wherever they go and whatever borders they cross. Every human being, both migrants and their hosts, are created in the image of God (*imago Dei*) – regardless of race, ethnicity, social class or gender – and therefore possesses inherent worth, dignity, rights and responsibilities. Daniel Carroll insightfully writes, "For those in the majority culture, it can yield a fresh appreciation of the immigrant's value and promise; for the immigrants, its message is an encouragement to forge ahead and an exhortation to live well as God's representatives."[17] God values foreigners or aliens as much as the "native-born" for he commands his covenant people to love their neighbors – including people on the move – as they love themselves (Lev 19:34). The concept of *imago Dei* is the unshakable founda-

---

16. Castor, "Transnationalism," 573.
17. Carroll, *Bible and Borders*, 17.

tion for all human relationships, while the love ethic represents its highest practical expressions.

Additionally, the "missional hermeneutic" of transnational migration reveals God's heartbeat for all people. God's love and offer of forgiveness extend to everyone, regardless of ethnicity or race. Although sin entered and distorted human nature, God did not abandon humanity; instead, God initiated his redemptive plan immediately after human disobedience. However, the groundwork for this saving and reconciling work began even before the foundations of the world (Eph 1:4–10). God's design to save people from the bondage of sin, reconcile them to himself, and call them to ethical living, missions, and ministry encompasses all peoples, including transnational migrants. Mobility does not revoke people's access to saving grace. God's love is inclusive, offering people a pathway to salvation and reconciliation regardless of their socioeconomic backgrounds, ethnic and racial relations, cultural and religious systems, and spiritual conditions.

Inclusion of Transnational Migrants in the Kingdom of God

Biblically speaking, not all transnational migrants are currently citizens of God's kingdom.[18] The Bible outlines the pathway to spiritual citizenship. Transnational migrants could relate to the kingdom of God in various phases: *potential, positional, incarnational,* and *missional*. These stages apply to all transnational migrants worldwide, as well as to all humanity.

The *potential* phase provides transnational migrants with an opportunity to encounter Christ before, during, or after their experience of mobility. Although these individuals are not yet members of God's kingdom, they can have access to the gospel through interactions with followers of Christ throughout their life's journey. They may be "outsiders" to God's kingdom, but they could be exposed to the gospel as they work and live with people who are already citizens of God's kingdom. Their potential to become citizens of God's kingdom depends on the degree of exposure they have to the gospel and how they respond to the claims of Christ over their lives.

The *positional* phase describes transnational migrants as members of God's kingdom by virtue of their positive response to the gospel, their exercise of faith, and their act of repentance in their personal encounter with Christ. Their spatial mobility or border crossing does not in any way alter or affect their status in God's kingdom. These are people on the move whose lives have

---

18. For further discussion on spiritual citizenship, see Casiño, "Changing Identity," 69–94.

already been transformed by the grace of God. The Spirit of the living God sustains their spiritual position and condition.

In the *incarnational* phase, transnational migrants learn to embody the good news in their lives, both as a mindset and as a lifestyle. They live, laugh, listen, interact, and work with nonbelievers in a place away from home. They actualize grace and love in their words and actions, showing compassion and care, serving the weak and the needy, and helping to meet the spiritual, physical, and practical needs of others. Transnational migrants who live incarnationally possess a strong sense of empathy and desire to be witnesses for Christ whenever an opportunity arises.

The *missional* phase shows how transnational migrants understand that they are called not simply to salvation but also to participate in God's work of reconciliation in the world. Missions and migration go hand in hand in the spread of the gospel.[19] Transnational migrants who follow Christ are in a strategic position to be salt and light in their family, community, and society. They also strive to proclaim the kingdom of God in practical, circumstantial, and meaningful ways.[20] Moreover, the transnational migrants need to be trained to embody the motives, message, and methods of Christian mission, announcing the good news of Jesus.[21] As Miriam Adeney observes with reference to refugees,

> Like the rest of us, they are called to action because God is not static. He is not quiet. God is a mover. He acts. He is at work in the world. Most gloriously he moved when the Word became flesh, took on the form of a human being, and humbled himself to the point of death – and then exploded right out of the tomb because God is God over death as well as life. Such a God is not still. No, he moves – because he loves.[22]

Major Implications

In the area of *theological education*, seminaries should add diaspora and migration studies to their curricula to provide leaders with tools for effective intercultural ministry, including ministry among transnational migrants.

---

19. Walls, "Mission and Migration," 3–11.
20. Chang, "Opportunity to Mission," 145.
21. For an extensive treatment of these themes, see Dodson, *Unbelievable Gospel*.
22. Adeney, "Place Called Home," 169.

Student-leaders need to grasp the realities involving transnational citizenship and responsibility, cultivate intercultural intelligence, and be prepared to face the numerous challenges and missional opportunities involved in interacting with transnational migrants and the global diasporas that represent a diversity of cultures. Reflecting on theological education and mission, D. A. Carson argues that "if we are to interact with the culture in which God has placed us, we must try hard to understand the culture and be discerning."[23]

In terms of *church's contemplation and action*, pastoral caregiving and counseling among transnational migrants should include aspects such as self-care, mental health, trauma and healing, and emotional intelligence. Ministry to transnational migrants should be integrative and holistic, covering three interrelated levels: pastoral, spiritual, and theological.[24] A significant practical action could be extending hospitality to transnational migrants. Tabitha McDuffee aptly notes that the biblical practice of hospitality "is not simply entertaining our friends and family for dinner; instead, it is loving and welcoming complete strangers, even those whom we are tempted to fear."[25] To welcome strangers is to participate in God's mission in the world. The stories of the Samaritan leper, the Samaritan woman, and the Good Samaritan convey the biblical motif of *shamar* (שָׁמַר; keep). The Samaritans – with their transnational identity and cultural ties with the heritage of both Jews and Gentiles – offer a glimpse of how followers of Christ should consider a migrant "as not only a brother or sister but also as oneself and as a part of one's mission."[26] In other words, to welcome strangers unconditionally based on the practice of *shamar* is the most practical form of contemplation and action on the part of the church.

Concerning *missions*, followers of Christ must become more aware of the plight of transnational migrants so that they may seize both evangelistic and discipleship opportunities. Human mobility in different parts of the world presupposes the movement of grace as an expression of the God who moves. God meets people in their movements, which facilitates mission in motion.[27] However, not many local congregations are aware of the challenges and opportunities for missions involving transnational migrants. Elias Medeiros cautions, "Local church leaders must never make the mistaken assumption that everyone in all of our churches fully understands and lives out Christ's command to make

---

23. Carson, "Biblical Theology of Education," 206.
24. See Groody, *Theology of Migration*.
25. McDuffee, "Becoming a Welcomer," 134.
26. Fong, "Christians' Roles," 600.
27. On this theme, see Matenga and Gold, *Mission in Motion*.

disciples of all nations."[28] Churches should know where transnational migrants live and work, connect with them, reach out to them, and serve alongside them. For too long, outreach efforts among transnational migrants by many receiving nations have not been intentional. J. D. Payne observes, "Transnational missions recognizes that reaching migrants in the host countries is critical to reaching people in their social networks across the globe."[29]

As far as *policy-making* goes, government leaders should be aware of the plight of transnational migrants. The church can initiate meaningful and productive conversations with those in government to advocate for effective and proactive policies that would benefit transnational migrants. These policies should be crafted and implemented to ensure that people on the move become good citizens of the land without abandoning their ethnic, cultural, and linguistic heritage. Laws should be enacted to ensure equal access to social services for both natives and migrants, while ensuring that policies leading to dependency and reliance on handouts are avoided. Reasonable policies on integration and assimilation would provide transnational migrants with the tools for success and functionality in their new society.

Conclusion

The plight and conditions of transnational migrants are not always ideal but can be improved. The church should view transnational migrants as potential members of the kingdom of God, who must also become good citizens of their adopted society. A call to action is long overdue. Now is the time to increase efforts in reaching out to transnational migrants with the good news that the kingdom of God offers. Whenever people move, the gospel also advances to make a life-changing impact on the lives of transnational migrants.

---

28. Medeiros, "Local Churches," 222.
29. Payne, *Strangers Next Door*, 126.

References

Adeney, Miriam. "A Place Called Home." In *Refugee Diaspora: Missions amid the Greatest Humanitarian Crisis of Our Times*, edited by Sam George and Miriam Adeney, 167–74. Pasadena: William Carey, 2018.

Brubaker, Rogers. "The 'Diaspora' Diaspora." *Ethnic and Racial Studies* 28, no. 1 (January 2005): 1–19.

Carroll R., M. Daniel. *The Bible and Borders: Hearing God's Word on Immigration*. Grand Rapids: Brazos, 2020.

Carson, D. A. "A Biblical Theology of Education." *Evangelical Review of Theology* 47, no. 3 (August 2023): 199–210.

Casiño, Tereso C. "Changing Identity and Disrupted Belongingness: A Theology of Nations, Citizenship, and Transnationalism." In *Reflections of Asian Diaspora: Mapping Theologies and Ministries*, edited by Sam George, 69–94. Minneapolis: Fortress, 2022.

Castor, Trevor. "Transnationalism, Identity, and Virtual Space: A Case Study of One Woman's Attempt to Negotiate Two Worlds." In *Scattered and Gathered: A Global Compendium of Diaspora Missiology*, edited by Sadiri Joy Tira and Tetsunao Yamamori, 569–78. Revised and updated. Carlisle: Langham Global Library, 2020.

Chang, Steven S. H. "Hybridity and the Gentile Mission in Matthew's Genealogy of Christ." In *A Hybrid World: Diaspora, Hybridity, and Missio Dei*, edited by Sadiri Joy Tira and Juliet Lee Uytanlet, 31–44. Pasadena: William Carey, 2020.

———. "From Opportunity to Mission: Scattering for the Gospel in the New Testament Story." In *Scattered and Gathered: A Global Compendium of Diaspora Missiology*, edited by Sadiri Joy Tira and Tetsunao Yamamori, 131–48. Revised and updated. Carlisle: Langham Global Library, 2020.

Cohen, Robin. *Global Diasporas: An Introduction*. Seattle: University of Washington Press, 1997.

Dodson, Jonathan. *The Unbelievable Gospel: Say Something Worth Believing*. Grand Rapids: Zondervan, 2014.

Faist, Thomas, Margit Fauser, and Eveline Reisenauer. *Transnational Migration*. Malden: Polity Press, 2013.

Fong, Paul C. "An Understanding of Christians' Roles in Human Migration through the Biblical Theme of Shamar: From Genesis to the Good Samaritan." *Religions* 14, no. 5 (May 2023): 600.

Groody, Daniel G. *A Theology of Migration: The Bodies of Refugees and the Body of Christ*. Maryknoll: Orbis Books, 2022.

Kim, Ji-hoon Jamie. "Transnational Identity Formation of Second-Generation Korean-Americans Living in Korea." *Torch Trinity Journal* 13, no. 1 (30 May 2010): 70–82.

Levitt, Peggy. "Transnational Migrants: When 'Home' Means More Than One Country." *Migration Policy Institute*, 1 October 2004. https://www.migrationpolicy.org/article/transnational-migrants-when-home-means-more-one-country/.

———. *The Transnational Villagers*. Los Angeles: University of California Press, 2001.

Matenga, Jay, and Malcolm Gold. *Mission in Motion: Speaking Frankly of Mobilization.* Pasadena: William Carey, 2016.

McDuffee, Tabitha. "Becoming a Welcomer: Practical Ways to Serve Refugees and Obey Scripture." In *Refugee Diaspora: Missions amid the Greatest Humanitarian Crisis of Our Times*, edited by Sam George and Miriam Adeney, 133–42. Littleton: William Carey, 2018.

Medeiros, Elias. "Local Churches in Missional Diasporas." In *Scattered and Gathered: A Global Compendium of Diaspora Missiology*, edited by Sadiri Joy Tira and Tetsunao Yamamori, 213–24. Revised and updated. Carlisle: Langham Global Library, 2020.

Ong, Aihwa. *Flexible Citizenship: The Cultural Logics of Transnationality*. Durham: Duke University Press, 1999.

Otto, Martin. *Church on the Oceans: A Missionary Vision for the 21st Century*. Carlisle: Piquant, 2007.

Payne, J. D. *Strangers Next Door: Immigration, Migration and Mission*. Downers Grove: InterVarsity Press, 2012.

Santos, Narry F. "Diaspora in the New Testament and Its Impact on Christian Mission." *Torch Trinity Journal* 13, no. 1 (May 2010): 3–18.

Sheffer, Gabriel. *Diaspora Politics: At Home Abroad*. New York: Cambridge University Press, 2003.

Walls, Andrew F. "Mission and Migration: The Diaspora Factor in Christian History" in *Global Diasporas and Mission,* eds. Chandler Im and Amos Yong. Oxford: Regnum, 2014, 19–37.

Werntz, Myles. "First words . . . Addressing Migration among Christian Audiences: A Modest Proposal." *Review & Expositor* 115, no. 3 (August 2018): 317–20.

You, Xiaoye. "Introduction – Making a Transnational Turn in Writing Education." In *Transnational Writing Education: Theory, History, and Practice*, edited by Xiaoye You, 1–18. New York: Routledge, 2018.

6

Hospitality and *Imago Dei* in the Bible

Yoon Jong Yoo

Introduction

This chapter explores recent exegetical studies of Genesis 1:26–28 concerning the *imago Dei*. It also shows how *imago Dei* is relevant to the issue of hospitality – as seen in Abraham's story in Genesis 18–19 – and contributes to migration theology. Migration theology is closely connected to the biblical tradition of hospitality. Hospitality is "the act of being friendly and welcoming to guests and visitors."[1] It should be noted that the emphasis on hospitality is present across every genre of the Old Testament – Torah, Nevi'im, and Ketuvim – as well as the New Testament. This affirms that although hospitality is not always given the attention it deserves, it is one of the most important themes of the Bible.

It is widely agreed that in the creation story of Genesis 1, the creation of human beings is the climax of God's creative work. In Genesis 1:26–28, humankind is created in God's "image" and "likeness," which is the most significant distinction between human beings and other creatures. This declaration contains a fundamental principle of God's relationship with humanity, affirming that *imago Dei* symbolizes fundamental human dignity, irrespective of race, belief, or culture. Although numerous studies have explored the meaning of *imago Dei*, a definitive resolution remains elusive. In the context of the ancient Near East, it is well-documented that a king was seen as possessing a divine image, thereby legitimizing kingship and authority to rule over the state. From

---

1. https://dictionary.cambridge.org/dictionary/english/hospitality.

an interpretative standpoint, being created in God's image and likeness implies that human beings are fashioned as co-regents who bear the responsibilities of rulers in managing God's created world. This declaration also points to the inherent dignity of every human being. An exegetical examination of the phrases "image" and "likeness" in Genesis 1:26 and "rule" and "subdue" in Genesis 1:28 sheds light on these aspects. Furthermore, this chapter demonstrates that as a ruler, a human being can either be a benevolent ruler or a tyrant, highlighting the potential outcomes of exercising this role. In the Christian tradition, Abraham is revered as a model of both action (Jas 2:21–24) and faith (Rom 4:13). He is often interpreted as a figure who exemplified hospitality to strangers (Gen 18), and hospitality is deemed as hosting angels (Heb 13:2). This underscores the significance of Abraham's hospitality, setting him apart from the people of Sodom, who lacked such hospitality.

This chapter proposes that Abraham serves as a model for those who succeed the first human beings created in God's image – that is, with *imago Dei* – and fulfills the royal obligations presented in Genesis 1:26–28 through his practice of hospitality toward strangers. It also suggests that the concepts of God's image (*ṣelem*) and likeness (*dĕmût*) in the creation story are transformed into justice (*mišpaṭ*) and righteousness (*ṣedekah*) within the context of salvation history. Consequently, this reveals the link between the concept of *imago Dei* in Genesis 1:26–28 and hospitality in Abraham's story.

Imago Dei and Royal Obligation in Genesis 1:26–28

The term *imago Dei* (God's image) originates from the account of the creation of human beings in the first chapter of Genesis:

> Then God said, "Let us make mankind in our image, in our likeness, so that they may rule over the fish in the sea and the birds in the sky, over the livestock and all the wild animals, and over all the creatures that move along the ground." So God created mankind in his own image, in the image of God he created them; male and female he created them. God blessed them and said to them, "Be fruitful and increase in number; fill the earth and subdue it. Rule over the fish in the sea and the birds in the sky and over every living creature that moves on the ground." (Gen 1:26–28)

The interpretation of Genesis 1:26–28 raises two key issues relevant to this paper. The first issue concerns the meaning and theological significance of *ṣelem* and *dĕmût*, typically translated as "image" and "likeness." This leads us to inquire about the meaning of these terms and, consequently, the meaning of *imago Dei*. The second issue involves understanding the meaning of the verb *rdh* (rule) in verses 26 and 28 and *kbš* (subdue) in verse 28. The meanings of these two words are crucial for comprehending the role of human beings in God's created world.[2]

Image (ṣelem) and Likeness (dĕmût)

The concept that a human being is created in God's image is mentioned only three times in the Old Testament (Gen 1:26–27; 5:1; 9:6). It is also found twice in the apocryphal writings (Wis 2:23; Sir 17:3–4) and twice in the New Testament (1 Cor 11:7; Jas 3:9). It is widely acknowledged that the two Hebrew words *ṣelem* and *dĕmût* are very difficult to define. The root of *ṣelem* denotes "something carved or hewn," indicating an "image, statue, and idol."[3] Consequently, it is commonly understood that being created in God's image implies a physical resemblance between God and a human being. This interpretation finds support in the terminology used in Genesis 5:3 – "he had a son in his own likeness" (*dĕmût*) and "in his own image" (*ṣelem*) – which suggests that Adam's son bore a resemblance (εἰκών in LXX, meaning "icon") to him. In other biblical texts, *ṣelem* is also used to describe the idolatrous images that were to be destroyed (Num 33:52; 2 Kgs 11:18; Ezek 7:20; 16:17; 23:14; Amos 5:26).[4] In two instances in Psalms (39:7; 73:20), *ṣelem* is paralleled with vanity and dream, conveying the notion of insubstantiality. In 1 Samuel 6:5, 11, *ṣelem* is used three times to represent the physical forms of tumors and mice. Notably, in the Old Testament, *ṣelem* predominantly refers to substantial images or statues. The word *dĕmût* – although considered less significant – is also a subject of controversy. It is derived from the root *dmh*, meaning "be like or resemble." Thus, *dĕmût* is translated as "likeness," implying a less degree of substantiality than the term "image." The use of *dĕmût* weakens the concept of the substantial understanding of *ṣelem*. The term *dĕmût* frequently appears in Ezekiel 1–10 (1:5, 10, 13, 16, 22, 26, 28; 8:2; 10:21–22), where the prophet never explicitly states that he saw God but, rather, expresses ambiguity in theophanic experi-

---

2. Misinterpretation and misapplication of these two words have led to destructive ecological behaviors. See White Jr., "Historical Roots," 1203–7.

3. *HALOT*, 1028–29. The root *ṣlm* does not occur in verbal form.

4. Hamilton, *Genesis: Chapters 1–17*, 134.

ences.⁵ Hence, it is sometimes suggested that the term *děmût* is employed to avoid attributing a concrete and substantial image to God.

The physical understanding of *ṣelem* and *děmût* aligns with the ancient Near Eastern texts. In an Aramaic inscription the words *dmwt'* and *ṣlm* – similar to the Hebrew words *ṣelem* and *děmût* – appear with the meaning "stone statue," which is the only occurrence of these words as a pair outside of the Old Testament.⁶ However, this physical understanding is considered anthropomorphism, which contradicts the theology of the so-called Priestly writings of the Bible, including Genesis 1:1–2:4a.⁷

It is important to note that the concept that a human being is created in God's image is also found in ancient Near Eastern texts. In these texts, it is common for a king to possess a divine image, which represents the king's authorized power in the royal ideology of ancient Egypt and Mesopotamia. A king with a divine image is seen as God's representative in the world.⁸ Consequently, it can be argued that the idea of a human being created in God's image and likeness in Genesis 1:26–28 is in line with the royal theology of the ancient Near East. Notably, while only a king possesses a divine image in ancient Near Eastern texts, Genesis declares that all human beings are created in God's image and likeness. This signifies that the Old Testament teaches that every human has a royal quality, whereas ancient Near Eastern texts convey that common people are created to carry out the work of minor gods.⁹ The ancient Near Eastern concept that only a king has a divine image is contrasted with the Old Testament declaration that every human being is created in God's image. This suggests that every human being is elevated to a position of kingship in Israel.

Although the exact meaning of God's image presented in Genesis 1:26 is not made explicit, numerous interpretations have been proposed to explain its definition, often overlooking biblical exegetical works. However, Claus Westermann provides a comprehensive summary of the identity of the image of God, which he says includes the following: (1) the supernatural likeness of human beings to God, (2) spiritual qualities or capacities, (3) the external form, (4) the whole person, encompassing both the corporal and spiritual aspects, (5) the person as God's counterpart, and (6) the person as God's representative

---

5. Hamilton, 136.

6. Millard and Bordreuil, "Statue from Syria," 140.

7. Although there is no scholarly consensus on the reliability of the documentary theory regarding the formation of the Pentateuch, most commentators agree that Genesis 1:1–2:4a has a strong connection with the anti-Babylonian context of the exilic period.

8. Dick, *Born in Heaven*, 8; Also, see Walls, *Cult Image*.

9. Walton, *Ancient Near Eastern Thought*, 203–10.

on earth.[10] While the Bible does not define what *ṣelem* and *dĕmût* mean, it is evident that being created in God's image and likeness is what distinguishes human beings from other creatures. Therefore, it is necessary to interpret *ṣelem* and *dĕmût* in a relational sense, rather than solely in a physical sense. It has also been suggested that God's image and likeness in a human being indicates that the human being, as a king, plays the role of an intermediary between God and other creatures.

Rule (rdh) and Subdue (kbš)

The relationship between human beings and other creatures is expressed in Genesis 1:26 and 1:28 through use of the verb *rdh* in verse 26 and the verbs *kbš* and *rdh* in verse 28. Therefore, it is necessary to determine the exact meaning of these verbs and consider whether they encompass exploitative forces or not. This requires investigating the precise meaning and usage of the verbs *rdh* and *kbš* in the Old Testament.

According to the *Theological Dictionary of the Old Testament*, the root *rdh* occurs twenty-seven times in the Old Testament, with twenty-five of these occurrences being in verbal form. The root has two different meanings: *rdh* I, meaning "rule," with twenty-two occurrences, and *rdh* II, meaning "take" or "seize," with three occurrences.[11] Among the twenty-two instances of *rdh* I, controversial passages such as Judges 5:13 (two occurrences) and Lamentation 1:13 are excluded,[12] leaving nineteen examples for interpretation. Apart from Genesis, *rdh* I appears seventeen times in various contexts: (a) relating to human relationships (Lev 25:43, 46, 53); (b) chief officers overseeing laborers (1 Kgs 5:16; 9:23; 2 Chr 8:10); (c) kingship over subjects (1 Kgs 4:24); Ezek 34:4; Ps 72:8; 110:2) or over other countries (Lev 26:17; Num 24:19; Neh 9:28; Ps 68:27); Isa 14:2, 6; Ezek 29:15). In analyzing the texts where *rdh* is used, Zobel notes that "most of the texts using *rdh* appear to be concentrated around statements concerning kings. In these contexts, *rdh* is usually constructed with b^e."[13] This suggests that the writer of Genesis deliberately chose royal vocabulary to describe the role of a human being as king over other creatures. It is impor-

---

10. Westermann, *Genesis 1–11*, 148–55.

11. H. J. Zobel, "rādāh" *TDOT* 13:330. The root II is attested in Judges 14:9 (x2) and Jeremiah 5:31. The exact meaning of Jeremiah is still controversial.

12. On the complexity and controversiality of the root *rdh*, see *HALOT*, 1190.

13. Zobel, "rādāh," *TDOT* 13:332–33.

tant to note that the verb *rdh* does not always carry a positive connotation. For instance, Ezekiel 34:4 conveys a negative force translated as "rule harshly."

It is worth noting that the word *kbš* conveys a more oppressive force than *rdh*. It occurs fourteen times in the Old Testament. Apart from Genesis, it appears in the following contexts: (a) referring to making someone a slave (2 Chr 28:10; Neh 5:5 [x2]; Jer 34:11, 16); (b) describing sexual abuse (Esth 7:8); (c) treading (iniquities) underfoot (Mic 7:19; Zech 9:15); (d) denoting military conquest of land (Num 32:22, 29; Josh 18:1; 2 Sam 8:11; 1 Chr 22:18). The word *kbš* represents "violence or subduing by force." Interestingly, the word *kbš* is not uncommon in royal vocabulary since it is used to describe a king's subduing of other lands (2 Sam 8:11; 1 Chr 22:18), although it does denote the use of violent force.

A Human Being with Imago Dei *and Royal Obligations*

As explained previously, Genesis 1:26–28 states that every human being is created in God's image and likeness. It describes every human being as having a divine trait, worthy of being regarded as a ruler. However, in the ancient Near East, especially in ancient Mesopotamia, divine image and likeness were attributes reserved only for kings. The Hebrew verbs *rdh* and *kbš* are used to describe the relationship between a human being and other creatures of the world. The verb *rdh* is strongly connected to a king's positive action of ruling over his subjects. Hamilton puts it like this: "Thus, like 'image,' exercise dominion reflects royal language. Man is created to rule. But this rule is to be compassionate and not exploitative. Even in the garden of Eden he who would be lord of all must be servant of all."[14]

Undoubtedly, being created in God's image and likeness is the fundamental reason human beings are regarded as distinct from other creatures in the world. This explains why a human being's role is described using royal vocabulary. As Hamilton says, "Man is created to rule, but this rule is to be compassionate and not exploitative." A human being, as a king, has the capacity to be either compassionate or exploitative in how they manage the world. The relationship between a human being as a king and other created creatures is described using the verbs *rdh* and *kbš*. Therefore, it is necessary to investigate the royal usages of these two verbs in the Old Testament to fully understand the role of a human being as a king in the created world.

---

14. Hamilton, *Genesis: Chapters 1–17*, 138.

Kingship was a prominent political system in the ancient Near East, dating back to around 3000 BC. Following the historical crisis caused by the Philistines, Israel also adopted a kingly order (1 Sam 8). As representatives of their states, kings were held responsible for the care of their people in military, economic, and political matters. However, like other monarchies, the kings of Israel and Judah often failed to fulfill the expectations placed upon them by God. Only a few kings, such as Hezekiah and Josiah, were considered good kings. Others, like Ahab of Israel and Jehoiakim of Judah, were regarded as despots or tyrants. It should be noted that kingship itself does not guarantee the fulfillment of God's words, the well-being of the people, or order in the world. To justify and legitimize kingship, royal ideologies were developed in the ancient Near East. The most common royal ideology was the theocracy, in which a king, instead of a god, held the authority to rule a state. Kings were considered adopted sons of gods in Mesopotamia and regarded as the true embodiment of the deity Horus in Egypt. By proclaiming sonship or divine characteristics, they were seen as intermediaries between the heavenly gods and the people of the land. In ancient Mesopotamia, the king, as an essential symbol of the social system, worked toward establishing and maintaining order. The core values of kingship, as noted in ancient Sumerian and Akkadian literary texts, were known as *kittum* and *mešarum*, which represented divine and cosmic order as the king's responsibility. A similar concept, known as *ma'at*, exists in ancient Egyptian texts. These terms *kittum*, *mešarum*, and *ma'at* are often translated as "justice."[15] However, their exact sense is difficult to grasp as they have broad connotations, encompassing the wholeness or completeness of the cosmic order.

In the Old Testament, a king's primary responsibility often revolved around "justice and righteousness." The concept that an ideal king is expected to administer justice and righteousness is particularly evident in the book of Isaiah, with its anticipation of a messianic king. Examples of this are seen in the following passages:

> Of the greatness of his government and peace there will be no end. He will reign on David's throne and over his kingdom, establishing and upholding it with justice and righteousness from that time on and forever. The zeal of the Lord Almighty will accomplish this. (Isa 9:7)

---

15. Whitelam, "King and Kingship," 44.

> See, a king will reign in righteousness and rulers will rule with justice. (Isa 32:1)

On the other hand, the prophet Jeremiah criticized Jehoiakim, a tyrant king of Judah, for neglecting to administer justice and righteousness and oppressing the righteous:

> Does it make you a king to have more and more cedar? Did not your father have food and drink? He did what was right and just, so all went well with him. He defended the cause of the poor and needy, and so all went well. Is that not what it means to know me? (Jer 22:15–16)

It is noteworthy that in Israel, the obligation to administer justice and righteousness was not confined to kings and leaders but extended to all people. The prophet Isaiah condemned the inhabitants of Jerusalem:

> "See how the faithful city has become a prostitute!
>   She once was full of justice;
> righteousness used to dwell in her
>   – but now murderers!" (Isa 1:21)

These examples indicate that the evaluation of Old Testament kings as either good or bad was based on their fulfillment of God's expectations – namely, justice and righteousness. Similarly, a human being, created in the likeness of a king, is called to care for all other creatures. A human being is created with the obligation to care for the fish, the birds, the livestock and all the wild animals, and all the creatures that move along the ground (Gen 1:28). A human being, like a king, has the option to be a compassionate ruler or an exploitative tyrant.

Abraham's Hospitality (Genesis 18–19)

In the Old Testament, Abraham is the first recorded person to practice hospitality. When Abraham encountered three men whom he did not recognize at the terebinths of Mamre, he invited them to stay, offering them water to wash their feet and urging them to rest under a tree. He instructed Sarah, his wife, to bake some bread for these visitors and selected a choice calf from his flock and gave it to a servant to cook. Then Abraham himself placed the food before these men. After eating, the visitors informed Abraham that Sarah would have a son (Gen 18:1–15).

After visiting Abraham, two of the visitors went to Sodom.[16] Lot, who was sitting by the gate of Sodom, saw them and greeted them with courtesy. He invited them to spend the night in his house and prepared a meal for them. Later that evening, the people of Sodom surrounded the house and demanded that Lot bring the men out so that they may "know them" (Gen 19:5 ESV).[17] Lot pleaded with the crowd, saying, "I beg you, my brothers, do not act so wickedly" (Gen 19:7 ESV). Instead of bringing out the men, Lot offered his two daughters, but the people of Sodom rejected the offer and, becoming aggressive, tried to break down the door. However, the two men who were inside the house protected Lot and slammed the door shut (Gen 19:8–11).

The cities of Sodom and Gomorrah were destroyed by YHWH's sulfurous fire, but Lot and his two daughters were spared because YHWH remembered Abraham. According to Genesis 8:23–33, Abraham questioned whether YHWH would spare the city for the sake of fifty innocent inhabitants in Sodom. The number Abraham suggested gradually decreased from fifty to forty-five to forty to thirty to twenty and, finally, to ten. Through his negotiations with YHWH, Abraham sought to ascertain whether YHWH would indiscriminately kill the innocent along with the guilty.[18] Thus, Genesis 18–19 show that hospitality is a crucial criterion that distinguishes Abraham and Lot from the people of Sodom. Abraham and Lot treated strangers with courtesy, while the people of Sodom attempted to forcibly abuse them sexually.

God's Justice and Righteousness and Abraham's Hospitality

After receiving Abraham's hospitality and before conversing with Abraham, YHWH revealed three hidden plans to Abraham. First, Abraham would become a great and powerful nation, and all the nations of the earth will be blessed in him. Second, YHWH explained the reason he chose Abraham. Abraham was called to command his descendants to keep the way of YHWH by practicing righteousness and justice.[19] Third, there is an investigation into

---

16. Genesis 18:2 mentions three messengers or angels but Genesis 18:22 suggests that Yahweh, stayed and conversed with Abraham while the other two messengers proceeded to Sodom.

17. The phrase to "know them" refers to a sexual relationship as in Genesis 4:1.

18. Hamilton, *Genesis: Chapters 18–50*, 24–25.

19. The phrase righteousness (*ṣedekah*) and justice (*mišpaṭ*) occur less frequently than *mišpaṭ* and *ṣedekah*. These two words can be used interchangeably, making it very hard to differentiate between the two. The term *ṣedekah* is often used for the personal dimension, while *mišpaṭ* is used in the context of the communal aspect. The reason for placing righteousness first over justice can be explained by the fact that Lot is judged based on his individual righteous-

the outcry against Sodom and Gomorrah and their grave sins. Practicing righteousness and justice were not only the crucial criteria in YHWH's choice of Abraham and his descendants but also the condition for becoming a great nation. The absence of these qualities was the reason for the destruction of Sodom and Gomorrah. Additionally, it contrasts Abraham's hospitality and the inhospitality of the people of Sodom, highlighting the connection between Abraham's blessing and the destruction of Sodom and Gomorrah with the theme of hospitality.

It is noteworthy that the words justice and righteousness appear for the first time in the Old Testament after the description of Abraham's hospitality. These words are regarded as the way of YHWH because they are divine attributes of God. For example, "The LORD loves righteousness and justice; the earth is full of his unfailing love" (Ps 33:5) or "To do what is right and just is more acceptable to the LORD than sacrifice" (Prov 21:3). The phrase "the way of YHWH" also appears for the first time in the Old Testament.[20] In relation to the relationship between the way of YHWH and justice and righteousness, Sarna says, "He (Abraham) is the repository of those eternal values of righteousness and justice that constitute 'the way of the Lord.'"[21] The fact that YHWH commanded Abraham to teach his descendants the way of YHWH by practicing justice and righteousness indicates that Abraham is the father of justice and righteousness, and that all Israelites, including the leaders of Israel, should practice justice and righteousness. It is explicitly stated that practicing righteousness and justice was YHWH's purpose in electing Abraham and his descendants. This suggests a close connection between *imago Dei* and righteousness and justice because these qualities are derived from YHWH.

Abraham as a King

As discussed above, justice and righteousness were viewed as the responsibilities of kings in the ancient Near East. In the context of the Abraham story,

---

ness rather than the justice related to society. Lot is spared due to his righteousness amidst the misdeeds of the people of Sodom. This incident illustrates that God judges people according to their individual righteousness."

20. In Hebrew, the expression is "*derek* YHWH," which literally means "way, road, or path" – see, for example, Proverbs 1:7. In the book of Psalms, the word "*derek*" is the typical term used in the wisdom psalms to signify keeping the law.

21. Sarna, *Genesis*, 131.

Hamilton associates justice and righteousness with the prophetic tradition.[22] On the one hand, there is no doubt that Abraham functions as a prophet in pleading for the lives of the people of Sodom (Gen 18:22–33). Additionally, in the story of Abimelek in Genesis 20, Abraham is explicitly referred to as a prophet who intercedes for Abimelek through prayer (Gen 20:7).

On the other hand, it can be argued that we also find a royal portrayal of Abraham in Genesis. Alexander insists that Genesis focuses on a divinely-promised royal "seed."[23] He designates Genesis 3–50 as "intimations of the royal line" and states that "although Abraham is never directly designated a king, he is sometimes portrayed as enjoying royal status."[24] God declared that Abraham would be called "the father of many nations"[25] (Gen 17:4–5); he also proclaimed that "kings will come from you" (Gen 17:6), a promise reiterated in Jacob's story (Gen 35:11). Xeravits argues that "the image of Abraham as a progenitor of rulers is complemented here by the view that he himself was a kind of royal figure."[26] The Septuagint reading of Genesis 23:6 reinforces the notion of Abraham as a royal figure: "a king from a god among us."[27] Additionally, it could be argued that Abraham, as a deliverer of righteousness and justice, also took on the role of a king of the ancient Near East in addition to his role of a prophet.

Hospitality as a Representation of *Imago Dei*

We have already discussed that being created in God's image signifies that human beings are created to be like kings. Against the background of the royal ideology of the ancient Near East, the declaration in Genesis 1:26–28 can be interpreted as a revolutionary shift in humanity's position and role. This declaration demonstrates that every human being is elevated to the status of a king; however, whether they become a compassionate king or a tyrant depends on their own choices. This raises a question: What criterion is used to judge

---

22. Hamilton, *Genesis: Chapters 18–50*, 19. Sarna also interprets Abraham from the prophetic perspective. See Sarna, *Genesis*, 131.

23. Alexander, "Royal Expectations," 198.

24. Alexander, *Servant King*, 30. Abraham as an individual defeats a coalition of five eastern kings. The Hittites refer to Abraham as "a prince of God" (Gen 23:6 ESV).

25. Alexander discusses various social roles of "father" including: prophet (2 Kgs 6:21), priest (Judg 18:19), king (1 Sam 24:11), or governor (Isa 22:20–21). See Alexander, "Royal Expectations," 201.

26. Xeravits, "Abraham," 32.

27. This can be translated literally, "You are God's prince among us." Xeravits, 32.

whether someone is a compassionate king or a tyrant? Every human being, as a king, faces two paths depending on their choices. Alexander points out, "On the one hand, there are those who enjoy a positive relationship with God and experience his blessing. On the other hand, there are those who distance themselves from God by their evil actions and, as a consequence, experience God's displeasure."[28]

When God called Abraham, he promised, "I will bless those who bless you, and whoever curses you I will curse" (Gen 12:3a). This shows that people's destiny depends on their attitude – either positive or negative – toward Abraham. It also indicates that Abraham possessed the divine trait expressed as the way of YHWH, which is fulfilled through practicing righteousness and justice. Abraham fulfilled the practice of righteousness and justice by treating strangers hospitably, whereas the people of Sodom, in abusing strangers, failed to practice righteousness and justice. Furthermore, Abraham's compassionate character is apparent in his negotiation with God to protect the righteous people in Sodom. The people of Sodom and Gomorrah are portrayed as tyrants, and the outcries against them are so loud that they reach YHWH's ears. This implies that hospitality to strangers was the means by which YHWH tested Abraham and the people of Sodom regarding their practice of righteousness and justice. Therefore, we may infer that practicing righteousness and justice is equivalent to practicing hospitality.

Conclusion

In examining the relationship between *imago Dei* and hospitality, this chapter establishes that *imago Dei* in the creation story evolves into the themes of righteousness and justice in the salvation history presented to us in the Abraham story. Genesis 18–19 also demonstrate that hospitality is a symbolic action that fulfills the requirement for righteousness and justice. It is noteworthy that Abraham's descendants are chosen to practice righteousness and justice. The covenantal community formed through circumcision to practice righteousness and justice includes not only Abraham's descendants but also slaves born into his household and slaves purchased from foreigners (Gen 17:12). This demonstrates that every human being possesses the *imago Dei* and may choose to act either as a compassionate king like Abraham or as a tyrant like the people of Sodom. There is a lesson here for Christians. As members of the royal priesthood, we must actively participate in the ministry of hospitality to

---

28. Alexander, *Servant King*, 25.

all people, including migrants scattered throughout the world: "But you are a chosen people, a royal priesthood, a holy nation, God's special possession, that you may declare the praises of him who called you out of darkness into his wonderful light" (1 Pet 2:9).

References

Alexander, T. Desmond. "Royal Expectations in Genesis to Kings: Their Importance for Biblical Theology." *Tyndale Bulletin* 49, no. 2 (1998): 191–212.

———. *The Servant King: The Bible's Portrait of the Messiah*. Vancouver: Regent College Publishing, 2003.

Dehsen, Christian D. von. "The Imago Dei in Genesis 1:26–27." *Lutheran Quarterly* 11 (1997): 259–70.

Dick, Michael B., ed. *Born in Heaven, Made on Earth: The Making of the Cult Image in the Ancient Near East*. University Park: Pennsylvania State University Press, 1999.

HALOT, *Hebrew and Aramaic Lexicon of the Old Testament*, edited by Ludwig Koehler and Walter Baumgartner. Leiden: Brill NV, 2000.

Hamilton, Victor P. *The Book of Genesis: Chapters 1–17*. NICOT. Grand Rapids: Eerdmans, 1990.

———. *The Book of Genesis: Chapters 18–50*. NICOT. Grand Rapids: Eerdmans, 1995.

Middleton, J. Richard. "The Liberating Image? Interpreting the Imago Dei in Context." *Christian Scholar's Review* 24, no. 1 (1994): 8–25.

Millard A. R., and P. Bordreuil. "A Statue from Syria with Assyrian and Aramaic Inscriptions." *Biblical Archaeologist* 45, no. 3 (1982): 135–41.

Sarna, Nahum H. *The JPS Torah Commentary: Genesis*, Philadelphia: Jewish Publication Society, 1989.

Szczerba, Wojciech. "The Concept of Imago Dei as a Symbol of Religious Inclusion and Human Dignity." *Forum Philosophicum* 25 (2020): 13–36.

Threlfall, Jonathan. "The Doctrine of the *Imago Dei*: The Biblical Data for an Abductive Argument for the Christian Faith." *Journal of the Evangelical Theological Society* 62, no. 3 (2019): 543–61.

Walls, Neal H., ed. *Cult Image and Divine Representation in the Ancient Near East*. Boston: American Schools of Oriental Research, 2005.

Walton, John H. *Ancient Near Eastern Thought and the Old Testament: Introducing the Conceptual World of the Hebrew Bible*. Grand Rapids: Baker Academic, 2006.

Westermann, Claus. *Genesis 1–11*. Translated by John J. Scullion, SJ. Minneapolis: Augsburg, 1984.

White Jr., Lynn. "The Historical Roots of Our Ecological Crisis." *Science* vol. 155, no. 3767 (1967): 1203–7.

Whitelam, Keith W. "King and Kingship." *Anchor Bible Dictionary* 4 (1992): 40–48.

Williams, David T. "'He Is the Image and Glory of God, but Woman...' (1 Cor 11:7): 'Unveiling' the Understanding of the *Imago Dei*." *Scriptura* 108 (2011): 314–25.

Xeravits, Géza G. "Abraham in the Old Testament Apocrypha." In *Abraham in Jewish and Early Christian Literature*, edited by S. A. Adams and Zanne Domoney-Lyttle, 29–42. London: Bloomsbury, 2019.

Zobel, H. J., "rādāh," in *Theological Dictionary of the Old Testament*, edited by G. Johannes Botterweck and Helmer Ringgren. Grand Rapids: Eerdmans (2004) 13:330–36.

7

Mission Through and Beyond the Chinese Diaspora in the Middle East: Two Case Studies

Jeanne Wu

Introduction

Earlier this year, a popular Chinese Malaysian Christian singer held an evangelistic concert in Dubai. Approximately 4,500 Chinese migrant workers and businesspeople attended this concert. It was reported that all ten Chinese churches in Dubai conducted a joint worship service that Sunday. In addition, a Chinese-speaking Christian media outlet based in Taiwan covered this event, praising its success and noting that about three hundred Chinese attendees raised their hands to receive Jesus that day. The preacher for these events was a megachurch pastor from Taiwan.[1]

This event was significant in several ways. First, it is an indicator of the large Chinese population in Dubai. Second, a joint worship service involving all Chinese churches is rare in any city, particularly in a Muslim country. Third, these events presented a typical transnational network of Chinese – that is, a Chinese Christian singer from Malaysia and a preacher from Taiwan – participating in evangelistic events aimed at reaching the Chinese community in Dubai. The enthusiasm shown by preachers and organizers on social media

---

1. Chinese news report: https://cdn-news.org/News.aspx?EntityID=News&PK=0000000 02c40ca4120747f26c0f5b44ca2eb2073492e09b0.

about hosting such an event in the Middle East reflects the increasing interest of Chinese Christians in this region.[2]

Since the 1990s, China has intentionally invested in and sought allies in the majority world – including Africa, Latin America, and the Middle East – to collaborate in economic and political activities. Apart from economic interests, there are also outreach efforts. In recent years, several of my Christian friends – all Taiwanese or Chinese Americans – have participated in a short-term mission (STM) to the Middle East in response to the refugee crisis of the 2010s due to the Syrian civil war and the activities of ISIS. For some, it was their first-ever STM trip. Later, I found out that many of them had been hosted by the same NGO registered in the Kurdistan Region of Iraq (KRI), which was founded by Chinese Christians in the diaspora. This is remarkable because it is an instance of the *Chinese* diaspora serving the *Middle Eastern* diaspora.

Throughout history, the Lord has used diaspora peoples to expand his kingdom. My previous research on Chinese American missions "*Mission through Diaspora*" (2016) revealed that most of the long-term missionaries and STM teams that Chinese American churches sent or supported were involved in ministries in China or the Chinese diaspora. This research also revealed the collaboration that takes place among the Chinese diaspora as they engage in missions. My previous research was carried out ten years ago, at a time when Chinese diaspora churches paid little attention to the Middle East, but now things have changed. How does the Chinese diaspora contribute to the Great Commission in the Middle East? I have lived and served in the Middle East for the past nine years and have often visited multiple countries across the region, including the UAE and the KRI. This updated research is based on my interviews with a founding pastor who planted several Chinese churches in the UAE and the director of an NGO in the KRI, as well as my observations during the visits to these ministries and my personal experience serving in the Middle East.

In his book *Global Diasporas: An Introduction* (1996), Cohen called the historic dispersion of Chinese "Trade Diaspora." Trading and business activi-

---

2. It is important to distinguish between various groups of Chinese people. The English word "Chinese" is an umbrella term that, in the Chinese language, encompasses various categories including the following: (1) National Chinese (*Zhongguoren* 中國人), (2) Chinese migrants or immigrants (*Huaqiao* 華僑), (3) ethnic Chinese who are descendants of Chinese immigrants (*Huayi* 華裔), and (4) a broad term that encompasses (1), (2), and (3) above (*Huaren* or *Tangren*華人或唐人). In addition, the term "overseas Chinese" (*Haiwai Huaren* 海外華人), which includes (2) and (3) above, is closest in meaning to the concept of the Chinese diaspora. In this paper, "Chinese" refers to the term described in (4) above – that is *Huaren*, a broad term that includes (1), (2), and (3).

Mission Through and Beyond the Chinese Diaspora in the Middle East

ties between China, South Asia, and Southeast Asia can be traced to the Tang dynasty (AD 618–907). During the Ming dynasty (AD 1368–1644), Chinese traders began building up communities around the South and East China Sea. In the nineteenth century, many *coolie* laborers went from China to North America as miners and railroad builders and established the first and largest Chinatown in San Francisco in 1848.

The modern Chinese diaspora began in 1949, with the founding of the People's Republic of China. Millions of mainland Chinese fled to Hong Kong and Taiwan in the late 1940s and early 1950s. Since the 1960s, new waves of Chinese migrants have been coming to North America. According to the 2022 Statistical Yearbook of the Overseas Community Affairs Council, the overseas Chinese population – including ethnic Chinese and their descendants – who emigrated from mainland China, Taiwan, and Hong Kong number 49.7 million globally[3] (See Table 1).

Table 1: Chinese Diaspora as of 2010 and 2022

Continent	Chinese Diaspora as of 2010 (in millions)	Chinese Diaspora as of 2022 (in millions)
Asia	29.82	34.62
Americas (North, Central, and South)	7.26 (North: 5.43)	9.77 (North: 7.46)
Europe	1.32	2.38
Oceania	0.95	1.77
Africa	0.24	1.18
Global	39.57	49.73

In an early article titled "Diaspora Missiology," Enoch Wan provides statistical data to demonstrate the moving people groups and the push and pull factors of migration. These people are immigrants, visitors, students, workers, refugees, and so on, and he views diaspora missiology as "mission on our doorstep,"[4] which means we can reach different people in our neighborhoods. Samuel Escobar says that "migration is an avenue for the evangelistic dimension of mission" and notes that migrants in transition, who are facing uncertainty, "are open to become believers, ready to assume a faith in a personal

---

3. Overseas Community Affairs Council of R.O.C. Accessed 22 November 2023, https://www.ocac.gov.tw/OCAC/Pages/VDetail.aspx?nodeid=30&pid=313.
4. Wan, "Diaspora Missiology," 3–7.

way."[5] A good example is the large number of conversions of mainland Chinese in the United States. From both sociological and psychological perspectives, Christianity meets their needs amid this transition and answers their questions about life.[6] Furthermore, diaspora missiology is more than outreach to migrants; it can also be mission *by* diaspora. Since the overseas Chinese have more religious resources and freedom than Chinese people in China, the mission movement is mainly through the Chinese diaspora. Wan identifies two missiological trends among the Chinese diaspora: "mission opportunities among them and the potentials in mission participation by them."[7]

Wan summarizes the strategy and practices of diaspora missions as (1) missions to the diaspora, (2) missions through the diaspora, and (3) missions by and beyond the diaspora.[8] The missions *to the diaspora* involve reaching out to new immigrants such as international students or workers; missions *through the diaspora* focus on new immigrants or migrants reaching out to their kinspeople in their country of origin or other countries; and missions *by and beyond diaspora* is the cross-cultural mission that takes place by the diaspora reaching out to people who are not their kinspeople.

Mission through the Chinese Diaspora in the Middle East

Over the past ten years, since China started the One Belt, One Road Initiative (also known as Belt and Road Initiative, BRI) in 2013,[9] migrants from China have increased significantly in Africa and the Middle East. According to the 2011 data of the Chinese Coordination Centre of World Evangelism (CCCOWE), the whole Middle East region hosted only 259,200 Chinese,[10] but now this number has increased to more than half a million, most of whom are in Saudi Arabia, Turkey, and the UAE.[11] In 2004, "Dragon City" – the largest Chinese goods trading market in the Middle East – was opened in Dubai, the most populous city in the UAE, in which the majority of the population are expatriate workers. Chinese in Dubai have increased dramatically since 2013. In 2002, there were roughly thirty thousand Chinese in UAE; this figure has

---

5. Escobar, "Migration," 19.
6. Yang, "Chinese Conversion," 237–57; Wang and Yang, "Evangelical and Ethnic," 179–92.
7. Wan, "Mission among the Chinese Diaspora," 38.
8. Wan, *Diaspora Missiology*, 138–40.
9. Chinese State website: http://english.www.gov.cn/beltAndRoad/.
10. CCCOWE, "The Statistics Data of Overseas Chinese Population and Chinese Church."
11. Chinese State report: http://www.chinanews.com.cn/m/hr/2017/01-06/8116463.shtml.

Mission Through and Beyond the Chinese Diaspora in the Middle East   101

now grown to more than two hundred thousand, with most of these people living in Dubai.[12] In 2020, the first-ever Chinese international school was opened in Dubai, with classes from kindergarten to twelfth grade, using a Chinese curriculum.[13] Contract laborers, professionals, and businesspeople from mainland China have built up their communities, and Chinese churches continue to grow and witness to their kinspeople in UAE.

In 1995, a Chinese mission sending agency was founded in California with a vision of "reaching our kinsmen, touching all nations." In other words, their outreaches are mainly through Chinese around the world and intended to reach out to the Chinese diaspora or to Chinese nationals in China.[14] Their mission fields include Latin America, Southeast Asia, the Middle East, Europe, and Africa, and they have more than one hundred staff. Recently, they began sending missionaries to work among refugees in the US, Asia, and the Middle East – that is, missions *beyond* the Chinese diaspora.

Pastor J – the founding pastor of many Chinese churches in the UAE – is a missionary with this Chinese diaspora-sending organization and has planted diaspora churches in diverse contexts during the past three decades. Born and raised in Hong Kong, he first planted Chinese churches in Macao in the late 1980s, and later in Mexico and Brazil in the 1990s. In 2007, after hearing about the spiritual needs of Chinese migrant workers and businesspeople in Dubai, he decided to move there. Within two weeks, he started conducting worship services. At first, he planted three separate congregations for Chinese laborers, businesspeople, and young professionals. Years later, these congregations merged. It is thanks to the outreach efforts of these Chinese churches that most of these church members became believers after their arrival in the UAE. In addition to attending worship services, some of these believers participate in small groups and outreach efforts to newcomers. They receive STM teams from China or Chinese diaspora churches and have vison to offer theology programs to train Chinese ministers. In many ways, conducting missions through the diaspora is similar to the mission work of the Chinese diaspora in North America and Europe.

It is apparent that mission through the Chinese diaspora in the context of the UAE has been fruitful. In thirteen years, Pastor J planted more than

---

12. Mao and Li, "迪拜华人简史" (Brief History of Chinese in Dubai) http://www.dubairen.com/45629.html.

13. Xinhua, "1st Chinese Public School outside China Opens in Dubai," *Xinhuanet*, 2 September 2020, http://www.xinhuanet.com/english/2020-09/02/c_139337746.htm.

14. Since I serve on the board of this mission agency, I am well-acquainted with their activities. For security reasons, the name of this agency will not be disclosed here.

ten small Chinese churches in the UAE and other Gulf countries. He was also successful in raising younger leaders in his churches. Now he is retired, and there are a handful of younger full-time and bivocational pastors serving in different congregations. For example, Pastor A, who is in his late thirties, was working as an engineer in the UAE and became a believer after he went to Pastor J's church. After several years of growing and serving in the church, he decided to be a full-time minister in one of the churches that Pastor J had planted. Pastor L, a middle-aged business owner, who also became a believer while in the UAE, is now a bivocational minister. Pastor A, Pastor L, and some other Chinese ministers preach in rotation in a dozen Chinese churches in the UAE and other Gulf countries.

Yet, this ministry is not without its challenges. For example, although the recent evangelistic concert and joint worship service mentioned earlier sounds encouraging and was organized with good intentions, Pastor J expressed concern about it because many Chinese churches in Dubai are not registered with the government. Unlike Chinese churches in North America and Europe that enjoy religious freedom, such events draw unwanted attention from the local government in the Middle East as well as from the Chinese government, thus jeopardizing future activities of the churches. Pastor J explained to me that "expats are only allowed to worship legally in church compounds in which they compete with dozens of nationalities for limited time slots and space." In this way, church work is limited and evangelism by expats and nationals is discouraged by the local authorities. Pastor J believes that "the local government intends to limit the development of expat churches," and he has received several warnings from local authorities regarding evangelistic work among the Chinese. As a result, although he has been very bold in his evangelistic efforts among his kinspeople in the UAE and other neighboring Gulf nations, he is hesitant to extend their ministries to their Muslim neighbors. Furthermore, outreach to the Chinese diaspora is prohibited by the Chinese government, which monitors its citizens' political and religious activities overseas; and this monitoring activity has intensified since the new Regulations on Religious Affairs was enforced in February 2018.[15] Pastor J confirmed that it is now more difficult to share the gospel with laborers and contract workers from China.

---

15. Laney Zhang, "China: Revised Regulations on Religious Affairs," https://www.loc.gov/item/global-legal-monitor/2017-11-09/china-revised-regulations-on-religious-affairs/.

Mission by and beyond the Chinese Diaspora in the Middle East

My previous research showed that China was the top destination for STM teams from Chinese churches in the United States.[16] However, since the new Regulations on Religious Affairs was introduced, the door to China has been shut and a new wave of persecutions and missionary expulsions have taken place. Thus, many Chinese diaspora churches are looking for new fields to continue their mission mandate. Meanwhile, the Middle Eastern refugee crisis has captured the attention of Christian churches, including Chinese churches, around the world. For example, the KRI is an autonomous and relatively safe region in the north of the country and hosts about 1.5 million Internally Displaced Persons (IDPs) and Syrian refugees after ISIS invaded parts of Iraq and Syria in 2014.[17] Many Chinese diaspora churches – including my home church, which is a medium-sized Chinese church in the United States – have now started to send STM teams to the Middle East.

In 2016, a group of American Christians – whose backgrounds are Taiwanese, Singaporean, or Hong Kong – founded a relief and development NGO in the KRI.[18] Mr. T, the founder and director of this NGO, is a Singaporean American Christian. This ministry serves Syrian refugees and Yazidi IDPs persecuted by ISIS through STM teams, whose members are mostly Chinese diaspora Christians. This NGO provides mission orientation and training in topics such as cross-cultural principles, basic theology, and missions. In 2016, this NGO brought five STM teams to the KRI; and since 2017, they have brought in more than ten teams annually, a number that keeps growing every year. Between 2018 and 2020, they brought short-term surgical teams that operated on forty-five patients. Their projects came to a halt in 2020 due to the pandemic but slowly resumed in 2021. In 2022, they hosted nine STM teams carrying out medical and educational services. These ministries have successfully brought many Chinese diaspora Christians to bless refugees in the KRI. This also provides a platform for long-term kingdom workers on the field to reach out to people facing severe need. Mr. T recruits younger Christians to his leadership team and employs many local people as translators, managers, and office staff.

---

16. Wu, *Mission through Diaspora*, 121–26.

17. UNHCR Iraq Refugee Crisis, https://www.unrefugees.org/news/iraq-refugee-crisis-explained/.

18. For security reasons, the name of the NGO will be not disclosed in this research.

Most STM teams from Chinese American churches were sent to China or Europe, where they ministered primarily to Chinese people.[19] In addition, Chinese churches tend to focus on spiritual needs and direct evangelism such as discipleship training and Bible teaching in same-culture settings, with relief and charity activities ranking lower in their priorities (see Table 2).[20] When STM team members (short-termers) lack local cultural and linguistic knowledge, carrying out discipleship training or Bible teaching in a cross-cultural context becomes challenging, especially given the language barrier. Therefore, for Chinese churches to send out STM teams to serve non-Chinese communities through charity and relief work represents a major paradigm shift. The refugee ministry gives them an opportunity to consider and adopt a holistic approach to mission and extend their mission to non-Chinese people. Furthermore, many short-termers in this ministry grow to love and care for a people group that is completely different from them in ethnicity, language, culture, and faith. This is a significant development in the context of Chinese diaspora mission.

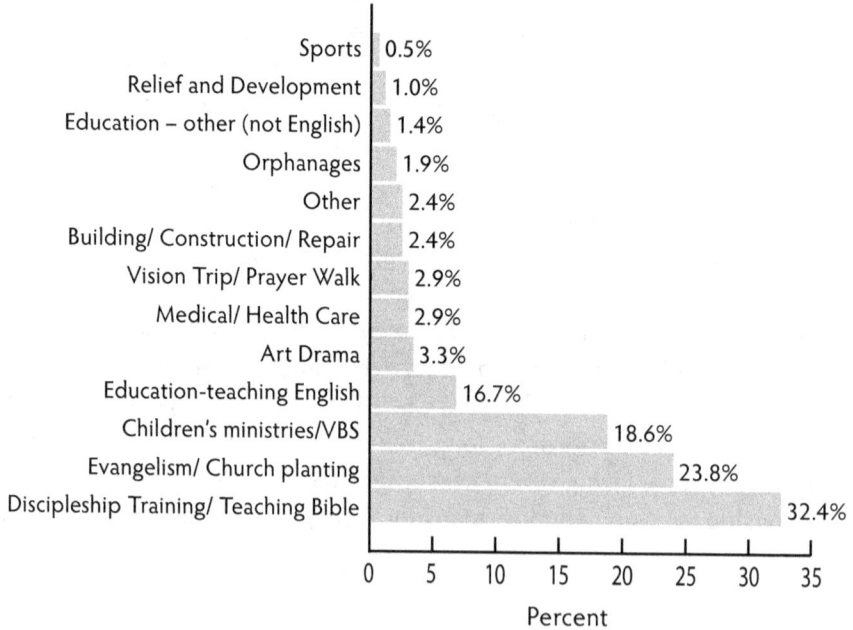

Table 2: STM focus of US Chinese churches

---

19. Wu, *Mission through Diaspora*, 121–26.
20. Wu, 129.

As for the prospect of turning STMs into long-term missions, this may require additional efforts by short-termers to learn to adapt to and appreciate the local culture. For example, a short-term medical team that returned to serve regularly actually brought their own Chinese chef to cook them Chinese food during the whole mission trip because they did not like the local food! This kind of mindset and approach may not work for long-term cross-cultural mission. In addition, language is also an issue. The short-term teams do not speak the local languages and, therefore, rely heavily on local interpreters. While this is workable for relief and medical work for a short time period, sustainable and fruitful long-term discipleship should be carried out in the heart language of the local people.[21] Another limitation is that even though the Kurdistan government has thus far been open and friendly to foreigners, this is still a Muslim context, where "proselytizing" Muslims is socially and culturally offensive.[22] Recent regional news coverage highlighted the suspicion and anger of the local community against a foreign NGO that allegedly tried to convert Yazidi IDPs.[23] It is reported that there are a few hundred foreign NGOs in the KRI; if the government starts to interfere with them, this could be a major blow to mission work.

Research Findings

As we research Chinese diasporas, it is evident that three developments will have a lasting impact on the diaspora missions of Chinese globally. First, the BRI of 2013 opened the door for Chinese contractors and businesspeople in South Asia, the Middle East, and Africa, and this dispersion is likely to see a significant increase in the coming years. Second, the new Regulations on Religious Affairs that began in 2018 shut the door on mission work in mainland China, resulting in a major shift in the mission force. Third, the global pandemic of 2020 that originated in China heightened suspicion and mistrust of Chinese people worldwide and resulted in border closure for three years. However, missiologists are now evaluating the effect of the rise of China. A veteran Malaysian Chinese missionary who served in Africa recently reported that as a result of the BRI, local Africans are not as friendly to Chinese people

---

21. See Becker, Adams, and Daniels, *Fruitful Practices*. http://www.fruitfulpractice.org/wp-content/uploads/2022/08/Fruitful-Practice-Videos-Worksheets-vimeo-links2.pdf.

22. Wu, "Jordan," 26–27.

23. Alex MacDonald, "Iraq: Evangelicals Spark Outrage by Praying 'to Break Power' of Yazidi Temple," https://www.middleeasteye.net/news/iraq-yazidi-american-christians-praying-temple-outrage.

as they were twenty years ago. In recent years, many Chinese contractors have poured into Africa to build new towns with shops, restaurants, and hotels for Chinese migrants. China's BRI is a "double-edged sword" as locals feel that the Chinese are exploiting poor countries by developing infrastructure in exchange for their natural resources, which they perceive as a form of colonialism. If Chinese Christians leverage China's economic or political power for mission work, they risk repeating the same mistakes made by Westerners during the colonial era.

Social scientists refer to the concept of transnationalism in discussions about globalization. To better understand diaspora in the age of globalization, we must appreciate the relationship between transnationalism and diaspora. Transnationalism may be defined as follows:

> The process by which immigrants build social fields that link together their country of origin and their country of settlement. Immigrants who build such social fields are designated "transmigrants." Transmigrants develop and maintain multiple relations – familial, economic, social, organizational, religious, and political that span borders. Transmigrants take actions, make decisions, and feel concerns, and develop identities within social networks that connect them to two or more societies simultaneously.[24]

Whether in New Testament times or in our era of globalization, diaspora collaboration in mission by utilizing transnational networks and resources is both common and natural.[25] Laurence Ma recognizes the significance of transnationalism in the Chinese diaspora, focusing on transnational activities such as trading and the globalization of "Chinese capitalism" among Chinese diasporic communities.[26]

In the case of ministry in the KRI, both the STM teams and the workers of Mr. T's NGO are drawn mainly from the Chinese diaspora from Southeast Asia, North America, Asia, and Australia. This encouraging turnout of workers is a result of the extensive recruiting and networking of the NGO director. Mr. T said, "We are highly active in recruiting. I am constantly talking to pastors, to organization leaders, and to our network." On the other hand, so far, Chinese nationals sent from mainland China have not been greatly involved in this ministry. Apart from some local staff, both the receiving side (NGO)

---

24. Schiller, Basch, and Blanc-Szanton, *Transnational Perspective*, 1–2.
25. Wu, *Mission through Diaspora*, 115–16.
26. Ma, "Space, Place and Transnationalism," 24.

and the sending side (STM teams and sending churches) consist primarily of Chinese Christians in the diaspora. One possible reason for this is that the founder of this NGO has not yet recruited short-term teams and long-term workers from mainland China – in contrast to the church-planting ministry in the UAE, which primarily involves mainland Chinese (except for Pastor J himself). The mission through the Chinese diaspora in the UAE also involves a transnational network. In addition to bringing in short-term Chinese teams from China and the United States, Pastor J mentioned that in a new church planted in a Gulf country, they had recruited a Chinese lady who had emigrated to New Zealand but later relocated to the Gulf country to lead the congregation there. Similarly, they also recruit ministers from China to serve in other church plants.

Transnational Leaders as Mission Catalysts

Both these ministries in the UAE and the KRI were initiated by catalytic leaders with significant diaspora experiences. Pastor J was born and raised in Hong Kong when it was still a British colony. After his marriage, he and his family moved first to Mexico and then to Brazil to plant churches among the Chinese diaspora and then later moved to the UAE in response to spiritual needs there. Mr. T was born and raised in Singapore, emigrated to the United States as a young adult, and participated in several short-term trips to the Middle East. Several years ago, he responded to the Lord's calling to start an NGO to serve Yazidis and Kurds in the KRI. When I visited these ministries, I noticed that both leaders switched freely between two or three languages as they interacted with different people. We see a biblical parallel in the way God specifically called Paul, a Jew in diaspora from Tarsus, who was bilingual, bicultural, and capable of reaching out to Gentiles and other Jews in the diaspora to expand the kingdom of God. In his letter to the Corinthians, Paul describes himself like this:

> To the Jews I became like a Jew, to win the Jews. To those under the law I became like one under the law (though I myself am not under the law), so as to win those under the law. To those not having the law I became like one not having the law (though I am not free from God's law but am under Christ's law), so as to win those not having the law. (1 Cor 9:20–21)

Furthermore, I also observe Filipino transnational ministry leaders being effective in ministries to migrant workers. Because of their linguistic abilities, transnational networks, cross-cultural skills, and pioneering spirit, it seems natural to them to start new missions and mobilize and recruit other Christians of their ethnicity to join them. Perhaps we should consider "the transnational Christian leader as a mission catalyst" as a diaspora mission paradigm.

Conclusion

In recent times, the landscape of Chinese diaspora mission has gradually changed due to political developments in China and the Middle East, which has closed some doors but also opened others. As the Lord says in the book of Revelation, "These are the words of him who is holy and true, who holds the key of David. What he opens no one can shut, and what he shuts no one can open" (3:7). This research highlights the new opportunities and challenges for Chinese diaspora mission in the Middle East.

References

Becker, John, Laura & Eric Adams, and Gene Daniels. *Fruitful Practices: A Guide for Learning from the Best Practices of Church Planters in the Muslim World.* Vision 5:9, 2019.

CCCOWE. "The Statistics Data of Overseas Chinese Population and Chinese Church." In *Chinese Church Today*《今日華人教會》Hong Kong: Chinese Coordination Centre of World Evangelism, no. 281 (2011): 8–10.

Cohen, Robin. *Global Diasporas: An Introduction.* London: UCL Press, 1997.

Escobar, Samuel. "Migration: Avenue and Challenge to Mission." *Missiology* 31, no. 1 (January 2003): 17–28.

Ma, Laurence J. C. "Space, Place and Transnationalism in the Chinese Diaspora." In *The Chinese Diaspora: Space, Place, Mobility, and Identity*, edited by Laurence J. C. Ma and Carolyn Cartier, 1–49. Lanham: Rowman & Littlefield, 2003.

MacDonald, Alex. "Iraq: Evangelicals Spark Outrage by Praying 'to Break Power' of Yazidi Temple," *Middle East Eye*, 21 April 2023.

Mao, Yiming, and Li Hwafei. 毛一鸣 & 李华飞. 迪拜华人简史 (Brief History of Chinese in Dubai), 2017. http://www.dubairen.com/44679.html.

Schiller, Nina Glick, Linda Basch, and Cristina Blanc-Szanton, eds. *Towards a Transnational Perspective on Migration: Race, Class, Ethnicity, and Nationalism Reconsidered.* New York: New York Academy of Sciences, 1992.

Wan, Enoch. "Diaspora Missiology." *EMS Occasional Bulletin*, vol. 20 (Spring 2007): 3–7.

———, ed. *Diaspora Missiology: Theory, Methodology, and Practice.* Portland: Institute of Diaspora Studies, 2011.

———. "Mission among the Chinese Diaspora: A Case Study of Migration and Mission." *Missiology* 31, no. 1 (2003): 35–43.

Wang, Yuting, and Fenggang Yang. "More Than Evangelical and Ethnic: The Ecological Factor in Chinese Conversion to Christianity in the United States." *Sociology of Religion* 67, no. 2 (2006): 179–92.

Wu, Jeanne. "Jordan, Home for Refugees: Two Challenges." In *Refugee Diaspora: Missions amid the Greatest Humanitarian Crisis of Our Times*, edited by Sam George and Miriam Adeney, 25–32. Pasadena: William Carey, 2018.

———. *Mission through Diaspora: The Case of the Chinese Church in the USA*. Carlisle: Langham Academic, 2016.

Xinhua, "1st Chinese Public School outside China Opens in Dubai," *Xinhuanet*, 2 September 2020, http://www.xinhuanet.com/english/2020-09/02/c_139337746.htm.

Yang, Fenggang. "Chinese Conversion to Evangelical Christianity: The Importance of Social and Cultural Contexts." *Sociology of Religion* 59 (1998): 237–57.

Zhang, Laney. "China: Revised Regulations on Religious Affairs," *Library of Congress*, 2007.

8

Migrant Mission Training in South Korea and Beyond

Hanna Hyun

Historical Context of Migrant Inflows in South Korea

Between 1954 and 1988, there was an influx of foreign laborers into South Korea through the United Nations Korean Reconstruction Agency (UNKRA), supporting the country's new industrialization and economic growth activities. The 1988 Seoul Olympics introduced the "economic miracle" of Korea to the world. Without international assistance, Korea would not have achieved progress along the Han River and demonstrated its substantial economic development or experienced the rapid expansion of Christianity. Furthermore, the cultural landscape of Korean society was profoundly altered by the influx of foreigners during the 1990s.

The implementation of the Industrial Training Program (ITP) by the Korean government in 1992 led to a significant influx of foreign laborers across diverse sectors such as agriculture, manufacturing, small-scale operations, and fishing. In the 1990s, foreign workers on E-9 visas for nonprofessional employment began to replace domestic factory workers. The majority of Southeast Asians, classified as low-skilled laborers in the homogeneous Korean culture, were forced to endure hardships as they adjusted to this predominantly Korean society. The term "3D jobs" refers to the dirty, dangerous, and difficult tasks carried out by these non-natives. Since the 1970s, there has been a rise in the number of intercultural marriages as unmarried Korean males living in rural areas sought marriage partners from neighboring countries such as China, Vietnam, Thailand, and the former Soviet Union. Between 1989 and 1992, a few

Korean churches launched outreach initiatives aimed at expatriates alongside their endeavors to send missionaries overseas.

The 2019 Seoul Declaration on Diaspora Missiology marked a new direction in missiological thinking about God's kingdom work in the world. In the early years of migrant missions, it was anticipated that God's mission through Korean diaspora churches would focus mainly on overseas missions. Today, however, various ethnic groups are playing a vital role in global missions. Many scholars argue that global migration necessitates diaspora missions and emphasize that to fulfill the Great Commission, it is imperative to implement a mission manifesto that encompasses mission to diaspora, mission through diaspora, and mission beyond diaspora across different geographical boundaries.

WMI and Its Foundational Principle of FAITH

In the 1990s, migrant ministries were sporadic, and only a few pastors participated in radical evangelism among industrial employees.[1] Initially, not many church-affiliated organizations engaged in missions to migrants. However, over time, more Christian organizations – including NGOs and local churches – began working hard to solve various difficulties and resolve grievances faced by migrant workers in the industrial field – for example, industrial accidents, assault, disease, wage arrears, fraud, and death. WiThee Mission International (WMI)[2] was founded in 1997 by Reverend Changsun (Barnabas) Moon and his wife, Jin-Suk, in response to the requirements of various organizations serving these migrant worker communities.

In the monocultural Korean society, migrant workers often experience prejudice, discrimination, and exclusion. Hence, missions to migrants must be carried out with an awareness of cultural differences and ethnic diversities, similar to the way overseas missionaries are required to undergo training in languages and integration into society. To achieve mission priorities, it was vital to develop a distinct approach to ministering to migrant laborers, refugees, and people in cross-cultural marriages. In the 1990s, the overseas mission was the only recognized cross-cultural mission paradigm. Therefore, when Rev. Moon initially began ministering to foreigners in South Korea in 1992, these

---

1. Seo, *Gospel for Workers*, 31–63.

2. WiThee, which combines the words "With" and "Thee," signifies "With the Lord" and "With you"; in accordance with Matthew 22:37–39, the purpose of WTI is "to demonstrate God's love to the migrant neighbours in Korea."

domestic missions were not immediately recognized as real mission work. At that time, missionary work was generally thought of as an overseas endeavor that focused on sending missionaries abroad, and helping migrants in the local neighborhood did not seem to count as "mission" in South Korea. However, Rev. Moon learned early on that migrants could be a medium for global missions, and his organization, WMI, has served as God's instrument in training many dispersed migrants in South Korea.

WMI began a Filipino congregation that later formed an independent fellowship for English speakers, attracting Africans from Ghana and Nigeria between 1998 and 1999. WMI is consistent about reaching migrants with the gospel of Jesus Christ so that they may be trained, commissioned, and sent back to their homelands or to other nations to fulfill the command to "make disciples of all nations" (Matt 28:19). WMI's operation focuses primarily on "foreign migrant workers," which shapes the scope and direction of its missional activities. WiThee is dedicated to collaborating with numerous associations and establishing international networks to train immigrant ministers from other countries, working together with them to devise efficient strategies for outreach and church establishment in the 10/40 window.[3]

Rev. Moon regards the following as pivotal verses for mission work: "Whatever you do, do it with all your heart, as working for the Lord, not for human masters" (Col 3:23) and "Your people will rebuild the ancient ruins . . . you will be called Repairer of Broken Walls" (Isa 58:12). His steadfast dedication to helping migrant congregations and local leaders catalyzed the growth and advancement of WMI. As a result, both the congregation and WMI experienced growth, and a curriculum for mission training specifically designed for migrants was developed during the 2000s. In addition, prompted by the intercultural marriage of his brother, Rev. Moon expanded his ministry beyond domestic regions and ventured into international missions, particularly in Nagaland, India. The Migrant Mission Training School (MMTS) course was further enhanced following the biannual Nagaland Mission Conference organized by WMI in collaboration with North Indian Christian leaders. By 2022, WMI had 102 linked missionaries serving in twenty-three nations spanning four continents: Africa, North America, Asia, and Europe.

WMI's mission strategies are Friendship, Assembly, Independence, Transformation, and Hubs (FAITH).[4] Friendship-building involves investing both time and monetary resources in migrant missions. By cultivating strong bonds

---

3. Moon, "Flow of Missionary Work."
4. Moon, "Foreword," *WiThee Mission International*, 2.

of friendship, one can develop reliable connections that facilitate engaging in profound spiritual dialogues with newcomers. Assembly is the next stage of acquainting a migrant with more companions or supportive collectives, enabling individual believers to flourish and have further opportunities to engage in godly relationships and discipleship. The interaction between migrant communities and local church organizations in the host country can create synergy, creating more opportunities to learn about other cultures and experience mutual growth. Independence is the third stage, in which ethnic communities within the host culture church can establish their own separate and autonomous community. Independent migrant churches have the flexibility and full responsibility to build and maintain their congregations. Transformation is the fourth stage, characterized by the reproduction and regeneration of new converts through a genuine process of transformation. Upon their return, the discipled migrants will engage in reverse missions in their home country. The final stage, the hub, has emerged as the latest strategic approach for engaging diaspora missions, with migrants taking on the role of disciple-makers. The WiThee headquarters in Korea serves as a conduit for establishing ties with other nations. The gospel has the potential to penetrate unreached communities within the native cultures as well as host and adopted cultures.

The Development of the MMTS Curriculum

WMI was one of the first mission organizations in Korea to launch a targeted mission to migrants. In 2006, the Employment Permit System (EPS) project was launched as a ten-year plan, and the number of foreigners exceeded one million, which was about 3 percent of the total population. Serving migrant workers became an urgent task for local churches. As a result, in 2007, WMI created the MMTS to train local churches and mission agencies to reach out to migrants and equip them to reach leaders in their home countries using the FAITH principles.

The MMTS curriculum differs from the Migrant Training or Migration Adaptation Training provided by the Korean government. Its purpose is to enhance the integration of migrants into South Korean culture and society. Therefore, its main focus is on providing Korean language classes to help newcomers to assimilate into the host nation, improve their language proficiency, and gain a deeper cultural understanding. Nevertheless, the MMTS also has clear and specific goals and priorities to engage migrants for evangelism.

The objective of the curriculum is to provide training to individuals who are currently engaged in or aspire to leadership roles within diaspora organizations in South Korea. Though small, WMI has had a significant impact on thousands of expatriates who came to South Korea for employment and education. The training course has been implemented for almost two decades and offers appropriate education for evangelism and discipleship to people on the move. Furthermore, the integration of global perspectives has led to a more balanced curriculum that emphasizes practical application over theory. This training is designed differently from conventional cross-cultural training methods.

The majority of the participants who complete the course are local church leaders, and the course is designed to help them reach migrants. The courses are divided into levels, with advanced courses – which are more missiology-oriented and strategic in nature – being offered following the successful completion of the foundational course. The curriculum was developed by qualified and experienced lecturers who are engaged in nonformal education. Rev. Moon's involvement in local migrant training in Korea and his global mission engagements and leadership expanded the organization globally. Some students complete their courses through academic programs in Jeonju Technical College, Juan International University, Hanyoung University, and Presbyterian University and Theological Seminary.

At the third Lausanne Congress in South Africa in 2010, "diaspora" was introduced as a strategic focus area for the global church. The Lausanne diaspora strategy acknowledges the gathering and scattering of peoples throughout the earth, as part of the mission of God, orchestrated by the Father, Son, and Holy Spirit. As an embodiment of Christ, local churches became the primary medium of God's operation in the world, and the strategic biblical discipline of "diaspora missiology" and "diaspora missions" became significant frameworks for global missions by empowering people on the move for God's redemptive mission.

The Global Diaspora Network (GDN) was established in October 2010 as a result of the Third Lausanne Congress convened in Cape Town, South Africa.[5] Lausanne catalyst Tetsunao Yamamori contacted Rev. Moon, who has had a mission among migrants since the 1990s. Inputs from Yamamori and Dr. Tereso C. Casiño shaped the development of the MMTS domestic courses for migrants in Korea to make them more global in their perspective. Rev. Moon's relationship with GDN board members helped to establish the foundational relationship between WMI and GDN, and WMI became an active participant in GDN initiatives and helped the MMTS to impact migrant missions around

---

5. See www.Global-Diaspora.com for more on GDN's vision and activities.

the globe. At the GDN's request, the scope of the curriculum was expanded to include courses on global training and discipleship. The main topics covered in the MMTS classic and advanced courses may be considered under three categories. First, the subjects relating to knowledge are (1) Global Mission and Its Flow, (2) Mission Theology, (3) History and Status of Migrant Mission in Korea, and (4) Policy and Law of the Government for Migrants and Multicultural Families. Second, the subjects relating to strategies and methods of migrant missions practice are (1) Mission on Migrant Workers, (2) International Students Mission, (3) Ministry on Migrant Families and Children, and (4) Mission among Refugees. Third, courses relating to advancement for field workers are (1) Establishing Migrant Mission, (2) Quality and Leadership of Migrant Mission Ministers, (3) Mission Operations and Network Building, and (4) Mission Field Report.

Diaspora organizations serve as intermediaries between the adoptive country and the home country or between the first and second adoptive countries. WMI's principles of FAITH, and the MMTS program can serve any mission agency targeting ministry through/beyond diasporas.[6] From its modest inception, the MMTS has evolved into a short-term, sustainable initiative with a curriculum tailored to the specific requirements of diaspora leaders within the country, as well as those engaged in outreach to expatriates across the peninsula. However, mobilizing international students and migrant workers has been difficult because most of them lack time as well as awareness of their diasporic identity. Therefore, migrants must be discipled before they are invited to participate in migrant missions. Migrant workers who are unaware of their diasporic identity must first open their eyes and learn to reidentify themselves as diasporas before they can join courses for migrant missions. Hence, foundational discipleship courses must first address diaspora identity and calling.

Therefore, WMI offers two tracks of training: the MMTS program for local practitioners to reach migrants and the WMI Bible Institution (WBI) training course to disciple migrants and shaped them into missionaries and ministers. WBI's prerequisite courses are designed for new migrant converts and non-Christians attending the ethnic fellowships to expand their knowledge and understanding of biblical foundations. The MMTS operates with the slogan "For the Migrants, through the Migrants, Beyond the Migrants." Considering the home-based migrant mission, the aim of training is to be locally inclusive, and focused on a particular group. Therefore, experts from various fields – including immigration policymakers, pastors, scholars, refugee

---

6. Wan, *Diaspora Missiology*, 138–40.

ministry workers, mission practitioners, embassy officials, and missiology professors – are invited as instructors and facilitators.

Evaluation of the MMTS Curriculum and Contents

The primary aim of this training course is to enhance intercultural sensitivities and competencies by incorporating them into the curriculum. This is crucial for bridging the gap between different languages and understanding the needs of migrants. During the intensive sixteen-week MMTS course, church leaders and Christian migrants invest time, energy, and resources to participate in fruitful and significant missionary endeavors such as providing shelters, becoming a more multiculturally friendly society, and supporting the educational goals of international students in South Korea.[7] The courses include varied pedagogical tools such as group discussions and presentations, class lectures, group visits to migrant mission sites, and practicums in the form of fieldwork and internships. The MMTS participants engage in person-centered reflection and review sessions concerning their local ministries with migrants.

The core curricula focus on three key areas: biblical-theological perspectives on migration, sociocultural elements, and strategic missions for migrants. Understanding social phenomena and evolving policies is necessary for acquiring knowledge through the study of society. Diasporic mission strategies and fieldwork-based training aim to equip migrants with advanced methods and tools for their missions. Additionally, discussions and reflections from a global perspective are designed to enhance knowledge and strategies. The MMTS students gain theoretical and practical understanding in relation to diaspora missions, learning how to engage with current Korean migrants and refugees and put into practice the theories of migration and diaspora missions obtained in their classic and advanced courses.

Following a WMI tradition within the MMTS courses, group leaders who have successfully completed these courses serve as mentors for new course participants. Through these courses, many churches gain practical knowledge about pertinent social issues, multiculturalism, skills in interfaith dialogue, and intercultural competency. Thanks to its courses, the MMTS has established local connections throughout South Korea, as a result of which WMI is now affiliated with hundreds of congregations, local mission agencies, and NGOs engaged in fieldwork and domestic migrant missions as well as diaspora mis-

---

7. Cronshaw et al., "Mission as Hospitality."

sions in many majority world countries.[8] To date, it is estimated that more than 870 individuals have been trained through the MMTS, and many graduates who have completed classic courses and diaspora missionary studies are now participating in field missions both at home and abroad.

After completing the course, students must pass a test to receive a Level 1 certificate in intercultural communication offered by the Korea Evangelical Missiological Society (KEMS). The growing interest in migrant training has raised expectations regarding the evaluation of existing migrant mission training programs. About 70 percent of the MMTS students are engaged in migrant missions, and 50 percent of migrant trainees serve in missions in their home countries or in local churches in their homeland or other nations. These MMTS students are mainly Koreans whose aim is to reach out to migrants for the task of diaspora missions.

To evaluate the MMTS course and identify connection points for global mission training through and beyond diasporas, the researcher distributed open-ended questions regarding the MMTS courses to assess their reliability and validity for migrant missions and intercultural competency. The courses were evaluated for their applicability in diverse settings such as global diaspora classrooms and formal institutional courses. The following queries were distributed to participants:

1. To what extent have local churches or organizations implemented and deployed the MMTS curriculum?
2. How many people have completed the MMTS training course in Korea?
3. What are the basic terms used to characterize the MMTS courses?
4. What are the guidelines for creating the MMTS courses focused on global diaspora missions?
5. How may the MMTS Korea-based training courses have been effectively adopted, recontextualized, and applied in different local settings?

---

8. WMI is connected to or affiliated with nearly 190 local churches, mission organizations, multicultural ministry centers, and institutions in Korea such as Bundang Church, Jangseok Church, Church of Love, Hansarang Church, and Hallelujah Church. The list also includes mission societies and organizations connected to WMI, such as Lausanne-GDN (Global Diaspora Network), Senior Missionary Korea, Paul Missionary Society, Onnuri M Centre, Daecheong Bridge Mission Centre, Worldwide Evangelization for Christ (WEC), Campus Crusade for Christ (Cru), Operation Mobilization (OM), Youth With A Mission (YWAM), KWMA (Korea World Missions Association), and KIMA (Korea Immigrants Missions Association).

This evaluation questionnaire was administered to key members of WMI, including group leaders, hosts, and curriculum managers. Overall, the respondents testified to the program's effectiveness. One respondent who had completed the MMTS training said this:

> Previously, there were numerous inquiries regarding my ability to engage in missionary endeavors, and I simply thought that I needed to go abroad. However, this is no longer the case. I understood the significance of migrant ministry in Korea and gained insight into how to start a global mission in domestic areas. Now, I already commenced my mission to migrants, so I am delighted to share a testimony of my change.

Summary and Recommendations to the MMTS

The researcher found that the MMTS courses have been revised for global engagement with migrants. Amid the COVID-19 pandemic, online and hybrid courses were initiated, and the publication of Rev. Moon's textbook – which includes detailed instructions and MMTS course topics – is scheduled for 2024. According to Rev. Moon, WMI's goals for 2023 and beyond are threefold: creating more systematic training courses, sustaining the organization, and ensuring sustainability through a natural succession process. The MMTS will offer an effective framework for training individuals in global diaspora missions by organizing courses into two distinct tracks: global migrants and domestic migrants.

WMI's migrant mission course was initially created to cater to the needs of missional target groups, including North Korean defectors, refugees, and migrant children. The focus of global training will be on integrating global diaspora mission through robust networks between local churches and transnational staff. To foster relationships between diaspora ethnic churches – such as those of Asians and Africans – and local churches in both Western countries and their home countries, it is imperative to reinforce networks and encourage collaboration among these entities. To ensure that these courses are effective, the training curriculum for domestic missions can be used to develop rubrics for evaluating migrants' comprehension of global theories and practices.

Based on the researcher's participant observation as a lecturer of the MMTS course and the collected data from thirty-two participants of open-ended questions, here is a summary and recommendations for implementing the training program more globally:

1. **Revise and publish the MMTS course materials**

   To enhance the reliability of the course content, the MMTS course materials should be collected, revised, and published in book form in both Korean and English.

2. **Balance textbook and lecture content**

   Students reviewed the assigned textbook – *Scattered and Gathered: A Global Compendium of Diaspora Missiology*[9] – which is the primary source material used in classes. However, since the lecture content is more locally focused, a balance is required between the textbook and lecture content.

3. **Highlight key points and practical applications**

   After each lecture, there is time allotted for group discussions. This time should be utilized to highlight the key points of the lecture and consider how these can be practically applied in the individual's field of ministry.

4. **Introduce short-term practicums or internships**

   After the completion of advanced courses, field-based assignments should be fulfilled through weekly or monthly short-term mission practicums or internships. This will allow trainees to gain experience in diverse fields, develop their intercultural skills, and enhance their understanding of dynamic roles in migrant missions.

5. **Offer consultation on relevant issues**

   WMI not only provides courses but also timely information about trends in migration policies and updates on ethnic group situations. This has enabled the MMTS course participants to expand their ministries and develop local-based plans for long-term migrant missions. The MMTS curriculum, shaped by diverse local contexts, should offer more consultation on relevant issues such as low wages, wage theft, medical treatment, legal matters, deportation, insurance, surgeries, the funerals of foreigners, and property issues.

---

9. Tira and Yamamori, *Scattered and Gathered*.

6. **Increased openness to diversity and multicultural environments**

   To enable Korean monocultural society to adapt to the growing need for multicultural families to integrate into mainstream society, training courses must be more open to diversity and a multicultural environment.

7. **Maintain consistency**

   To ensure greater consistency in the content and quality of lectures, professionals in the relevant subjects must ensure that they provide the same content in both their lectures and course materials.

8. **Include migrants' perspectives**

   While lectures by specialists provide valuable information, the MMTS courses should include additional sessions to address the pressing needs of migrants – for example, by allocating time for migrants, refugees, internationals, and multicultural families to share their narratives.

9. **Compile course materials into a book**

   MMTS course materials should be compiled into a book, focusing specifically on summarizing Rev. Moon's specialized tactics in the MMTS course textbook.

10. **Greater flexibility and diversity**

    Respondents emphasized the need for greater flexibility and diversity in class schedules and teaching methods, including the use of multilingual materials and settings that better serve the needs of mission trainers working with the global diaspora.

11. **Use online platforms for international training**

    To provide courses to an international audience in different countries, platforms such as Zoom or Microsoft Teams should be used for online training.

12. **Useful for formal theological training**

    When the MMTS was used to launch nonformal education at local churches, the assignments and the reflective presentations by leaders were based on the experiences of practitioners. However, academic institutions will be able to find linking points so that the contents and pedagogical tools for formal theological curricula can be implemented in the future.

Conclusion

While multiple ethnic backgrounds and diverse cultural conflicts make it difficult to provide unified and integrated courses in global contexts, the primary aim of migrant training in Korea was to overcome the host country's hidden self-centric worldviews and monocultural prejudices. The trends of global migration, climate change, and conflicts are beyond the scope of local church missions as these transcend domestic realities. These factors will result in an increase in global migration because of the ecological crisis, economic uncertainties, asylum seekers, the refugee crisis, internally displaced persons, widows affected by civil wars, and international conflicts. The FAITH principles of the MMTS will enhance creativity and inclusivity in global migrant training. Global leadership training for migrants will be designed to be more diverse, multisite, reflective, multiethnic, contextualized, and flexible in content.

Over the course of migratory history in Korea, pioneering organizations such as WMI encountered many adversities. Yet, under the steadfast leadership of Rev. Changsun Moon, WMI has established connections with hundreds of local churches and mission agencies that are actively engaged in aiding domestic migrants in South Korea. By equipping local church leaders for diaspora missions in Korea and around the world, WMI has expanded the MMTS course through the application of diaspora theology and a global mission perspective. Since the global diaspora movement launched the GDN, countless locally based mission organizations have requested practical and relevant mission training for reverse missions and transnational networks, and the significance of diaspora missions is now well-established. It is time for churches to awaken and heed God's gentle call to be more involved in his harvest work among the diaspora and to follow his lead in engaging in "mission at our doorstep."[10] As they do so, churches will be able to observe how God guides and prepares our

---

10. Kim, *Divine Conspiracy*, 151.

missional paths across the margins and peripheries and enables us to participate in these missions.[11]

References

Cronshaw, Darren, Hanna Hyun, Peter Laughlin, Titus S. Olorunnisola, and Stephen Parker. "Mission as Hospitality with Refugees and Other Migrants: Exploring Ross Langmead's 'Guests and Hosts' in Australian Churches." *Mission Studies* 40, no. 1 (2023): 150–76.

Hyun, Hanna. "Making a Place for the Theological Foundation of 'Migration and Refugee': Review of Daniel G. Groody's Perspective and Hospitality as a Metaphor of Mission." *Theology of Mission* 55 (2019): 428–58.

Kim, S. Hun. *Divine Conspiracy*. Seoul: Arilac, 2022

Kim, S. Hun, and Wonsuk Ma, eds. *Korean Diaspora and Christian Mission*. Eugene: Wipf & Stock, 2011.

Moon, Changsun. "The Flow of Missionary Work for Migrants in Korea and the Progress of Ministry." *Journal of Mission Insight* (2016): 66–74.

———. "Foreword." *WiThee Mission International: A Strategic Model for Diaspora Missions in the Twenty-First Century*, by Tereso C. Casiño. Anyang: WiThee Mission Korea, 2015.

Seo, Deok-Seok. *A Gospel for Workers: Cho Chi Song, Yeongdeungpo Urban Industrial Mission, and Minjung*. Minneapolis: Fortress, 2023.

"The Seoul Declaration on Diaspora Missiology." *Lausanne Movement*, 2009. https://lausanne.org/content/statement/the-seoul-declaration-on-diaspora-missiology.

Tira, Sadiri Joy, and Tetsunao Yamamori, eds. *Scattered and Gathered: A Global Compendium of Diaspora Missiology*. Carlisle: Langham Global Library, 2020.

Wan, Enoch. *Diaspora Missiology: Theory, Methodology, and Practice*. Portland: Institute of Diaspora Studies, 2011.

WMI. *The Introduction of WiThee Mission and MMTS*. Anyang: WiThee Mission Korea. 2000.

https://www.moj.go.kr/immigration/1569/subview..do (Accessed on 3 July 2023).

https://www.immigration.go.kr/immigration_eng/index.do. The September 2023 Monthly Statistics of Korean Immigration and Foreign Policies by Korean Immigration Service (Accessed on 20 December 2023).

https://www.withee.org. This is the WMI's official website (Accessed on 3 June 2023).

https://www.global-diaspora.com/withee-internationals-migrant-mission-training-school-for-the-migrants-through-the-migrants-beyond-the-migrants/.

---

11. Hyun, "Making a Place," 439.

9

Justice Issues among Labor Migrants in Asia

Denison Jayasooria

Introduction

This paper focuses on the theme of labor migrants. In addition, we will review human rights violations and describe appropriate interventions to secure justice through United Nations mechanisms as well as other national human rights avenues for the protection of both documented and undocumented labor migrants. We recognize that labor migration is a dynamic global concern and a key area for human rights concerns.

The 2022 World Migration Report (WMR) estimates that there were 169 million labor migrants in 2019, of which 113.9 million (67 percent) were residing in high-income countries, 49 million (29 percent) in middle-income countries, and 6.1 million (3.6 percent) in low-income countries.[1] The WMR highlights that irregular migration in Southeast Asia is motivated by the same factors as formal migration. For example, smuggling occurs in Malaysia for migrants from the Philippines, Bangladesh, and Indonesia. A similar situation exists in Thailand for migrants from Myanmar, Cambodia, and Laos.

The report reveals that within Asia, 75 percent of trafficking victims are from Southeast Asia, with a significant number being trafficked for labor and sexual exploitation. The 2022 WMR documents the issue of migrants – including migrants sold at slave markets – being trafficked, tortured for ransom, and

---

1. United Nations, *World Migration Report 2022*, 36, https://publications.iom.int/system/files/pdf/WMR-2022.pdf.

exploited across a range of industries. The report also highlights the role of organized crime groups in these activities.

In this chapter, the term Faith-Based Organization (FBO) is used inclusively to refer to Christian and other religiously motivated organizations. This term was first used by the Work Bank[2] in recognition of the distinct strategic values of such organizations. The World Bank's engagement with faith communities was initiated in 1998 by James Wolfensohn, who was its president at the time. Mission organizations working with migrants can also be referred to as faith actors who have a legitimate space to interact with other civil society, voluntary, and not-for-profit bodies in championing the concerns of migrant workers.

Migrant Workers' Experiences of Exploitation

Migrant workers become victims of exploitative employers and recruitment agencies.[3] Depending on their status as migrant labor – with or without documentation and with or without regular work – they are vulnerable to exploitation and may fall victim to criminal organizations that use deceptive means to hold migrant workers captive and exploit their labor. Migrant workers may be exploited using control tactics such as charging exorbitant recruitment fees, putting people into debts, withholding wages, confiscating or destroying documents, and threats of violence, arrest, or deportation.

A sizable section of migrant workers who risk facing exploitative working conditions and discrimination are migrant domestic workers. Many of these domestic workers are in irregular situations, lacking access to basic economic, social, and cultural rights and also exposed to sexual and gender-based violence. Such workplace human rights violations are well-documented in "Behind Closed Doors" – a publication of the office of the UN High Commissioner for Human Rights, which highlights the risks faced by domestic workers in their workplaces.[4] These risks include being forcibly confined, being deprived of privacy, food, and sleep, being subjected to sexual and gender-based violence, and even being prevented from contacting their families and friends. Furthermore, abuse may also take place during the recruitment process. FBOs must

---

2. World Bank Group, "Faith Based and Religious Organizations," https://www.worldbank.org/en/about/partners/brief/faith-based-organizations.

3. Integral Human Development, "Exploitation of Migrant Workers," https://migrants-refugees.va/2022/07/12/exploitation-migrant-workers/.

4. UNHCR, "Behind Closed Doors," https://www.ohchr.org/sites/default/files/Documents/Publications/Behind_closed_doors_HR_PUB_15_4_EN.pdf.

document the experiences of migrant workers they encounter so that they can recognize patterns and identify those responsible for such abuse. This will enable FBOs to be more effective in their advocacy for individuals or groups and in addressing specific violations.

The Work of the International Labour Organization

The International Labour Organization (ILO) was established in 1919 and became a specialized agency of the UN in 1946. "The founders of the ILO recognized the importance of social justice in securing peace, against a background of the exploitation of workers in the industrializing nations of that time."[5] Furthermore, as an international body with a mandate for labor migration, ILO sets international standards and secures formal agreement between states, employers, and employees. The ILO's regional priority is captured in the document "Protecting Migrant Workers in Asia and the Pacific,"[6] which shows how ILO can help countries in the region manage risks such as exploitation and discrimination.

Labor migration has positive economic benefits for migrant workers and their families – for example, in Bangladesh, Nepal, and the Philippines, migrant worker remittances have helped reduce the incidence of poverty. However, the ILO notes that these development benefits are only possible if there are "effective and enforceable protection mechanisms to ensure equality of treatment and access to decent work opportunities for migrant workers."[7] In addition, abuses must be prevented.

There is no doubt that the ILO plays a unique role as a tripartite organization representing governments, employers, and workers. It builds consensus among these stakeholders and ensures better working standards in managing migrant labor. Today, of the 193 member states of the United Nations, 187 are ILO members. Therefore, FBOs must become familiar with the ILO's migrant labor standards, create local awareness, and advocate for local compliance with ILO's global standards. While this advocacy includes engaging with national governments and the relevant human resource or labor ministries, winning public opinion on this issue is also important.

---

5. International Labour Organization, "History of the ILO," https://www.ilo.org/about-ilo/history-ilo.

6. International Labour Organization, "Protecting Migrant Workers," https://www.ilo.org/asia/decentwork/adwd/WCMS_098140/lang--en/index.htm.

7. International Labour Organization, *Protecting Migrant Workers*, 4, https://www.ilo.org/wcmsp5/groups/public/---asia/---ro-bangkok/documents/publication/wcms_098142.pdf.

Another matter that must be considered is the role of working with trade unions. In most countries, trade unions usually support citizen workers in more formal employment settings and tend to perceive migrants or undocumented migrant workers as a threat to their jobs. The ILO has initiated a project involving trade unions that is focused on migrant workers.[8] This project aims to protect the rights of migrant workers through labor organizing, empowerment activities, enhanced cooperation, and trade union support in both countries of origin (Myanmar, Indonesia, and Nepal) and destination nations (Malaysia and Thailand).

Forming collectives and networks among migrant workers is an effective way of providing support, including advocacy and legal assistance, especially in cases of abuse and exploitation. Many FBOs and mission organizations already provide support to migrant workers in their communities. However, in addition to spiritual services, a more holistic intervention that includes legal aid, legal counsel, and legal representation might also be appropriate. Such an approach would complement current social service approaches and also move toward a more advocacy-focused and empowerment-focused approach.

The Convention and Lobby Member States

The *International Convention on the Protection of the Rights of All Migrant Workers and Members of Their Families* came into force on 18 December 1990. This convention incorporates the results of over thirty years of discussion. Only fifty-seven countries are parties to this convention, which is a relatively low figure compared to other human rights conventions. Of the fifty-seven member states, several are from Asia, including Bangladesh, Indonesia, the Philippines, and Sri Lanka. Additionally, eleven countries are signatories but 129 other countries have taken no action. In contrast to other core conventions, many member states are reluctant to comply with international standards. Countries that usually advocate for human rights – for example, the USA, the UK, and the Scandinavian countries – are not even party to this convention.

Therefore, there is an urgent need for FBOs and civil society to play an advocacy role in creating awareness about this convention and the mechanisms available through the UN for the protection of migrant workers. This convention on migrant workers has been described as "a global diplomatic deal to guarantee dignity and equality in an era of globalization" and one that "protects

---

8. International Labour Organization, "Migrant Workers Organizing," https://www.ilo.org/global/topics/labour-migration/projects/WCMS_315557/lang--en/index.htm.

the human rights of migrant workers at all stages of the migration process, in the country of origin, the country of transit and the country of employment, by imposing ensuing obligations on States parties."[9]

Like all other international human rights instruments, the convention sets standards for the laws and judicial and administrative procedures of individual member states. Governments of states that ratify or accede to the convention commit to apply its provisions by adopting the necessary measures. They also pledge to ensure that migrant workers whose rights have been violated are able to seek effective remedies.[10] Articles 76 and 77[11] empower the Committee on Migrant Workers (CMW) to receive complaints from state parties and individuals about alleged violations of the convention.

A Call to Engage with the Special Rapporteur

The Human Rights Council established Special Procedures by an independent group of experts on human rights.[12] There are about forty-five thematic and fourteen country-specific special rapporteurs, who serve on a nonpaid basis and have a three-year mandate. Their duties include engaging in advocacy, raising public awareness, providing advice for technical cooperation, and contributing to the development of international human rights standards.

The special rapporteur on the human rights of migrants is an independent expert position created in 1999 by the United Nations Human Rights Council.[13] The current special rapporteur – who has held this position since 2017 – is Felipe González Morales, Professor of International Law at the Diego Portales University, Santiago, Chile. The special rapporteur has a twofold mandate. First, to examine ways and means to overcome obstacles to the full and effective protection of the human rights of all migrants at all stages of migration. Second, to formulate recommendations for strengthening the promotion, protection, and implementation of the human rights of all migrants. The special rappor-

---

9. United Nations, *International Convention*, https://www.ohchr.org/en/instruments-mechanisms/instruments/international-convention-protection-rights-all-migrant-workers.

10. United Nations, "Background," https://www.ohchr.org/en/treaty-bodies/cmw/background-convention.

11. United Nations, "Communications Procedures," https://www.ohchr.org/en/treaty-bodies/cmw/communications-procedures.

12. United Nations, "Special Procedures," https://www.ohchr.org/en/special-procedures-human-rights-council.

13. United Nations, "Special Rapporteur," https://www.ohchr.org/en/special-procedures/sr-migrants.

teur acts on information submitted to him regarding alleged violations of the human rights of migrants and submits an annual report to the Human Rights Council about the global state of protection of migrants' human rights, any major concerns, and good practices that have been observed.

Access to Justice for Migrants

The human rights challenges faced by migrants is best described by the special rapporteur on the human rights of migrants, Felipe González Morales. He himself conducted a study entitled "Human Rights of Migrants," dealing with effective access to justice for migrants.[14] In this context, access to justice includes the right to information and interpretation, legal aid and representation, consular assistance, and access to remedies and redress. Morales also identified the obstacles migrants might face in accessing justice and advocated for the establishment of "firewall" protections to safeguard this right.

In addition to clear guidelines based on international law that affirm the fundamental rights that are inherent to every person, states have an obligation to guarantee the human rights of all individuals, irrespective of their nationality or migration status, including the right to access to justice and due process. Effective access to justice includes the right to legal aid and legal representation. These human rights provisions are enshrined in the *Universal Declarations of Human Rights* (UDHR) – for example, Article 8 holds that "everyone has the right to an effective remedy by the competent national tribunals for acts violating the fundamental rights," and Article 10 upholds the right to "a fair and public hearing by an independent and impartial tribunal."[15]

Diversifying Regularization Mechanisms

The special rapporteur, in a report to the Human Rights Council titled "How to Expand and Diversify Regularization Mechanisms and Programs to Enhance the Protection of the Human Rights of Migrants," writes about the vulnerability of "undocumented migrants" – a term that refers to "irregular migrants" or "migrants in irregular situations." According to the special rapporteur, "under

---

14. https://documents-dds-ny.un.org/doc/UNDOC/GEN/N18/298/96/PDF/N1829896.pdf?OpenElement (2018).

15. https://www.un.org/en/about-us/universal-declaration-of-human-rights.

international law, States are also obliged to protect the human rights of persons resorting to irregular migration pathways."[16]

Therefore, it is necessary to regularize processes and procedures that ensure that migrants fully enjoy their human rights – civil and political rights as well as economic, social, and cultural rights. This would include improving migrants' access to social protection, which includes health care, decent work, education, adequate living conditions, and family reunification. The special rapporteur has made many significant recommendations, three of which are:

1. Rethink and change the way migration is spoken about, especially when harmful narratives on migration are inserted into the public discourse.
2. Strengthen the legal framework for the protection of all migrants in line with international human rights standards.
3. Put an end to the criminalization of irregular migrants and promote solidarity toward migrants to change the narrative on migration and combat xenophobia, racism, and discrimination.

Engaging with National Human Rights Institutions

There are twenty-six national human rights institutions in Asia, established by the respective governments at the national level. The Asia Pacific Forum[17] is a grouping of all such organizations in Asia. Within the Association of Southeast Asian Nations (ASEAN), the ASEAN Intergovernmental Commission on Human Rights (AICHR)[18] consists of eleven national human rights commissions.

National human rights institutions set up by national governments play a critical role in promoting and protecting human rights within their own countries. These institutions base their mandate on foundational frameworks such as the UDHR and other UN declarations. The Paris Principles[19] provide guidelines to measure the level of autonomy and independence of these national human rights institutions. With regard to migrants, in a 2023 study

---

16. https://documents-dds-ny.un.org/doc/UNDOC/GEN/G23/075/40/PDF/G2307540.pdf?OpenElement.

17. Asia Pacific Forum, https://www.asiapacificforum.net/about/.

18. ASEAN Intergovernmental Commission on Human Rights, https://aichr.org/.

19. European Network of National Human Rights Institutions. "UN Paris Principles," https://ennhri.org/about-nhris/un-paris-principles-and-accreditation/.

entitled "Migration Management for the Most Vulnerable Groups within ASEAN,"[20] the AICHR recognizes that labor migration is a complex process and emphasizes the need to establish a management system that protects the rights of all parties. The report acknowledges that each of the main actors and stakeholders have rights and responsibilities within the multidimensional labor migration management system.

One key recommendation of the AICHR report is to make provision for greater involvement by Civil Society Organizations (CSO) in the labor migration management process, especially through the ASEAN Committee, to implement its "Declaration on the Protection and Promotion of the Rights of Migrant Workers." In this context, it was also noted that cooperation between the government and local CSOs can help to protect migrant workers, especially women. Such an approach will facilitate confidence building, especially public perception of the contributions of migrant workers in society. Therefore, faith-based and mission-based organizations working among migrant workers must build friendships and strengthen their partnerships to improve societal perceptions and influence structural changes in society. National human rights institutions such as the Human Rights Commission of Malaysia[21] have a complaints mechanism that enables a faith-based mission organization to report human rights violations, which the commission will then investigate. FBOs must utilize such mechanisms to strengthen the positions of migrant labor.

Tracking National Development Agendas through the Sustainable Development Goals

In September 2015, 193 countries agreed to the 2030 agenda for 17 universal Sustainable Development Goals (SDG).[22] Every four years, each member state submits a Voluntary National Review Report[23] at the annual High-Level Political Forum (HLPF) at the UN headquarters in New York. Goal 8 focuses on decent work for all, and target 8.8 is to "protect labour rights and promote safe and secure working environments for all workers, including migrant workers, in particular women migrants, and those in precarious employment." The specific SDG indicator 8.8.2 also seeks to "measure the level of national compliance

---

20. https://aichr.org/wp-content/uploads/2023/08/AICHR-Thematic-Study-on-Migration-Migration-Management-for-the-Most-Vulnerable-Groups-within-ASEAN.pdf.
21. SUHAKAM, https://suhakam.org.my/activities/.
22. United Nations, "17 Goals," https://sdgs.un.org/goals.
23. United Nations, "Voluntary National Reviews," https://hlpf.un.org/vnrs.

with fundamental labour rights." In addition, in SDG 16, target 16.2 focuses on eliminating exploitation, violence, and trafficking, while 16.3 promotes equal access to justice for all.

FBOs, along with CSOs, can play an important role at the national level when a Voluntary National Review (VNR) report is being prepared. Organizations dealing with migrant concerns could focus on SDG targets 8.8.2 and 16.3 by providing inputs as well seeking to secure status reports from their governments. Furthermore, FBOs can participate in regional and global events such as the High-Level Political Forum through the UN Major Groups mechanism such as the NGO Major Group or the Asia Pacific Regional Civil Society Engagement Mechanism.[24]

Best Practices among CSOs and FBOs

A Google search reveals that there are many Christian organizations working on migrant issues and concerns. Three such organizations have been recognized for their best practices in matters pertaining to advocacy and justice. These examples should encourage FBOs and mission agencies to adopt a holistic and pro human-rights approach to strengthen the positions and protection of migrant workers.

Migrante International

Migrante International (MI)[25] operates in twenty-four countries through two hundred member organizations dedicated to working with overseas Filipinos and their families. It is a global alliance of grassroots migrants' organizations, focusing on people's struggle for democracy, justice, and peace. MI actively defends and promotes the rights and welfare of overseas Filipino workers and aims to eliminate all forms of discrimination, exploitation, and abuse in the workplace. MI has five core activities: rights and welfare programs, campaigns and advocacy programs, education and research, networking and lobbying, and fostering international solidarity.

---

24. United Nations, "Major Groups," https://hlpf.un.org/sites/default/files/2022-06/MGoS%20Review%20Evaluation%20of%20Engagement.pdf.

25. Migrante International, https://migranteinternational.org/.

Do Bold[26]

Do Bold is a nonprofit organization dedicated to advancing human rights, promoting human dignity, and ensuring decent work for all migrant workers, particularly migrant workers in the Gulf countries. This organization seeks to fight modern slavery and empower the vulnerable. Its vision is to ensure that all migrant workers have access to dignified work, enjoy legal protection, and have access to justice and remedies if violations do occur. To achieve these objectives, Do Bold engages in data collection, designing human-centered solutions, and community building. Their approach focuses on empowering individuals and communities to assert their rights and includes the provision of legal representation to facilitate access to justice.

COATNET

Christian Organizations Against Trafficking in Human Beings (COATNET) is a network of forty-five Christian organizations (Catholic, Anglican, and Orthodox), dedicated to fighting labor exploitation and human trafficking. This network, which is coordinated by Caritas International, operates in thirty-nine countries and collaborates with other faith-based and civil society organizations (FBOs and CSOs) worldwide.[27] Caritas provides many services to support migrants, uphold their rights, and help them live in dignity. The organization also advocates for better legislation to protect migrants and operates centers that provide hotlines, shelters, legal help, and job training for migrants.

Caritas has produced a useful tool for its members and partners, titled *Doing Advocacy: Guidelines for Caritas International Members*. This toolkit provides guidance on methods for conducting advocacy, specifically aimed at challenging injustice and oppression. It focuses on using evidence to influence decision-makers in order to ensure the full protection of human rights for migrant workers.[28]

Practical Intervention Strategies

After discussing migrant issues and possible remedies at length, some practical interventions may help us develop effective action strategies. These actions can be carried out by local communities, particularly FBOs and CSOs. First,

---

26. Do Bold, https://www.dobold.org/our-work/.
27. COATNET, https://www.caritas.org/what-we-do/migration/human-trafficking/.
28. https://www.caritas.org/2014/01/christian-organisations-tackle-labour-exploitation/.

it is essential to understand the complex issues faced by migrant laborers, who are fellow human beings seeking fair compensation for their work. They have rights and must be treated with dignity. Second, migrant workers, like all workers, have both rights and obligations. Therefore, any exploitative practices are unacceptable.

Third, in addition to social services and support already provided to migrant workers in the local community – such as hospitality and religious services – it might be necessary to offer other services such as counseling and legal aid. This could involve support in the form of accompanying and assisting migrants as they engage with the national labor enforcement authorities regarding labor rights. Another possible activity is raising awareness about migrant workers' legal rights through public awareness programs for businesses and industries about fair and just treatment for migrant workers. In this context, FBOs can document the experiences of migrant workers they are working with, which could include recording conversations with the permission of the migrant worker. Such documentation might reveal patterns of abuse, which would help to bring perpetrators to justice and ensure justice for victims.

Fourth, when encountering human right violations such as abuse, violence, or extortion of money by an enforcement agency, the FBO could register a complaint with the National Human Rights Council or a relevant body monitoring human rights violations in the country – for example, a CS like Amnesty International.

Fifth, engaging with national parliamentarians or parliamentary committees is another avenue through which to raise awareness about human rights violations of migrant laborers, including active engagement with both traditional media and social media platforms.

Sixth, it is important to identify the national focal point for migrant workers. In most countries, this could be one agency or involve multiple agencies, but knowing the relevant agency and establishing a relationship with them is crucial. In Malaysia, for example, there are two key agencies – namely, the Ministry of Human Resources, with its labor enforcement unit, and the Ministry of Home Affairs, which deals with work permits and immigration concerns.

Seventh, working on the SDGs and engaging with UN-related mechanisms, such as the International Labour Organization (ILO) or the Special Rapporteur, is essential. It is important to understand the system and the agencies involved in order to effectively engage with them when needed.

Conclusion

Around the world, communities of faith, especially Christian mission organizations, have been active in extending care and compassion to migrant workers. In addition, we must also come to the forefront in the ministry of advocacy, speaking up and on behalf of migrant workers (Prov 31:8–9). It is important to utilize all available avenues and mediums for this purpose. Just as the apostle Paul asserted his rights as a Roman citizen (Acts 16:37), as citizens of our nations, let us do our utmost to improve the lives of all people, especially migrant laborers.

References

ASEAN Intergovernmental Commission on Human Rights. https://aichr.org/.
Asia Pacific Forum. https://www.asiapacificforum.net/about/.
Caritas. "Christian Organizations Tackle Labour Exploitation." https://www.caritas.org/2014/01/christian-organisations-tackle-labour-exploitation/.
Do Bold. https://www.dobold.org/our-work/.
European Network of National Human Rights Institutions. "UN Paris Principles and Accreditation." https://ennhri.org/about-nhris/un-paris-principles-and-accreditation/.
Human Rights Commission of Malaysia (SUHAKAM). https://suhakam.org.my/activities/.
ILO. "Protecting Migrant Workers in Asia and the Pacific." 2015. https://www.ilo.org/asia/decentwork/adwd/WCMS_098140/lang--en/index.htm.
Integral Human Development. "Exploitation of Migrant Workers and Tools for Protection." *Work for All*, 12 July 2022. https://migrants-refugees.va/2022/07/12/exploitation-migrant-workers/.
International Labour Organization. "History of the ILO." https://www.ilo.org/about-ilo/history-ilo.
———. "Migrant Workers Organizing through Cooperation with Trade Unions." https://www.ilo.org/global/topics/labour-migration/projects/WCMS_315557/lang--en/index.htm.
———. *Protecting Migrant Workers (Asian Decent Work Decade Resource Kit)*. Bangkok: ILO, 2011. https://www.ilo.org/wcmsp5/groups/public/---asia/---ro-bangkok/documents/publication/wcms_098142.pdf.
Migrante International. https://migranteinternational.org/.
UNHCR. "Behind Closed Doors: Protecting and Promoting the Human Rights of Migrant Domestic Workers in an Irregular Situation." New York; Geneva: United Nations, 2015. https://www.ohchr.org/sites/default/files/Documents/Publications/Behind_closed_doors_HR_PUB_15_4_EN.pdf.
United Nations. "The 17 Goals." https://sdgs.un.org/goals.

———. "Background to the Convention." https://www.ohchr.org/en/treaty-bodies/cmw/background-convention.

———. "Communications Procedures." https://www.ohchr.org/en/treaty-bodies/cmw/background-convention.

———. *International Convention on the Protection of the Rights of All Migrant Workers and Members of Their Families.* 1990. https://www.ohchr.org/en/instruments-mechanisms/instruments/international-convention-protection-rights-all-migrant-workers.

———. "Major Groups and Other Stakeholders." Department of Economic and Social Affairs, 2021. https://hlpf.un.org/sites/default/files/2022-06/MGoS%20Review%20Evaluation%20of%20Engagement.pdf.

———. "Special Procedures of the Human Rights Council." https://www.ohchr.org/en/special-procedures-human-rights-council.

———. "Special Rapporteur on the Human Rights of Migrants." https://www.ohchr.org/en/special-procedures/sr-migrants.

———. "Voluntary National Reviews." High-Level Political Forum on Sustainable Development. https://hlpf.un.org/vnrs.

———. *World Migration Report 2022.* https://publications.iom.int/system/files/pdf/WMR-2022.pdf.

World Bank Group. "Faith Based and Religious Organizations." https://www.worldbank.org/en/about/partners/brief/faith-based-organizations.

10

Changes to Immigration Policy and Korean Immigration Society

Kangmuk Ghil

Introduction

South Korea's experience with the unfamiliar social phenomenon of a post-war surge in foreign migrants has led to a new debate on migration. In 2007, sixty years after independence, the number of migrants reached one million for the first time. By the end of December 2019, just twelve years later, the number of foreign migrants, including naturalized citizens, exceeded 2.52 million. In 2001, the United Nations classified Korea as a late immigrant society, along with Germany and Taiwan. The Ministry of Justice predicted that by 2021, the migrant population would rise to three million, which is about 5.8 percent of the total population.

Current Status of Migrants

As of the end of April 2023, the number of foreign residents was 2,354,083. Although this figure decreased temporarily due to the global COVID-19 pandemic, it is now rising again. There are 1,237,616 long-term migrants (registered foreigners), 506,195 foreign nationals with domestic residence, and 610,272 short-term foreigners. It is an increase of nearly12 percent from previous year and accounts for 4.89 percent of the national population.[1]

---

1. See a report with slightly different numbers – Park Hye Ri, "Multicultural Era Nears as Foreign Population Exceeds 2.5M." See https://www.korea.net/NewsFocus/Society/view?articleId=245554.

Table 1: Top five migrant-sending countries and their population

Country of migrants	Population	Percentage
China	886,405	37.7
Vietnam	256,750	10.9
Thailand	207,169	8.8
United States	169,653	7.2
Uzbekistan	81,972	3.5

In terms of regions, 715,550 migrants (57.8 percent) live in the Seoul metropolitan area, 230,941 (18.7 percent) in the Yeongnam region, 146,230 (11.8 percent) in the Chungcheong region, and 101,583 (8.2 percent) in the Honam region. All 17 cities and provinces have seen an increase in foreign resident populations. The number of Korean spouses (marriage migrants) and foreign students has been steadily increasing to 172,254 and 206,746, respectively. Korean universities are aggressively promoting themselves to attract international students to face the demographic cliff resulting from the shrinking of the college-age population.

In the past, most migrants were single individuals, but in recent years, there has been a growing trend of migrants settling with their families, resulting in a growing number of children and adolescents from various migration backgrounds. Notably, the number of immigrants to Korea is increasing and the types of residencies have become more diverse. In the future, immigrants in Korean society are expected to surge.

Table 2: Composition of Migrants (Source: Ministry of Interior and Safety 2021)

Migrant Category	Population	Percentage
Foreign workers	460,000	21
Marriage immigrants	170,000	8
Foreign students	140,000	7
Foreign nationality compatriots	350,000	16
Other foreigners	580,000	27
Naturalized people	200,000	9
Children from multicultural families	260,000	12

Since around 2005, there has been greater diversity in the types of foreigners entering Korea – for example, marriage immigrants (F-6), foreign workers (E-9), foreign students (D-2, D-4), and compatriots (F-4, H-2). F-4 visa is for Overseas Koreans, designed for people of Korean descent who have previously held Korean citizenship but have since renounced it, while an H-2 visa is a working visit, allowing temporary employment for specific categories considered special cases. With the increasing number of long-term foreign residents such as marriage migrants and foreign national compatriots, Korea's policy on foreigner management and control has shifted toward integration. As the country becomes more multiracial and multiethnic, promoting social integration has become an important national policy to ensure that this diverse population does not become a source of conflict.

Immigration Influx and Policy Responses[2]

An examination of South Korea's current immigration laws and systems in response to the rapid influx of migrants reveals significant implications for ministry in this era of migration.

Prior to 1988, South Korea did not allow foreign labor for basic skills, but with the hosting of the Seoul Olympics, the country began to permit foreigners to enter the country for employment purposes. Under a system called "industrial technology training," businesses with overseas subsidiaries were allowed to employ up to 1 percent of their permanent workers for three-month training periods at their domestic offices. Subsequently, the Ministry of Justice introduced an "Industrial Technical Trainee System" that extended this training period to one year. Under this system, a company could employ up to fifty trainees or 10 percent of the number of permanent workers, whichever was greater. From 1992, under the Kim Young-Sam administration, the industrial trainee program thrived in response to growing demand for labor from small and medium-sized enterprises. Trainees from ten countries – including China, Vietnam, and the Philippines – came to South Korea, and it was permissible to extend the training period for up to three years. However, these trainees were paid low wages – on the basis that they were categorized as "trainees" under this system – and this led to wage disparities between trainees and other workers. As a result, many trainees left the workplace, which led to an increase in the number of illegal migrants. Allegations of human rights violations have consistently been raised against the treatment of these trainees who, despite their trainee status, functioned as regular workers.

In August 2003, the Ministry of Employment and Labor implemented the Employment of Foreign Workers Act, which introduced an employment

---

2. Adapted from Ghil, "A Study on the Effectiveness and Influencing Factors....," 2021.

permit system based on the principle of short-term rotations of three years. In September 2012, the Dedicated Worker System was established, allowing employees who had worked continuously for the first four years and ten months without changing workplaces to leave Korea and then reenter the country three months later and work at the same place. This effectively allowed workers to stay in Korea for up to nine years and eight months, which led to sharp disagreements over the question of social integration of foreign workers from sixteen countries who have stayed in Korea for approximately ten years.

Marriage Immigration and Multiculturalism

In addition to the influx of foreign labor, the number of marriage migrants entering Korea to marry Korean men began to increase after the year 2000, following implementation of the rural bachelor wedding program in 1988. Since the 1990s, there has not only been a dramatic increase in the number of international marriages but also greater diversity in the number of countries represented in these marriages, with Korea now having such marriage-related ties with 127 countries.

Table 3 shows that the number of Southeast Asian women immigrating to Korea through marriage to Korean men has increased dramatically since 2000. This represents a unique form of international migration that crosses borders through marriage, which is typically regarded as a private sphere. Marriage migration into Korean society has usually been categorized as economic migration, which blurs the line between immigration and marriage. This was a structural problem that was bound to give rise to conflicts between marriage migrants and their Korean spouses who sought economic benefits through their marriage to Korean nationals. These problems, combined with the language barrier between international couples, amplified conflicts and sometimes led to social problems such as domestic violence, desertion, and divorce. Ideally, immigration policies should address these issues arising from marriage migration, However, South Korea, viewing these issues as part of family policy, has responded with a welfare-oriented multicultural policy.[3]

---

3. This is evidenced by the significant drop in the number of marriages since the immigration policy decision to strengthen the screening process for issuing marriage licenses after 1 April 2014.

Table 3: Marriages to foreigners by nationality (2009–2019)[4]

	2000	2001	2003	2005	2007	2009	2011	2013	2015	2017	2019	Ration	YOY % Increase
KOR M+FOR F	6,945	9,684	18,751	30,719	28,580	25,142	22,265	18,307	14,677	14,869	17,687	100.0	6.5
Vietnam	77	134	1,402	5,822	6,610	7,249	7,636	5,770	4,651	5,364	6,712	37.9	5.9
China	3,566	6,977	13,347	20,582	14,484	11,364	7,549	6,058	4,545	3,880	3,649	20.6	-0.6
Thailand	240	182	345	266	524	496	354	291	543	1,017	2,050	11.6	31.4
Japan	819	701	844	883	1,206	1,140	1,124	1,218	1,030	843	903	5.1	-8.5
Philippines	1,174	502	928	980	1,497	1,643	2,072	1,692	1,006	842	816	4.6	-4.2
USA	231	262	322	285	376	416	507	637	577	541	597	3.4	5.3
Cambodia	1	2	19	157	1,804	851	961	735	524	480	432	2.4	-5.1
Others	837	924	1,544	1,744	2,079	1,983	2,062	1,906	1,801	1,902	2,528	14.3	16.1
KOR F+FOR M	4,660	4,839	6,025	11,637	8,980	8,158	7,497	7,656	6,597	5,966	5,956	100.0	-2.2

4. Marriage figures from Korea Statistics 2020. www.kostat.go.kr. KORM+FORF stands for Korean male married to a foreign female and KORF+FORM stands for Korean female married to a foreign male.

Surge of Foreign Nationals

As international migration has become more prevalent, the number of foreigners living in South Korea has increased annually. As foreigners enter and settle in the country, an expansion in policy targets and areas of concern is inevitable. In addition to immigrants themselves, their spouses, children, and extended family members may also enter the country, necessitating policies that address issues such as welfare, employment, and education. It was only after the 2005 migrant crisis that France and Germany began to establish legal and institutional foundations for systematizing social integration policies for settled foreigners. Learning from the immigration policy failures of other, more advanced, countries, South Korea is adopting various policy measures to prevent future conflicts.

The influx of foreigners into South Korea and the evolution of policies can be seen as having five distinct phases. The first phase (1948–1980) was a traditional phase of "controlling foreigners" during which the entry and exit of foreigners was managed primarily by the government of South Korea. In 1961, the Immigration Control Act – which became the basis for foreigner control – was enacted, and the administration of immigration control was transferred from the Ministry of Foreign Affairs to the Ministry of Justice.

The second phase (1980–2000) was the "residence management phase." During this period, the hosting of the 1988 Seoul Olympics helped to establish diplomatic relations with former socialist countries such as Mongolia, the Soviet Union, and China. Other significant developments during this period were the introduction of foreign labor in 1991 and the enactment of the Overseas Koreans Act in 1999.

The third phase (2000–2007) can be described as the "residency management phase," which took into consideration the human rights of foreigners. From 2000 onward, the number of foreigners entering and staying increased, and the system switched to "human rights-oriented residence management." In 2002, a permanent resident status was established, and in 2003, the existing foreign industrial trainee system was converted to an employment permit system.

The fourth phase (2007–2013) focused on the "social integration of migrants." In 2007, the number of foreigners living in Korea exceeded one million for the first time, prompting the government to promote policies that helped migrants to integrate into Korean society and fully utilize their abilities, as well as to create a social environment where Koreans and foreigners understand and respect each other.[5] In 2007, a visit-work program was implemented

---

5. Article 1, Treatment of Overseas Koreans Act.

for Chinese compatriots, allowing them to visit and work in Korea. During the same year, the basic law on the treatment of overseas Koreans was enacted, and World Day was designated as a national holiday and celebrated for the first time. In 2008, the Multicultural Family Support Act was enacted. A year later, a pilot program – the Korea Immigration Integration Program – was launched, introducing a point system for qualifying for permanent residency. In 2011, South Korea began permitting multiple nationalities; and in 2013, the Refugee Act was enacted. During this period, the First Basic Plan for Foreigners was prepared.

In the final phase, the Second Basic Plan for Foreigners (2013–2017) was implemented, followed in 2018 by the Third Basic Plan for Foreigners (2018–2022). The budget for foreigners has also increased, and efforts have been made to establish a stable budget system financed by foreigners' residence fees and criminal fines to promote long-term policies such as social integration and environmental improvements in densely populated areas.

Social Integration

The rapid increase in the number of foreigners residing in Korea has made it imperative to prevent social conflicts and ensure social safety. This influx of migrants has resulted in issues such as migrant solidarity, ghettoization, slums, and security concerns. Moreover, in the light of the security threat from North Korea, which makes it imperative to ensure national unity and security for Korean nationals, the influx of foreigners and immigrants presents further challenges for South Korea. In response to confrontations in the Korean Peninsula, South Korea began to prepare a Korean-style social integration policy with the following goals: first, to promote shared values of democratic order and foster essential social skills; second, to establish a societal framework in which diverse members live together harmoniously and promote understanding of diversity so that socially disadvantaged people such as migrants do not suffer unfair discrimination and prejudice due to differences in language, culture, and appearance; and third, to create a social environment where diversity is a source of national competitiveness in an era characterized by internationalization and openness.

Immigration Policy: Concepts and Objectives
The Environment of Immigration Policy

International migration declined after the global COVID-19 pandemic. Countries facing labor shortages due to travel restrictions, border closures, and suspension of immigration services are now implementing various strategies to utilize low-skilled workers and attract highly educated migrants, talented professionals, and investors through measures such as temporary entry of foreign workers, renewal of residence status, and change of status. Policies must adapt to accommodate the growing number of industries utilizing digital technologies, as well as the increasing use of noncontact methods in immigration administration and migrant education.

While the number of forced migrants worldwide is at a record high of 89.3 million, a report by the UNHCR exposes the limitations of resettling refugees in third countries[6] due to the impact of COVID-19 and calls for a balanced approach to accepting refugees in line with the external policy environment and international obligations. South Korea's immigration preference is steadily increasing. In July 2021, following the unanimous decision of the UN Conference on Trade and Development, South Korea was upgraded from a developing to a developed country, and in 2022, it ranked eighth in the Global Attractiveness Index (GAI). There is a growing trend among young people to immigrate to Korea due to popularity and the influence of K-content. Considering these developments, the country's immigration policies for employment and student immigration should be revised in line with the country's status and current immigration preferences. The productive-age population is sharply declining, as evidenced by 30,500 deaths outpacing 27,200 births in 2020. In 2021, South Korea's total population dropped by 0.2 percent, or 90,000 people, bringing the population to 51.74 million, marking the first population decrease. Figure 4 shows the severity of the population crisis based on the projected composition.[7]

In 2020, the population ratio in the metropolitan area reached 50.2 percent, with increasing concentration in urban centers and a gradual rise in regional depopulation due to overall population decline. In 2021, following the enactment of the Special Act on Balanced Development, the government designated eighty-nine regions as experiencing a population decline. The Presidential Committee for Balanced National Development initiated a regional growth plan to nurture strategic industries in fourteen nonmetropolitan areas. To deal

---

6. Third country refers to international protection provided for lawful stay in a third country other than where the person may originate from or where he currently sought refuge in.

7. Statistics Korea. www.kostat.go.kr/.

with regional depopulation, the government is implementing immigration-based regional revitalization initiatives in collaboration with local governments.

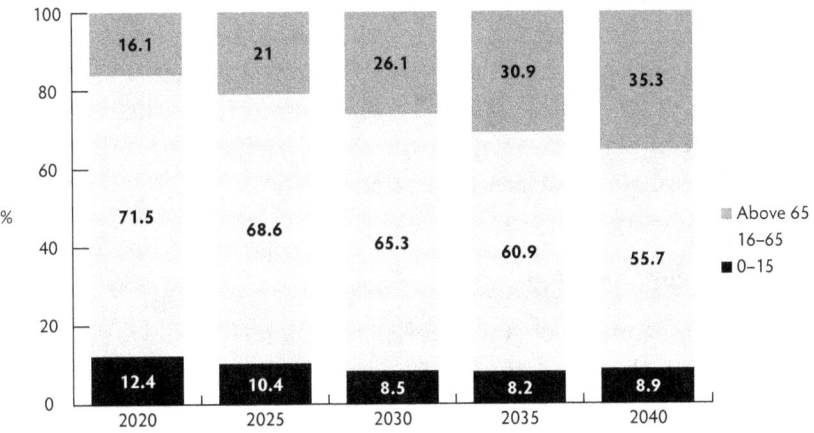

Figure 4: Population composition by age group (2020–2040)

The Concept of an Immigration Policy

In demography, immigration refers to the movement of people across national borders, which changes population size. The immigration policy of a country aims to control both the quantity and quality of population migration by regulating the entry and exit of nationals and foreigners. The reason both quantity and quality must be managed is that the influx of migrants is inevitably linked to all social aspects, causing long-term ripple effects in various fields such as economy, welfare, security, public order, and culture. Therefore, immigration policy can be viewed as a human resource management policy that determines criteria such as "who to admit into a country," "how to settle them," and "who is to be recognized as a member of the nation." A national immigration policy controls and manages a country's borders, taking into consideration all aspects of politics, economics, society, and culture. Due to the complexities involved, immigration policy demands a comprehensive approach that covers the management of legal and illegal migration, settlement and integration of migrants, as well as nationality and citizenship issues. This policy is intertwined with areas such as foreign relations, national security, labor, trade, skills development support, health, education, housing, welfare, and taxation policies.

Therefore, immigration policy has a broad and diverse agenda. It focuses on migrants and shapes a complex relationship between them and the nationals of the host country throughout various stages, from issuing visas to entry, residency, and the acquisition of permanent residence and citizenship. It must not only address the present but also consider the future life of a country, the spectrum of policy agendas in immigration-receiving countries can only be formed through the participation and collaboration of many national bodies, calling for a comprehensive approach to immigration policy, rather than a segmented response in each entity separately.

Goals of Immigration Policy

Over time, immigration policy has evolved from border control to the management of resident aliens and the integration of migrants into society. Migration control refers to actively excluding or artificially reducing undesirable groups in a country with the goal of promoting national interests. These national interests include economic, social, and cultural interests and must take into account both present and future circumstances since the effects of the present migrant influx also have significant sociocultural implications for the future.

In addition, another important consideration of immigration policy goals is to foster greater acceptance of migrants by the people of the host country. With the spread of globalization, migration naturally increases. Migration impacts the socio-economic development and growth for both the migrants and the host country. Besides it will change the people of the host country. Therefore, policies that mitigate anti-immigrant sentiments among the citizens have become necessary and increasingly important in recent years.

In South Korea, several governmental agencies are responsible for immigration administration: a) the Ministry of Justice (MOJ), which is responsible for the entire process of entry, stay, and integration of migrants; b) the Ministry of Employment and Labor (MOEL), which manages unskilled foreign workers in South Korea, including the limits of immigration and employment permits; c) the Ministry of Gender Equality and Family Affairs (MOGEF), which conducts various programs for married immigrants and their families; d) the Ministry of the Interior and Safety (MOIS), which works with local governments to provide accommodation and support to migrants; and e) the Ministry of Education (MOE), which focuses on the influx and management of international students and the adaptation and integration of multicultural students.

Recent Immigration Policy Changes in Korea
Launching of a Regionalized Visa Pilot

As some regions experience population decline due to falling birth rates and aging populations, and as attracting population inflows becomes more difficult, there is an urgent need to promote visa policies that support regional revitalization and reflect local needs. A pilot project will initially be implemented in areas with declining populations, where residents are likely to be more receptive. In 2020, there were 6.19 million businesses in the Seoul-Incheon-Gyeonggi metropolitan area, representing 85 percent of the national total of 7.3 million. The goal is to create a cycle of population growth and inflow by focusing on residents in densely populated metropolitan areas and addressing specific regional needs through visa policies developed in partnership with local governments.

The government is advancing a policy to offer residency benefits to talented individuals and families of foreign nationals who graduate from local universities and settle in depopulated areas. This initiative aims to reduce the concentration of foreigners in metropolitan areas, contributing to the balanced development of the country. It also encourages immigrant settlement in harmony with local residents, boosting the local economy through increased production and consumption. Additionally, the policy will enhance the competitiveness of local universities by attracting more international students, further stimulating the economies surrounding these institutions. This pilot project, which covers 28 regions—including six metropolitan and four basic areas—will accommodate migrants based on the unique characteristics of each region. It will also implement new governance practices that involve citizens, the government, and local businesses, promoting the rights and interests of residents while managing immigration responsibly and inclusively.

Fast-Track Permanent Residency and Naturalization of Outstanding Talents

In an era of globalization, migration is bringing about changes in nationality and permanent residency for foreign talented individuals who will lead the fourth industrial revolution in Korea as it competes with advanced nations. First, a new program has been launched to expedite the granting of permanent residency and nationality to master's and doctoral students in science and technology from five universities. To attract more global talent, this program links permanent residence and nationality, shortening the current six-year process to three, even for those who are not yet employed. Second, the government is exploring ways to provide customized services to stem the outflow of talented science and technology graduates who are leaving Korea by providing long-term residency options at their educational institutions.

Address Labor Shortages in Agricultural and Rural Areas

Over the years, as the gap between urban and rural areas widens, the problem of labor shortages in rural areas has become more serious, especially when compared to densely populated metropolitan areas. This situation has forced companies established in rural areas to relocate to nearby cities in search of labor, resulting in a vicious cycle that leads to local economic downturns, making migrant residency policies necessary.

In 2022, there were a total of 19,718 seasonal workers, and by the first half of 2023, this number increased to 26,788 workers nationwide. By May 2023, an additional 12,869 seasonal workers were added to this number. In addition, the existing five-month stay period for migrants was extended by three months, allowing migrants to participate in agriculture, fisheries, and seasonal manufacturing activities. This helped to resolve labor shortages in rural areas that were not covered by the current employment permit system.

Encourage International Students to Work

The number of foreign students studying in higher education institutions has been growing steadily, from 16,832 in 2004 to 166,892 in 2022. To attract and integrate foreign talents into local communities after their graduation, it is important to ensure that they have excellent Korean language skills. Through collaboration between universities, local governments, and industries, international students are given opportunities to work in specialized sectors after graduation. The Ministry of Employment is promoting a plan to increase job opportunities for international students who have not found jobs after graduation by converting their study visa (D-2) into a work visa. The ministry is also considering the creation of a specialists category (E-7) for international students who have difficulty finding employment.

Develop Multiculturalism in Korea

The National Multicultural Acceptance Survey – conducted by the government every three years – is being conducted for the third time with five thousand adults (aged 19 to 74) and five thousand youth (middle and high school students). The key areas covered in this survey include diversity, cultural openness, national identity, stereotypes, discrimination, expectations of one-sided assimilation in relationships, feelings of rejection and avoidance, willingness to engage, dual evaluations of universality, and global citizenship behavior.

In 2021, the multicultural acceptance score of adults was 52.27, which was 19.12 points lower than that of adolescents (71.39). The survey revealed that acceptance scores were higher among lower age groups. Both adults and adolescents report that participation in multicultural education has a positive effect on improving acceptance. The acceptance score of participants in multicultural education was 4.85, which was 2.38 points higher than that of nonparticipants. The government is promoting immigration impact assessments to prevent or reduce discrimination against migrants and enhance understanding of immigration issues. This initiative aims to increase opportunities for exchange and communication, thereby increasing the acceptance of immigrants within Korean society. The Presidential Committee of National Cohesion is promoting a national-level social integration policy that seeks to address blind spots caused by fragmented services by establishing a Korean-style immigration policy and providing clear direction for the integration of migrants in our society, with a special focus on ensuring that children with migrant backgrounds can settle down and grow up in a stable and healthy environment.

Suggestions for Migrant Ministry
Ministry in an Immigrant Society

As the composition of the nation and society changes, a paradigm shift is necessary in the local church and its ministries. First, there must be a shift in awareness. Migrant ministry is God's mission for us at this time. It is not a matter of choice. As the population declines due to low birth rates, the Korean church is aging. With fewer young people expected in the church in the next generation, this raises concerns about the changing dynamics within the church. In the context of ultra-low fertility, it becomes increasingly difficult to pass on the faith to future generations. Therefore, churches must collaborate with migrants in our society and engage in both local and global missionary work. It is encouraging to note that in recent years, missionary work and education have been increasingly responsive to changing times and social changes, leading to dynamic ministry approaches appropriate to the current situation.

Mission in the Age of Migration and Multiculturalism

Jesus envisioned global evangelization through his twelve disciples, and God has allowed the Korean church to be a significant player in global evangelization by ministering to foreign workers, compatriots, marriage migrants, and international students who come to this country. Each migrant is a seed of the gospel that can be planted in their families and the families they have left behind in their country of origin. Therefore, the Korean church must develop a pastoral concern that is sensitive to the needs of the migrants of our land and develop a missionary strategy where migrants themselves are the main actors. This is the diaspora missiology paradigm of mission to the migrants and through the migrants.

Married migrants are an important social class because they are here to stay. Unlike foreign workers who are required to return to their countries of origin after five years, marriage migrants are settled migrants (naturalized or permanent) who can be channels of evangelization to their country of origin. As the mothers and fathers of the next generation of Korean children, marriage migrants play a key role in passing the gospel to future generations. When an individual's salvation is connected to the salvation of their family, a missional strategy specifically for marriage migrants should be developed.

Develop Awareness and Multicultural Ministry Manuals

Developing a church community's understanding of migrants and developing appropriate services is important for migrant ministry. They need to develop diverse approaches to help migrants grow holistically and healthily as children of God, fostering their development as interdependent disciples rather than merely assimilating them into Korean society.

Recently, the term "multicultural" has been used in various contexts – for example, multicultural children, multicultural youth, multicultural soldiers, multicultural schools, and multicultural families. However, we should not label migrants as *multicultural* but, rather, as people who can integrate into existing churches and society. Any categorization of people as multicultural can be discriminatory and stigmatizing as it undermines their inherent worth and dignity.

Mission encompasses evangelism, education (nurture), social service, and fellowship. Migrant ministry involves practical ministry that changes the fabric of the community, creating a pathway for personal and church growth. The apostle Paul cites Jesus as having said, "It is more blessed to give than to receive" (Acts 20:35). Migrant ministries integrate a passion for evangelism with sound theological reflection and practice, which helps individuals to grow into disciples of Christ and churches to grow into healthy communities.

There is an urgent need to develop a ministry manual that helps to ensure balance within ministry in the areas of soul-winning, social reform, and service. In addition, educational programs are necessary to improve church members' sensitivity toward the unique cultural and religious backgrounds of migrants within the church community so that they can better understand the challenges faced by them.

Cooperation between Churches and Migrant Organizations

Migrant ministry can be more effective when carried out in partnership with government agencies, the church, and related organizations. Currently, there is an increasing trend of migrant and multicultural family ministries at the local church level in Korea. Most migrant-related organizations in Korea are run by small churches and missionary organizations, who share information as well as human and material resources. Since most of their members are migrants, these migrant organizations often face financial difficulties. Nevertheless, they are actively involved in multilingual worship, evangelism, providing shelter for the homeless, integration into Korean society, cultural education, medical assistance, and community conflict resolution. For greater impact, it is important to benchmark missionary practices and share experiences and information on migrant ministry.

Conclusion

Korean society is rapidly evolving into an immigrant and multicultural society, and this is an inevitable social phenomenon. The local church plays a vital role within such a society. The church must fulfill its social responsibility to serve these migrant and multicultural communities in society. The church should not exist for its own sake but to share the responsibilities and problems of the community. Transcending race, color, and culture, the local church – with Jesus Christ as its Lord and head – must become a servant to migrants in society.

Migrant ministry is not a product on a department store shelf; nor is it an optional special mission or a flashy adornment to enhance the reputation of the local church. Rather, it is the church's natural and obedient response to God's call and the changes in society. The current trend of increasing migration in Korea opens up new horizons for the Korean church's ministry and global mission. The declining birth rate and an aging society have raised a red flag about the continued viability of the Korean church. Instead of seeing the church solely as the traditional Korean church made up only of Koreans, the church must embrace the Great Commission alongside migrants in Korea as it evolves into a new, multicultural Korean church.

The pioneering migrant ministries must collaborate with local churches in areas such as migrant counseling, crisis management, education, training, joint research, and ministry development to address key challenges and implement targeted ministry strategies. Successful ministry models and practices, as well as the challenges involved in such ministries, should be disseminated among all Korean churches.

A migrant ministry paradigm is appropriate for a multicultural migrant society. Such a paradigm is a blessing that broadens an individual's spiritual horizons and perspectives, enhances inclusiveness within the church, and enables the church to become more Christ-like. Missions lie at the heart of the gospel and are the fundamental reason for the church's existence.

References

Ghil, Kang-Muk. "A Study on the Effectiveness and Influencing Factors of Frontline Officials' Collaboration on Immigration Policy." PhD Diss., Kyeonghee University, 2021.

Ri, Park Hye. "Multicultural Era Nears as Foreign Population Exceeds 2.5M." See https://www.korea.net/NewsFocus/Society/view?articleId=245554.

Statistics Korea, www.kostat.go.kr/.

11

Embracing Migrants and Refugees in Malaysia

Ng Oi Leng

Introduction

Malaysia hosts millions of foreign nationals, many of whom are from restricted access nations – the so-called unreached people groups, who can now be reached within our own country. Malaysia relies heavily on its migrant workforce, especially blue-collar workers, as well as IT experts, businesspeople, and professionals. In addition, there are millions of undocumented migrants who have become stateless, especially in East Malaysia. In addition, the Ministry of Higher Education (MOHE) granted student visas to between 130,000 and 170,000 thousand international students for 2022.[1] This unique situation can be viewed as either a threat or an opportunity. By intentionally engaging with and discipling these unreached groups, the Malaysian church can become a powerful force for change, both locally and globally.

In an effort to make the world a better place for all, the United Nations introduced the 17 Sustainable Development Goals (SDG) designed to transform our world by 2030,[2] and the Malaysian government has responded positively to these goals. Will these efforts really change the world and change Malaysia? As Christians, we believe that God has revealed his own superior plans and goals for transforming our world. Perhaps we can call these "Sustainable Discipleship Goals."

---

1. ICEF, 2022. https://monitor.icef.com/2023/02/malaysia-exceeds-target-for-new-international-student-applications-in-2022/.
2. United Nations, "17 Goals," https://sdgs.un.org/goals.

The church is called to disciple nations and bring God's shalom to our broken world. Through Christ's death and resurrection, all things on earth and in heaven are reconciled to God (Col 1:19–20). The ultimate goal of discipleship is far more than saving souls and growing the church; it involves seeing the beauty, goodness, and righteousness of God's kingdom being manifested on earth, transforming poisoned cultures, unjust systems, and corrupt practices, and blessing people from all nations, including those who do not yet know the truth. Our Lord teaches us to pray consistently for God's kingdom to come and his will to be done on earth (Matt 6:9–10). Therefore, the church must actively participate in initiatives such as the SDGs as part of its discipleship mandate, empathizing with the needy and marginalized, prioritizing community development and transformation, and acting as an agent of blessing for nations in transit.

The Malaysia Diaspora Network (MDN) seeks to connect and partner with mission organizations, the United Nations office in Malaysia, government agencies, embassies, corporations, humanitarian organizations, and international networks – such as the Refugee Highway Partnership and the Global Diaspora Network – to share knowledge and resources for greater impact on services and advocacy both locally and regionally.

> He has showed you, O mortal, what is good. And what does the LORD require of you? To act justly and to love mercy and to walk humbly with your God. (Mic 6:8)

The Vision of the MDN

Jesus used parables to teach his disciples about the kingdom of God. It is worth paying special attention to these parables as we engage in the work of mission and discipleship. The kingdom of God begins with the sower who sows abundantly in various types of soil (Mark 4:3–8). When the good seed falls on the good soil, it bears much good fruit. So, the primary work of the kingdom of God is sowing, not reaping. The sowing must be done in the field, not in the church. And not all who hear the gospel will bear fruit.

The parable of the growing seed (Mark 4:26–29) illustrates that after the seed is scattered on the earth, it germinates and grows naturally, day and night, without human intervention. These two parables remind us that conversion and growth are primarily the work of the Holy Spirit and that we must learn to trust him more.

Marana's Story

After the month-long Ramadan, the joyous festival of Aidil Fitri is celebrated. Marana[3] is a hospitable man and has invited many friends of various faiths to his home. This year, he has even more reason to celebrate. He proudly tells of his daughter's success in the 2022 IGCSE (Cambridge High School Exam) and announces with great excitement his decision to return to his home country. With a big grin on his face, he tells of his hope to acquire a business and start a cell phone repair shop. This is a skill he learned and honed from some Christian brothers. His wife can cook, so she plans to run a food stall while continuing to grow her multi-level marketing business, which she was introduced to by a Christian couple. He explains, "God is good, and you all have helped my family."

Twenty years ago, Marana came to Malaysia with his wife and a daughter, seeking greener pastures. Shortly after, the couple had two more children, born in Malaysia. As noncitizens who did not possess valid documents, his children only had the option of attending a madrasa (religious school) run in the community *surau* (a place for Muslim's to pray). In 2015, Marana discovered the ElShaddai Refugee Learning Centre (ERLC) in Klang. Despite criticism from his community, he enrolled his children in this Christian refugee learning center. Seven years later, his daughters had completed their IGCSE and applied for scholarships to study at a university in their home country. Because of this family's involvement in the learning center, teachers and members of the church visited Marana's home regularly, befriended the family, prayed for them, and demonstrated God's love in practical ways such as helping them to acquire skills and develop business networks.

Marana's courageous decision to send his children to the ElShaddai Centre broke the ice and bridged the chasm between this Christian organization and the Muslim diaspora communities. The ElShaddai Centre soon became the learning center of choice for many families from the *kampung* (village). The children were ministered to daily at the school, while their families also received visits and assistance. During the COVID-19 pandemic, with the help of the embassy, news of ElShaddai's work began to spread among other Muslim communities in different parts of Malaysia. Through the MDN, new learning centers were established, some in the most unexpected places in Malaysia.

When Marana plucked up the courage to look beyond his own community and reach out to the ElShaddai Centre, God's shalom blessed not just his own

---

3. Not his real name.

family but also others in his *kampung* and, eventually, similar ethnic communities in different parts of the country.

The ElShaddai Refugee Learning Centre, which is the leading organization of the MDN, works with people from twenty different nations in Malaysia: Indonesians, Myanmar, Afghans, Somalis, Sudanese, Suluk and Bajau from the Philippines, Sri Lankans, Pakistanis, Rohingya, Yemen, Syrian and so on. Over the last fifteen years, many testimonies have emerged from these diverse ethnic communities. Those who open their hearts to welcome this ministry frequently discover God's shalom come upon them. The goal of this movement is to see contextualized discipleship movements emerging within these communities.

Holistic Integral Approach to Community Transformation

> The kingdom of heaven is like yeast that a woman took and mixed into about sixty pounds of flour until it worked all through the dough. (Matt 13:33)

The easiest way to engage with communities is to meet their felt needs. In Malaysia, marginalized diaspora groups such as refugees, irregular migrants, and stateless people have no safety nets. They face challenges due to lack of legal work rights, limited access to regular schooling for their children, and inadequate access to subsidized health care. While it is important to advocate for systemic change within an appropriate legal framework, that remains a long-term goal. In the meantime, we must get to work. To bring changes within these communities, we must prioritize long-term development projects over rescue and relief efforts.

The ElShaddai Centre's ecosystem for empowering the diaspora is founded on the 4 Es: Evangelism, Education, Economy, and Environment programs:

1. Evangelism: The evangelism approach is contextual discipleship to catalyze discipleship movements within diaspora communities. Discipleship includes activities that promote the spiritual, physical, social, and emotional well-being of the whole person, inculcating values that broaden minds, enlighten hearts, and transform lives.

2. Education: Education is informal but systematic and includes all forms of academic and nonacademic activities. Academic programs range from preschool through primary and secondary education to online college courses. Nonacademic education includes Christian and mission trainings, health care and life skills, community

protection programs, coaching and sports, and vocational training. Partnership is key to providing quality education at the lowest cost, often making use of church buildings and other revitalized vacant or abandoned places within communities to conduct classes. Graduates receive training as teachers and are then sent to support mission-minded teachers at other community-run learning centers.

3. Economy: Economic activities include various social enterprises and microfinance activities that are aimed at creating jobs and providing livelihoods within the community. Examples include the sewing center in the Afghan community, an air-conditioning service enterprise, a fish farm, and bakery projects operated in partnership with refugee communities.

4. Environment: Environmental conservation is important in marginalized communities facing extreme poverty, particularly among the stateless people in Sabah. Some specific areas of concern are waste disposal, clean water, and sanitation.

At the heart of the 4E approach is the mobilization of the Malaysian church to recognize this kairos moment in diaspora mission and the opportunity to reach those who are most unreached and even considered "dangerous to reach" in our land. The Malaysian church, blessed with both human and financial resources, is like a sleeping giant waiting to be awakened by God's prophetic voice and to take on Christ's mandate to evangelize the world through local mission by reaching people on the move. Brother Andrew Ng, founding chairman of both the ElShaddai Centre and the MDN, organizes the biennial National Diaspora Symposium (NDS) in an effort to gather all workers in the field to share experiences and resources and to rally churches to initiate diaspora mission work in their respective regions.

The NDS Malaysia

The keynote speaker at the first NDS in September 2015 was Enoch Wan, a leading diaspora missiologist who has written many books on the subject. For many within the church, including those engaged in migrant ministries, this was an opportunity to learn about diaspora missiology and the different dimensions of diaspora mission. Following this groundbreaking NDS, Malaysian seminaries began to offer diaspora mission courses. The second NDS took place in 2017, with T. V. Thomas, chair of the GDN, as the plenary speaker. His sharing was practical and realistic, stirring many hearts and prompting even some who had been sitting on the fence to get involved. Slowly but surely the influence of these two missiologists led to greater commitment to local cross-cultural missions by church mission leaders.

The MDN steering committee persevered and organized the third NDS in 2019. This time, the plenary speaker was Kevin Higgins – president of William Carey International University – who spoke on contextualized discipleship and insider movements. His reminder that there were others who had gone before us in this model of discipleship greatly encouraged the MDN. Then the COVID-19 pandemic intervened, disrupting the momentum of the NDS. However, with the closing of borders and the difficulties in placing returning missionaries, many churches began to take seriously mission at their front door steps. This shift in focus, along with increased outreach efforts that led to favorable and trusting relationships within communities, contributed to the growth of diaspora outreach efforts by the ElShaddai Centre and other members of the MDN.

In September 2023, the MDN conducted the fourth NDS, with the theme "Building Bridges, Closing Gaps." This NDS did not feature a plenary speaker but, instead, included eight workshop topics facilitated by different practitioners. Every participant contributed actively by engaging in discussions about how to close gaps that prevented the church from prioritizing diaspora mission. These gaps might include unfounded fears, prejudices, misinterpretations of Scripture, and misplaced priorities. The solutions proposed by participants will be compiled into a document that will be printed and distributed to various churches for their reference.

ElShaddai Centre: A Model of Diaspora Mission in Malaysia

To effectively and sustainably disciple the diaspora communities locally, ElShaddai Centre operates as a humanitarian NGO, a mission agency, and a church. It functions like a living organism on a mission, eagerly sniffing out potential expansion opportunities, being intentional and passionate about strategically engaging with communities that are often overlooked by the church, carefully navigating the narrow path between local authorities and irregular communities, and often being perceived as chaotic and reckless in its approach. Strategic leadership in an organization of this nature is both an art and an act of faith. The guiding compass behind these efforts is the organization's ethos, a shift from the conventional mission mindset and an unwavering and clear vision to disciple the nations without leaving their homeland.

The leadership of ElShaddai Centre has identified some elements that they deem significant for building sustainable diaspora ministries, and these will now be discussed. First, be open to partnerships, and do not work alone. The major stakeholder in the partnership must be Jesus, and it is vital to also partner with the body of Christ and especially with recipient communities. Partnerships can be messy. As George Verwer rightly said in his book "Messiology," God, in his mercy, grace, and mystery, often does great things in the midst of the mess.[4] Second, adopt a missional and incarnational mindset. Instead of taking the people to church (attractional approach), take the church to the communities. In solving issues and resolving bottlenecks, think of decentralization rather than consolidation. Trust the Holy Spirit and let go, let God, and let others. Third, build a fluid, organically functioning system. Always plan for change when dealing with people on the move – urgent calls to action are the norm even in development programs. Finally, create an apostolic environment that focuses on equipping, participating, and sending people. Embrace diversity, not only of people but also of talents, gifts, and approaches to different tasks. With the help of expert partners, build a strong foundation for each ministry within the ecosystem, always keeping our eyes on Jesus, the Savior and initiator of our faith, who will bring his work to completion.

Risks and Challenges

Due to years of intimidation by political propaganda, the Malaysian church has fallen back on self-preservation and been hesitant to engage in outreach to the majority. However, the pressing needs on the ground and the government's dependence on NGOs to provide essential services have created opportunities for direct engagement with communities. Quality humanitarian services, transparent operations, and genuine relationships help to reduce suspicion on the part of the authorities. The government's endorsement of the UN Sustainable Development Goals and its ratification of the UN Convention on the Rights of the Child – which upholds the civil, political, economic, social, health, and cultural rights of all minors below eighteen years – authorize NGOs to operate learning centers and engage in education of various forms to empower communities holistically.

---

4. Verwer, *Messiology*, 2016.

Conclusion

> Ask me, and I will make the nations your inheritance,
> the ends of the earth your possession. (Ps 2:8)

Malaysia, a nation with a population of just thirty million, hosts many different nations. God has granted the Malaysian church a great opportunity to reach out to these nations and disciple them. This resonates with the concept of inheriting nations that is mentioned in Psalm 2:8, and when diaspora people come to faith and are discipled well, they have the potential to take the gospel to the ends of the earth.

References

ICEF, Monitor. "Malaysia exceeds target for new international student applications in 2022." https://monitor.icef.com/2023/02/malaysia-exceeds-target-for-new-international-student-applications-in-2022/ Accessed 1 November 2024.

United Nations. "The 17 Goals." https://sdgs.un.org/goals.

Verwer, George. *Messiology*. Chicago: Moody Publishers, 2016.

12

The Transnational Filipino Families: Pastoral and Missiological Issues

Noel A. Pantoja

Introduction

Over the past century, Filipinos have been migrating to various countries around the world. This migration has been driven by a multitude of factors, including political, economic, educational, and personal reasons. The global Filipino diaspora spans approximately two hundred countries, with millions of Filipinos now living overseas. This trend of overseas employment has created a strain on families that are left behind and also posed many unforeseen challenges for their local churches. This chapter explores the pastoral and missiological issues faced by churches in the Philippines because of these transnational Filipino families.

The Overseas Filipino Migration

The Commission on Filipinos Overseas (CFO) estimated there were approximately 13 million Filipinos residing in foreign countries around the world as of 2020.[1] Since the total Filipino population is around 110 million, this number is significant. The sheer number of Overseas Filipino Workers (OFW) highlights the importance of understanding and addressing the unique needs

---

1. See Commission on Filipinos Overseas (CFO). https://cfo.gov.ph/ (Accessed 1 February 2024).

and challenges of this diaspora. The Philippines is recognized as one of the largest sources of migrant workers in the world. In 2023 alone, approximately 2.3 million Filipinos left the country to work abroad.[2] The primary destinations for Filipino migrants include the United States, Saudi Arabia, Japan, Australia, Germany, Italy, Canada, and the United Arab Emirates. Economic opportunities and better prospects for employment abroad are the key factors driving this migration trend.

This trend of large-scale labor migration from the Philippines began in the mid-1970s when the country's population surged and there was a widespread lack of local employment opportunities. The government promoted overseas employment to secure foreign currency for its debt repayments. The oil boom in the Middle East and the rapid growth of many cities in Asia drew many Filipinos to explore employment opportunities abroad. In both the Middle East and Asia, there are significant numbers of Filipinos working as seafarers or domestic helpers. The more educated professionals – such as nurses, engineers, and computer professionals – seem more inclined to seek opportunities in Europe and North America.

Remittances sent by Filipinos overseas play a crucial role in the Philippine economy. In 2023, remittances amounted to a staggering total of US$39.1 billion.[3] The financial contributions of overseas Filipinos have a significant impact on the livelihoods and well-being of their families in the Philippines. These remittances also contribute significantly to the revenue of Filipino churches and their missionary activities. These overseas workers also contribute to the Philippines through the transfer of knowledge and skills and by creating goodwill toward the Filipino people globally. Since overseas jobs are more lucrative and provide upward social mobility, more and more young Filipinos aspire to secure employment abroad.

Philippine Government Programs

Due to the growing number of migrants from the Philippines and the rising levels of their remittances, the Philippine government has been proactive in addressing issues faced by these migrants. The programs and services initi-

---

2. PhilStar, 2023. https://www.philstar.com/headlines/2024/04/12/2347168/historic-2023-ofw-deployment-moves-philippines-labor-migration-forward-pandemic.

3. Migration Data Portal, 2023. https://www.migrationdataportal.org/international-data?focus=profile&i=remit_inflows&t=2023&cm49=608.

ated by the Philippine government to address the needs of OFWs include the following:

1. Regulation of Deployment: The government regulates the deployment of OFWs through the Philippine Overseas Employment Administration (POEA), ensuring that recruitment agencies follow ethical practices and comply with labor laws to protect the rights and welfare of OFWs.

2. Pre-departure Orientation Seminar (PDOS): Before leaving the country, OFWs are required to attend a PDOS conducted by the POEA. This program provides them with information on their rights, responsibilities, and cultural orientation in their destination countries.

3. Overseas Workers Welfare Administration (OWWA): The OWWA provides social and welfare services to OFWs and their families. It offers various programs such as livelihood assistance, education and training scholarships, health care benefits, and repatriation assistance.[4]

4. Assistance to Nationals (ATN) program: The Department of Foreign Affairs (DFA) operates the ATN program, which assists OFWs in distress or those facing legal issues abroad. This program assists in repatriation, provides legal aid, and offers other support services.

5. Overseas Filipino Bank (OFB): The government established the OFB to cater specifically to the banking needs of OFWs. The OFB offers tailored services in relation to remittances, loans, and savings accounts.

6. Reintegration Programs: The government offers various reintegration programs aimed at supporting OFWs upon their return to the Philippines. These programs include livelihood and skills training, entrepreneurship support, and financial assistance to help them reintegrate into the local economy.

7. Bilateral Agreements and Diplomatic Relations: The Philippine government actively engages in bilateral agreements and maintains diplomatic relations with other countries to protect the rights and

---

4. https://owwa.gov.ph/.

welfare of OFWs. These agreements focus on labor standards, social security, and the prevention of abuse and exploitation.

These comprehensive measures encompass regulatory measures, support services, and diplomatic initiatives to ensure the welfare and protection of OFWs both at home and abroad.

Pastoral Needs of Transnational Filipino Families

While some countries provide a pathway for family reunification or sponsorship for family members to join migrants working overseas, most Filipinos migrate alone, especially to the Middle East or when migrating as unskilled workers to Asia or Europe. Therefore, family disintegration is a serious issue among transnational Filipino families. The absence of one or both parents due to overseas employment often leads to children being left behind with grandparents or extended family members. This absence can profoundly impact the emotional, psychological, and social development of such children.

Studies have shown that children left behind by migrant parents are more vulnerable to problems such as drug addiction, early pregnancy, and involvement in criminal activities. The lack of parental guidance and support can leave children feeling neglected and disconnected, causing them to seek solace in unhealthy patterns of behavior. In Filipino culture, family units are usually closely knit, but these strong bonds have weakened significantly in recent decades due to the prolonged absence of one of the parents, especially during children's crucial developmental years. Overseas employment may also reshape and reconfigure gender roles, authority structures, and relational bonding. The sudden influx of money and improved economic status may also disrupt the sense of belonging for the next generation as they relocate to better neighborhoods or attend better schools. With increased disposable income and the new choices available – but without the benefit of parental guidance – young people often end up making poor choices, which often permanently alter their futures and haunt them for many years.

The role of nannies and relatives in caring for the children of overseas Filipino parents is crucial, but these present their own set of challenges. Nannies may struggle to provide the same level of emotional support and guidance that parents do, which can further exacerbate the issues faced by transnational Filipino families. In the case of Filipino domestic helpers and maids working abroad, they care for the children of their employers in foreign lands while being unable to do the same for their own children. Gerardo B. Lisbe Jr., who has explored the family dynamics of transnational Filipinos, offers eight ways that local churches can respond to the challenges faced by OFWs.[5]

The Response of Filipino Churches

The Philippine churches represented by the Philippine Council of Evangelical Churches (PCEC) and the Philippine Mission Association (PMA) are actively involved in providing pastoral care and spiritual support to OFWs and their families back home. Here are five actions taken by these churches:

First, because of the growing need among family members separated because of their vocational choice to work in another country, there is a greater demand for pastoral care and counseling among Filipino Christians who have family members working abroad. Therefore, churches are seeking more help and training to offer counseling services to address emotional, spiritual, and relational issues faced by overseas Filipinos and their families. These churches provide a safe space for individuals to share their struggles and seek guidance.

Second, many churches organize special worship services and fellowship times specifically tailored to the needs of overseas Filipinos and often conducted in their native language. These services create a sense of community and fellowship, helping Filipinos to connect with their cultural and spiritual roots.

Third, through organizations like the PMA, Filipino churches are sending missionaries to countries that have significant Filipino populations. These missionaries minister to their scattered brethren in foreign lands and equip them to reach others in their host lands. They also provide spiritual guidance, discipleship training, and support to overseas Filipinos by establishing local churches and ministries.

Fourth, Filipino churches pray regularly for the well-being and safety of overseas Filipinos. They organize regular prayer gatherings, prayer chains, and intercessory groups dedicated to lifting up the concerns and needs of overseas Filipinos. Some of these prayer meetings are conducted online, allowing overseas Filipinos to share their needs and be prayed for. This has nurtured a deeper sense of virtual community between overseas workers and their home churches, making these overseas workers feel deeply cared for and encouraged by their home churches.

Fifth, the diaspora churches are encouraged and equipped to actively engage in outreach and evangelism efforts within overseas Filipino commu-

---

5. Lisbe Jr., "Transnational Family Dynamics of Overseas Filipino Workers," 55–72.

nities. They conduct missions, evangelistic events, and Bible studies to share the gospel and provide spiritual guidance to those in need.

Missiological Issues in Transnational Filipino Families

Despite the challenges faced by transnational Filipino families, there is a significant presence of born-again Christians among overseas Filipinos. It is estimated that approximately one million overseas Filipinos have encountered Christ and embraced the Christian faith. Filipino Christians are strongly inclined toward migration, and those who have gone abroad have often experienced a revival in their Christian faith in foreign lands. This spiritual renewal has led to the establishment of many new Filipino churches all over the world and has also instilled a fresh missionary zeal among churches in the Philippines.

However, there is a pressing need for missional, ministerial, and theological training within the Filipino Christian community. Many overseas churches are led by pastors who lack formal training, which can result in a shallow understanding of the Scriptures and an inability to provide a deep spiritual foundation for new believers. Most diaspora churches are led by lay people, and some of these function merely as social clubs, without any ecclesial connections or the proper spiritual nurturing that is necessary for missional living. These lay leaders have limited time and resources to draw from to address the complex sociocultural and family challenges faced by transnational families.

The lack of accountability and networking within independent churches is another significant missiological issue. Without proper "spiritual covering," accountability structures, and coordination, new believers may struggle to receive the necessary support and guidance for their spiritual growth and life transformation. Building strong networks and fostering a sense of community is essential for the long-term sustainability and impact of Filipino Christians in diaspora communities. Additionally, the needs of the next generation – who are growing up in foreign lands with limited linguistic and cultural skills to navigate immigrant churches and their governance – are often not addressed. Another serious issue is the relational strain experienced by married OFWs, often leading to emotional or sexual infidelity and even extramarital affairs. There is an urgent need for diaspora churches to train pastors to address such situations of family breakdown and to provide counsel on how families can overcome the barriers created by overseas employment and thrive despite geographical distances and time zone differences. It is critical to offer confidential and culturally sensitive family ministries and counseling services for struggling families in diasporic locations.

Conclusion

Transnational Filipino families face significant pastoral and missiological challenges due to the migration of Filipinos overseas. Critical concerns that must be addressed include family disintegration, the absence of parents, and the vulnerability of children left behind. Additionally, to ensure the spiritual growth and transformation of life of overseas Filipinos, it is critical that there be missional, ministerial, and theological training, as well as accountability and networking within these diaspora churches. By recognizing and addressing these issues, we can work toward building stronger communities, fostering a sense of belonging and purpose among overseas Filipinos and ensuring the well-being and flourishing of transnational Filipino families. Despite the growing awareness and efforts made to address the concerns of transnational families, much more needs to be done, especially given the upward trend in global migration. It is crucial that the training of pastors and missionaries incorporate the specific issues that impact transnational families.

References

Commission on Filipinos Overseas (CFO). "About Us." https://cfo.gov.ph/about-us/. Accessed 1 February 2024.

Commission on Filipinos Overseas (CFO). "Stock Estimates of Overseas Filipinos." 2021. https://cfo.gov.ph/yearly-stock-estimation-of-overseas-filipinos/. Accessed 1 November 2024.

Department of Foreign Affairs (DFA). "PH Attends Training Course for ASEAN Countries Police Officers." https://dfa.gov.ph/dfa-news/dfa-releasesupdate/18753-assistance-to-nationals. Accessed 1 February 2024.

Lisbe, Gerardo B., Jr. "Transnational Family Dynamics of Overseas Filipino Workers." In *Interconnections of Asian Diaspora: Mapping the Linkages and Discontinuities*, edited by Sam George, 55–72. Minneapolis: Fortress, 2022.

Migration Data Portal. "Annual remittance inflows in 2023." https://www.migrationdataportal.org/international-data?focus=profile&i=remit_inflows&t=2023&cm49=608. Accessed 1 November 2024.

Overseas Workers Welfare Administration (OWWA). https://owwa.gov.ph/. Accessed 1 November 2024.

Philippine Overseas Employment Administration (POEA). "About POEA." https://dmw.gov.ph/archives/programs/programs&services.html. Accessed 1 February 2024.

United Nations. "International Migration 2019." Department of Economic and Social Affairs, 2019.

Philstar. "Historic 2023 OFW deployment moves Philippines' labor migration forward from pandemic" | Philstar.com. https://www.philstar.com/headlines/2024/04/12/2347168/historic-2023-ofw-deployment-moves-philippines-labor-migration-forward-pandemic. Accessed 1 November 2024.

13

Love [Your City]: Diaspora Churches Start and Support City Movements

Jacob Bloemberg

> Seek the shalom of the city to which I have sent you, and pray to the Lord for it, for in the shalom of the city you will have shalom. (Jeremiah 29:7; paraphrase mine)

"It's not fair, Lord! This isn't America; this is Hanoi!" My frustration was palpable, a blend of agitation and genuine dismay. I found it disheartening that the Lord had led me to yet another book from the USA, one brimming with ideas that seemed utterly impractical in my reality – namely, the context of Hanoi, the capital of Vietnam.

The book in question – *To Transform a City* by Eric Swanson and Sam Williams – opens with an intriguing story about how to love Boulder. The authors belonged to a group of pastors from various corners of Boulder, Colorado – a notably liberal university town – who regularly gathered to seek divine guidance for church-planting opportunities within the city. In a profound yet simple revelation, they sensed God's guidance through two words: Love Boulder. This directive was clear – it was not about reaching, converting, or changing Boulder but solely about loving the city.[1] Embracing this vision, these pastors engaged with the city's mayor, inquiring earnestly how the church could assist with Boulder's unique challenges. This marked the beginning of

---

1. Barth, *Good City*, 25.

a collaborative effort in community service projects, all aimed at reflecting God's glory (Matt 5:16).

Back in 2011, this concept seemed remote and unattainable to me. The situation in Hanoi was completely different. Unlike Boulder, Colorado, where pastors stood united in prayer for their city, such unity was absent in Hanoi. Even in a hypothetical scenario where such unity existed, the likelihood of being granted an audience with the mayor was slim. And in the rare event that such a meeting did take place, what guarantee was there that the mayor would openly discuss the city's challenges with us? Furthermore, given our status as a small religious minority, why would he consider our assistance valuable?

A Diaspora Journey to Start a City Movement

Since arriving in Hanoi in 1997 to support orphanages for a Christian NGO, my family and I had experienced firsthand the constraints faced by Christians in the city. At that time, Protestant Christians accounted for a mere 0.1 percent of Hanoi's seven million (now ten million) inhabitants. The aftermath of Vietnam's war had created a deep divide between the state and the church

Over a decade, the Hanoi International Fellowship (HIF), born in the living room of an expatriate in 1995, had experienced growth and been relocated to various hotel ballrooms over the years. By 2005, HIF faced an identity crisis, having become an overly inward-looking group of expatriate Christians. Although our outreach seemed limited by our context, we felt God urging us to shift our focus outward. Around that time, I participated in a conference by the Missional International Church Network (MICN) that seemed to address our pressing question: How could an international church be missional in our context? HIF's leadership appointed me as its pastor and authorized me to implement the MICN's vision. Despite my earlier frustrations with Swanson's book, the "Love Boulder" story inspired HIF to launch the "Love Hanoi" campaign in 2012.

Drawing from the Love Hanoi campaign and my doctoral research, I have developed a framework comprising five steps to foster citywide movements. This paper uses these steps as a guide and records my journey from beliefs and habits to practice, collaboration, and, finally, transformation.

Step 1: Principles

The journey toward citywide movements begins by establishing a solid theological foundation. This involves developing principles that support an expansive relational ministry that can transcend various boundaries. Initially, the focus is on a theology of and for the city. This is followed by broadening the scope to encompass a theology of place. Next, we explore the Hebrew concept of shalom. Finally, a theology of the kingdom equips us to work effectively across diverse boundaries, striving for the shalom of the cities where God has placed us.

A Theology of the City: The biblical narrative that begins in a garden culminates in a city. This trajectory shows that God's plan is not a regression to Eden but a progression toward the new Jerusalem. From the outset, cities were part of God's design, and he is described as the "architect and builder" of the heavenly "city with foundations" (Heb 11:10).

As Ray Bakke aptly puts it, we need "a theology as big as the city."[2] This goes beyond simply conducting a word study on cities in the Bible. We need a theology that addresses the multifaceted issues of urban life. The Scriptures offer insights into God's vision for cities, particularly through Jerusalem and the anticipated new Jerusalem. According to the divine blueprint, cities are hubs of worship, justice, culture, creativity, invention, education, economy, and governance. While resembling the prosperity of some modern cities, these cities will be devoid of crime, evil, idolatry, poverty, inequality, and injustice.

A Theology of Place: From the outset, God created humans in his image and with a physical form. Since human beings needed a suitable environment – a place for living, sustenance, and companionship – God "planted a garden in the east, in Eden" and placed the first man there, to continue and collaborate on God's creation project (Gen 2:8). Through this action, God revealed himself as the original place maker or a homemaker – a role reflecting his divine nature.

For God, this act of place-making and city-building was never God's plan B but always his primary intention. God envisioned sacred spaces in which humanity could coexist with him. This journey of divine place-making that began at Eden and continued in the tabernacle, the temple, the incarnation, and the church will culminate in the new Jerusalem. This is a venture that God embarked on, continues to engage in, and will always keep pursuing. This vision of God portrays a state of perfect harmony between God, humanity, and creation – an ideal that once existed and will one day be restored. It embodies the essence of perfect peace, encapsulated in the Hebrew concept of shalom.

A Theology of Shalom: Shalom represents a holistic peace, a sense of completeness or wholeness that the English word "peace" does not fully capture. In Jeremiah 29:7, shalom is variously translated as "peace and prosperity" (NIV, NLT), "welfare" (ESV, NRSV), "well-being" (MSG), or simply "peace" (KJV).

---

2. Bakke, *Theology*, 30.

Bryant Myers, who defines shalom as peace in relation to God, others, self, and nature, comments that shalom means "just relationships (living justly and experiencing justice), harmonious relationships, and enjoyable relationships."[3]

Andre Van Eymeren interprets shalom as human flourishing, which he describes as the individual's well-being within their community, which encompasses all elements essential for healthy living. Van Eymeren recommends viewing shalom as "completeness, wholeness, or wellbeing in the present."[4] Echoing God's directive to the Israelites in Babylonian exile, today's diaspora church is similarly called to "seek the shalom of the city to which I have carried you into exile and to pray to the Lord for it, because as it experiences shalom, you too will have shalom" (Jer 29:7; paraphrase mine).

A Theology of the Kingdom: The prophet Daniel glimpsed God's kingdom through his interpretation of King Nebuchadnezzar's dream and his own vision of the four beasts. He foresaw a kingdom unlike any other – including Israel – that was ruled by "a son of man" (Dan 7:13) and revered by all nations eternally. Daniel's prophecy began to unfold when Jesus came, declaring the kingdom's arrival and identifying himself as "the Son of Man." Jesus taught us to pray for the coming of this kingdom: "Your name honored; your kingdom come; your will done – on earth as in heaven!" (Matt 6:9–10; paraphrase mine).

The good news encompasses not just salvation but restoration. It announces the rectification of societal wrongs, the upliftment of marginalized groups, and the reestablishment of Jubilee principles for universal equity. The kingdom's reach was wherever Jesus went. This authority bestowed upon Jesus was then entrusted to his followers, who received the mandate to "go and make disciples of all nations" (Matt 28:19). This vision of God's kingdom, which has been understood in various ways, unites believers across the world.

In the final chapters of the book of Revelation, the themes of city, place, shalom, and kingdom converge (see Figure 1). The narrative that began in a garden, the original holy of holies, culminates in the ultimate holy of holies – the city. Nations enter this city, bringing their cultural treasures as offerings to the king. God's ultimate dwelling with his people from every nation, tribe, and tongue ends in the City of Peace. Designed by the Great Architect, this city becomes a place where shalom prevails and the King of Kings reigns supreme.

Even now, I can vividly recall how I was riding my scooter through Hanoi's bustling boulevards when a realization struck me: I lacked a biblical theology tailored for my city. Immersed in Bakke's book, I was at a loss to understand

---

3. Myers, *Walking with the Poor*, 97.
4. Van Eymeren et al., *Urban Shalom*, 16.

what the Bible might say about the urban challenges of Hanoi. As I sped from point A to point B, it struck me that my engagement with the city was primarily for my own or my ministry's benefit. Although not inherently wrong, this focus did not consider how I – and the church – could positively impact society. I began to ponder: If I were to leave or if HIF were to cease to exist, would Hanoi be any better off? Amid the busy traffic, I repented and embarked on a journey into urban theology.

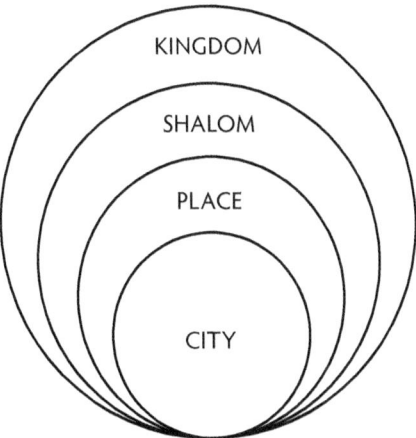

Figure 1: The four theologies in relation to each other

Step 2: Posture

Our nonverbal cues often convey more about us than our words. The way we position ourselves physically and metaphorically when interacting with others reveals our true thoughts and beliefs. Regrettably, the posture of Christians toward each other and the city has often been less than positive. Church leaders, consumed by the demands of church life, tend to adopt a church-centric view. Moreover, churches can sometimes resort to escapism, viewing themselves as outsiders in society, which may lead to defensiveness or aggression toward the public and even toward other churches.

Diaspora churches risk becoming inward-looking as expatriates seek comfort in shared culture, distancing themselves from local society. To initiate or support a citywide movement, diaspora Christians must adopt an integrated approach toward the city, their community, and those who are impoverished. Instead of seeing themselves as going *to* or doing things *for* the city, or simply being *in* the city, churches must transition to being an integral part of the city, collaborating actively *with* it (see Figure 2).

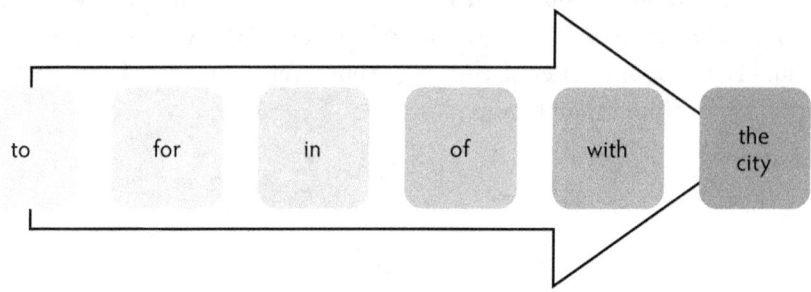

Figure 2: The church-integral posture

This shift in posture resonates with my personal experience. During HIF's initial decade, we were primarily a church of expatriates who had come *to* the city. Despite sponsoring projects *for* and *in* the city, we had no meaningful relationship with the city government. When I became the pastor, I recognized that our church was merely existing within the city. I realized that we needed to repent of our escapist stance and become more outward-focused. However, it was not until the Love Hanoi campaign that we truly began to see ourselves as an integral part *of* the city, working *with* the city.

Step 3: Process

Once a diaspora church decides to pursue the peace of its host city and collaborate with local leaders for this purpose, a question arises: How and where do we begin? Mark Gornik reinterprets Nehemiah's story through the lens of community development.[5] Drawing from Wallace's six stages of cultural revitalization, Gornik aligns Nehemiah's account with these stages (See Table 1). This framework serves as an excellent basis for a sermon series to kickstart your Love [Your City] campaign, similar to what HIF did with Love Hanoi.[6]

---

5. Adapted from Gornik, *To Live in Peace*, 133–45.

6. For other outlines and retellings of Nehemiah, see *Renewing the City: Reflections on Community Development and Urban Renewal* by Robert D. Lupton and *City of God, City of Satan* by Robert C. Linthicum.

Table 1: Nehemiah Outline and Stages of Cultural Revitalization[7]

Wallace's Stages	Nehemiah	Gornik's Titles
Reformulation	1:1–10	Hearing call
Communication	1:11–2:20	Beginning to take on the odds
Organization	3:1–32	A community becomes organized
Adaptation	4:1–7:4	Overcoming difficult obstacles
Transformation	7:5–10:39	New commitment to community
Routinization	11:1–13:31	Taking on new challenges

Like Wallace's model, community development is a cyclical process of continuous action. Christian Community Development (CCD) practitioners have developed an eight-phase cycle to guide churches and groups in vision implementation (see Figure 3). This is not a one-time event but a sustained process; repeated cycles foster community development and city transformation, ideally leading to the realization of God's kingdom.

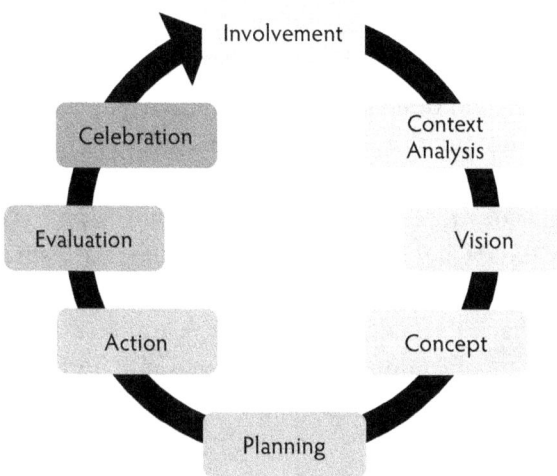

Figure 3: The cycle of CCD[8]

Asset-Based Community Development (ABCD) – an approach that involves collaborating with the local community and utilizing local resources – is crucial. This method focuses on enhancing and building upon existing

---

7. Adapted from Gornik, *To Live in Peace*, 133–45.
8. Adapted from Reimer, "Community Transformation," 29.

strengths within the community. However, churches and nonprofits sometimes make the mistake of focusing only on the negative aspects of the community and positioning themselves as the sole solution. Seed (new ministry idea) projects offer a practical starting point for community engagement. In my book *Love [Your City]: 5 Steps to Citywide Movements*, I list 40 ideas of projects for initiating citywide movements.

Replicating this process in Hanoi posed significant challenges due to our event-oriented culture, a transient church community, and governmental restrictions on church-led community projects or collaboration with international Christian NGOs. Nevertheless, some churches have successfully carried out initiatives such as street cleanups, support for leprosy camps, and the establishment of rehabilitation centers that have helped thousands of addicts.

Step 4: Partner

"Let us start rebuilding" was the community's collective response to Nehemiah's proposal (Neh 2:18). Working shoulder to shoulder, the people rebuilt Jerusalem's wall in just fifty-two days (Neh 6:15). Similarly, we can rebuild our cities through partnerships with the government, neighbors, and fellow citizens, irrespective of their backgrounds or lifestyles. Such collaborative processes also offer valuable opportunities for community building and sharing life stories.

Launching and supporting a citywide movement is, as Missio Nexus aptly puts it, "too big to do alone and too important not to do together!"[9] Partnership is pivotal in citywide movements, and mastering this aspect is essential for a successful Love [Your City] campaign. Understanding the distinction between networks and partnerships is crucial to avoid misplaced expectations and frustration. Phill Butler succinctly defines these terms: Network is "Any group of individuals or organizations, sharing a common interest, who regularly communicate *with each other to enhance their individual purposes.*" Whereas Partnership is "any group of individuals or organizations, sharing a common interest, who regularly communicate, *plan and work together to achieve a common vision beyond the capacity of any one of the individual partners.*"[10]

Partnerships cannot be forced; instead, they must be cultivated. While we cannot compel people to partner together, we can inspire and create environments conducive to partnership formation through networking. Networks,

---

9. Learn more about Missio Nexus at www.missionexus.org.
10. Butler, *Well Connected*, 261.

as Butler notes, are "incubators for partnerships."[11] The more you invest in enhancing your network's quality and reach, the greater the potential for partnerships that contribute to city transformation. Butler's City Ministry Network Model demonstrates how resources flow through partnerships for urban ministry projects, which is essential for developing your Love [Your City] network (see Figure 4).

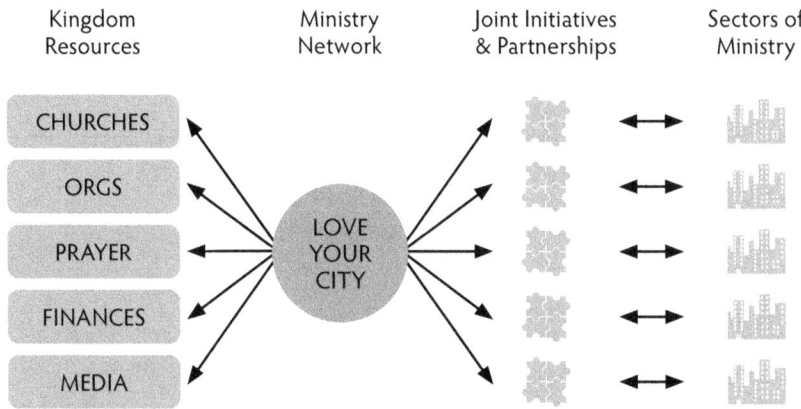

Figure 4: City Ministry Network Model[12]

At HIF, we focused on networking to encourage both local and international partnerships for the Love Hanoi movement. We hosted conferences and workshops, bringing together partner organizations for presentations and training. These events often culminated in spontaneous partnerships to tackle city issues. After a decade of nurturing this network and growing partnerships, the leadership of the Love Hanoi Network is now transitioning from HIF to local leaders. As a diaspora church, HIF is now one among many partners in this collaborative effort.

Step 5: People

Phill Butler accurately observes that "*people* determine the success or failure of any collaborative effort. *By* people, *with* people, and *for* people – that is the essence of partnership."[13] At each stage, a citywide movement needs diverse

---

11. Butler, 261.
12. Adapted from Butler, 277.
13. Butler, 202. Emphasis added.

leaders to guide the processes and partnerships. Drawing from Butler's insights, Glenn Barth elaborates on the stages of citywide movements.[14] Understanding these stages, along with the required leadership functions and skills, can greatly assist in starting, growing, and sustaining a movement, as well as avoiding stagnation and frustration (see Table 2).

Table 2: Stages of Development for Organizations Serving City Movements[15]

Stage	Function	Skill
1. Exploration	Catalyst Visionary	Relational Communication Convening
2. Formation	Visionary	Communication Facilitating Management Creative thinking
3. Operation	Management	Decision-making People-building Motivational
4. Realization	Prayer	Doing the right things at the right time
5. Transformation	Discipling	Presence-based prayer
6. Replication	Teaching	Training Coaching

While it is important not to blindly replicate movements undertaken in other cities, there is also no need to completely reinvent the wheel. Leadership skills evolve as a movement matures. Sometimes, a single leader can adapt and grow along with the movement; other times, different leaders are needed at various stages. It is crucial that leaders recognize when to evolve and when to pass the baton to avoid stagnation of the movement.

In my role, my strengths lie in creating vision and catalyzing action, as well as administrative skills. The best decision I made was to hire a manager for Love Hanoi's operations. Love Your City now employs several part-time staff, and each city network will eventually require its own catalytic leader and management support staff. Integrating prayer movements and events into our annual strategy is a key element in our approach. The five steps described above have

---

14. Barth, *Good City*.
15. Adapted from Barth, *Good City*, 41.

enabled us to develop a training program for initiating new citywide movements. This calls for the mobilization of trainers who will, in turn, train others.

These five steps to citywide movements can guide your diaspora church in starting a Love [Your City] campaign in your city:

1. **Principles:** Develop a theological framework for urban ministry.
2. **Posture:** Adopt a Christlike posture toward the city, the community, and the marginalized.
3. **Process:** Understand where to start, what to do next, and the importance of repeating processes.
4. **Partner:** Learn to collaborate across sectors, building networks that incubate partnerships.
5. **People:** Recognize the leadership skills necessary for different stages of citywide movements.

Conclusion

What was the outcome in Hanoi? Interestingly, some now say, "That happened in Hanoi, but it can't happen in our city!" As the Love Hanoi campaign gathered momentum, the expatriate community noticed and invited us to set up a Love Hanoi booth at their annual charity bazaar – a new opportunity for our church. Our African band members and singers performed at this bazaar and quickly became the highlight of the event. This initial success was replicated in subsequent years. The following activities illustrate the progress and impact of Love Hanoi over the years.

- We organized a Charity Christmas Concert with a silent auction to fund a new roof for a children's home. To our delight, the national TV station broadcasted the event as the Love Hanoi Christmas Concert, giving us national media exposure.
- Building relations with the government became crucial as our church moved into an office tower. Inspired by the Love Boulder story, I consistently asked in meetings, "How can we as Christian foreigners love Hanoi?" This approach significantly enhanced our church's reputation with the government.
- We collaborated with local and Korean churches for a joint Easter concert, inviting government officials for permit reasons. Surprisingly, the chief of police attended. He later joined HIF's Christmas concert and invited us to celebrate Christmas at the police headquar-

- ters' theater in December 2014, featuring performances by police cadets and church groups.
- By 2015, the pastors were collaboratively working and praying, even visiting government officials for the lunar new year. Remarkably, the chief of police, now the mayor of Hanoi, had fostered a positive relationship with us.
- In 2016, churches united to celebrate 100 years of Protestantism in Hanoi. Encouraged by the event's success, we agreed to an even larger celebration the following year.
- The Billy Graham Evangelistic Association reached out to us for organizing a festival in 2017. The Love Hanoi Festival drew over 30,000 attendees from Hanoi and North Vietnam, with more than 4,500 individuals committing to Christ. In preparation, the Love in Action Committee coordinated 17 community service projects, involving 3,600 participants.
- Love in Action continued to expand its network, inspiring churches to actively serve their communities. During the pandemic, it facilitated national online conferences for shared learning experiences. The Vice Minister of Home Affairs praised Protestant pastors and Christians for their dedicated service to communities amid the COVID-19 crisis.
- In 2020, the "Love [Your City]" book was published internationally. Three years later, its Vietnamese version was released, featuring a foreword by the former Vice President of the Government Committee for Religious Affairs.
- Annual Christmas festivals, collaboratively organized by various churches and an American evangelist, attract around 10,000 attendees. These events, complete with bazaar booths and family activities, see at least 5% of attendees choosing to follow Jesus as Lord and Savior.
- In 2023, Love in Action was rebranded to Love Your City, now registered as a social enterprise to help start and support citywide movements.

Today, pastors across Vietnam are saying, "We want God to work in our city as he is working in Hanoi!" God's wisdom in igniting a citywide movement through a diaspora church has inspired other cities to seek similar transformation everywhere![16]

References

Bakke, Raymond J. *A Theology as Big as the City*. Downers Grove: InterVarsity Press, 1997.

Barth, Glenn. *The Good City: Transformed Lives Transforming Communities*. Tallmadge: S. D. Myers Publishing, 2016.

Bloemberg, Jacob. *Love [Your City]: 5 Steps to Citywide Movements*. Bloomington: WestBow Press, 2020.

Butler, Phil. *Well Connected: Releasing Power, Restoring Hope through Kingdom Partnerships*. Waynesboro: Authentic Media, 2005.

Gornik, Mark R. *To Live in Peace: Biblical Faith and the Changing Inner City*. Grand Rapids: Eerdmans, 2002.

Myers, Bryant L. *Walking with the Poor: Principles and Practices of Transformational Development*. Revised and Expanded Edition. Maryknoll: Orbis Books, 2011.

Reimer, Johannes. "Community Transformation, Peace and Church Growth." Micah/PRN Global Series, 2019.

Swanson, Eric, and Sam Williams. *To Transform a City: Whole Church, Whole Gospel, Whole City*. Grand Rapids: Zondervan, 2010.

Van Eymeren, Andre, Ash Barker, Bryan McCabe, and Chris Elisara, eds. *Urban Shalom and the Cities We Need*. Birmingham: Urban Shalom, 2017.

---

16. For more on Love Your City movements in Hanoi, Vietnam, see www.bloemberg.org or www.loveyourcity.vn.

14

Asian Students Going Abroad and International Students in Asia

Leiton Chinn and Lisa Espineli Chinn

Introduction

This paper highlights the two-way flow of students between Asia and other countries. Due to constraints of space, the paper limits its focus to countries from the Asia-Pacific region that send and receive the greater number of international students. For over a century, the United States has been the most popular destination for Asian students. During the academic year 2022/2023, 53 percent of foreign students in the US were from China and India, and while these two countries headed the list, South Korea, Vietnam, Taiwan, and Japan were among the top eight sending nations.[1]

China's First Hundred recounts the story of 120 students sent by the Chinese Educational Mission (CEM) to study in America during the period 1872–1881.[2] Upon returning home, they transformed China with the knowledge they gained abroad. These students embody the mission of the International Student Ministry (ISM): to empower foreign students as temporary diaspora who make an impact in their home countries – or wherever life may lead them. Over the next one hundred years – that is, up to the 1980s – the flow of international students from Asia has been predominantly to Western educational institutions in North America, Europe, Australia, and New Zealand.

Over the last thirty years, however, there has been a significant increase in the number of international students moving into the Asia-Pacific region –

---

1. Open Doors, *2023 Report*.
2. LaFargue, *China's First Hundred*.

either from other continents or from within the wider Asian context – to attend Asian schools. The trend of leaving Asia to study abroad has given way to a new trend, with increasing numbers of students either entering or remaining in Asia for their education, reflecting a dual and dynamic shift in international student mobility trends. The 2015 research publication of the Institute of International Education predicts that "the 21st Century will be the Asian Century, it is natural that more and more international students will enroll in Asian universities . . . just as the American Century led to a natural shift of international students studying in American universities."[3]

An article in the December 2019 issue of ICEF (International Consultants on Education and Fairs) Monitor – "Closer to Home: Intra-regional Mobility in Asia" – summarized at least ten factors that contributed to this emerging trend and commented that "the idea that a Western degree is automatically better and more advantageous than one obtained in Asia is losing ground. Asian students now have an array of appealing options within their region for study."[4] One of the reasons given for studying in Asia is that Tokyo and Seoul – two of the top three "best cities for students" in the world – are in Asia.[5]

The influx of diaspora students into and within Asia are part of the "new normal" of the post-pandemic reality. But this accelerating trend came to an abrupt halt in March 2020 when the World Health Organization (WHO) declared COVID-19 a global pandemic. In May 2023, three years later, the WHO announced that the global pandemic was over, leading to the reopening of formerly closed borders and a surge in "study abroad" globally. When the pandemic began, there were nearly six million international students worldwide, and the Holon Global Student Flow Project – which forecasts global student mobility – anticipates that this number will grow to nine million by 2030.[6] It is projected that by 2025, nearly 80 percent of the growth in the international student market will come from Asian countries.[7] Nevertheless, the United States remains the primary destination for Asians studying abroad.

---

3. Bhandari and Lebefure, *Asia*, 18.

4. ICEF, "Closer to Home", 2019. https://monitor.icef.com/2019/12/closer-to-home-intra-regional-mobility-in-asia/.

5. Stacey, "London Best Student City," https://thepienews.com/london-best-student-city-2024/.

6. Holon Global Student Flows, "US International Education," https://www.holoniq.com/notes/us-international-education-in-2030-6-charts-top-20-source-countries-and-preliminary-forecast.

7. Hogan, "79% of International Student Growth," *The PIE*, https://thepienews.com/news/79-international-student-growth-come-asian-countries/.

Asian Students as Diaspora in the United States

The first recorded Chinese international student was Hong Rong (also called Yung Wing or Jung Hung),[8] who graduated from Yale College in 1854. His efforts led to the formation of the Chinese Educational Mission (CEM).[9] Upon returning to China, CEM students contributed to the modernization of China.[10] Rong is listed first among the ten outstanding Chinese Christian returnees (1850–1950), among whom are pioneers in various fields such as modern education, medicine, media, diplomacy, public leadership, roles for women, civic organizations, and social work.[11]

Niijima Jo (Joseph Hardy Neesima) graduated from Amherst College in 1870. He returned to Japan and founded a small school – Doshisha English School – in Kyoto in 1875. By 1889, this school had become the center for Christian education in Japan, and today, Doshisha University is an educational hub with nine campuses ranging from kindergarten to graduate school.[12] Moung Kyaw, the first Burmese international student at Colgate University in New York, graduated in 1868. He became a Christian and returned to Burma as a missionary.[13] Masakazu Toyama and Eijiro Ono were students at the University of Michigan in the 1870s. Toyama became president of Tokyo Imperial University and later served as Japan's Minister of Education. Ono completed his doctorate in 1889 and returned to Japan to establish and manage the political school at Doshisha.[14]

Hikoichi Orita graduated from Princeton University in 1876. He returned to Japan and served as head of the Third Higher School for many decades.[15] This school merged with other schools to form the University of Tokyo.[16] Four students of the CEM attended Columbia University. Among them was Hong Yen Chang. He was the first Chinese graduate of Columbia Law School and

---

8. Hamrin and Bieler, *Salt and Light*, 14.
9. LaFargue, *China's First Hundred*, 23.
10. Hamrin and Bieler, *Salt and Light*, 26.
11. Hamrin and Bieler, 1.
12. Moore, "History of Amherst College," https://www.amherst.edu/academiclife/departments/asian/japanese_language/Amherst_Japan/node/5388.
13. Nguyen and Jeffres, "Moung Kyaw," https://200.colgate.edu/looking-back/people/moung-kyaw-colgates-first-international-student.
14. Center for Japanese Studies, "President Angell," https://ii.umich.edu/cjs/history-of-cjs.html.
15. Graham, "Princeton Portrait," *Princeton Alumni Weekly*, https://paw.princeton.edu/article/princeton-portrait-samurai-distant-land.
16. UTokyo, https://www.u-tokyo.ac.jp/en/about/history.html.

later joined the Chinese Diplomatic Service and served as chargé d'affaires at the Chinese embassy in Washington, DC. On 1 January 2021, Columbia Law School's Center for Chinese Legal Studies was named the Hong Yen Chang Center for Chinese Legal Studies.[17]

Han Chiao-shun (Charles "Charlie" Jones Soong) was the first international student at Trinity College – now Duke University – from 1881 to 1882. He transferred to Vanderbilt for theological studies and then returned to Shanghai as a missionary with the North Carolina Annual Conference of the Methodist Episcopal Church (South) from 1886 to 1892. Later, as a layperson and a businessman, he was a generous supporter of the American Bible Society and founded the YMCA in Shanghai. He and his family are regarded as "China's First Family." Soong was an ardent supporter and close friend of Sun-Yat-sen, who became his son-in-law by marrying Soong's daughter Ch'ing-ling. His other daughter married Chiang Kai-shek, and his third daughter married the Chinese finance minister, who was considered the richest man in the world at that time. Soong's three sons held powerful positions in government and finance. All six children were educated in the United States.[18]

Stanford University's first international student was Tokyo's Keinosuke Otaki, who graduated in 1894 with a degree in zoology.[19] As many as two hundred Japanese students came to New Brunswick, New Jersey, from the late 1860s to 1912. Most of them attended Rutgers Grammar School and, if successful, went on to study at Rutgers College (now Rutgers University). Kusakabe Taro was the first to attend Rutgers College and excelled in mathematics, physics, Latin, and English. Unfortunately, before his graduation, he died of tuberculosis in 1970, at the age of twenty-five. Taro had a local friend and tutor, William E. Griffis, who eventually went to Fukui, Japan, to teach. Griffis became a scholar of Japan and an influential figure in the country's modernization, exemplifying the significant impact international students may have upon students of the host nation.[20]

In 1883, twenty-one-year-old Anandibai Joshi graduated from the Women's Medical College of Pennsylvania, now known as Drexel University College of

---

17. Columbia Global Centers, "Columbia and China," https://globalcenters.columbia.edu/content-beijing/columbia-and-china-history.

18. "Charles Soong," https://library.duke.edu/rubenstein/uarchives/history/articles/soong.

19. Hennessy, "Foreign Students," *Stanford Magazine*, https://stanfordmag.org/contents/why-foreign-students-are-so-important.

20. Chadwick, "Rutgers," https://sas.rutgers.edu/news-a-events/news/newsroom/student-news/3404-a-tragic-death-and-a-fateful-journey-how-rutgers-and-japan-forged-an-enduring-connection-2.

Medicine. She was the first woman doctor in India. In 1888, Sumantrao Vishnu Karmarkar arrived in Connecticut from India for divinity studies at Hartford Seminary and completed his studies at Yale. His wife, Gurubai Karmarkar, also attended the Women's Medical College of Pennsylvania and graduated in 1892.[21] They returned to Mumbai and served as missionaries with the American Marathi Mission,[22] engaging in evangelistic preaching and medical work among children affected by famine.[23]

Yu Gil-jun was a Korean intellectual, writer, politician, and reformist, who was part of the first official Korean delegation to the United States in July 1883. He studied at Governor Dummer Academy in Byfield, Massachusetts, in 1884. The political situation in Korea forced him to return home, where he advocated for the modernization of Korea. Later, he dedicated his efforts to the Korean Independence Movement.[24]

For China, the Boxer Rebellion of 1900 and the subsequent establishment of the Indemnity Scholarship Fund, the Communist takeover in 1949, the death of Mao Zedong and the rise of Deng Xiaoping in 1978, and the Tiananmen Square incident in 1989 all affected the flow of Chinese students to American schools.[25] For Japan, the untold story of the Government Account for Relief in Occupied Areas (GARIOA),[26] Fulbright scholarships, and the economic boom from 1984 to 1991[27] impacted the number of Japanese international students in the US. For the Philippines, the Pensionado Act 854 (1903–1943)[28] and Fulbright scholarships led to an increased number of Filipino international

---

21. Rajghatta, "Indian Students," http://indpaedia.com/ind/index.php/Indian_students_in_the_USA.

22. Pripas-Kapit, "Educating Women Physicians," https://escholarship.org/content/qt9gh5b9j1/qt9gh5b9j1_noSplash_9b8d0d9e73787d59ab1cf063070e5c93.pdf.

23. Virdhi-Dhesi, "Gurubai Karmarkar," https://scroll.in/article/661289/photos-of-the-amazing-life-of-gurubai-karmakar-woman-doctor-in-19th-century-mumbai.

24. Kim, "Yu Gil-jun," https://sites.bu.edu/koreandiaspora/individuals/boston-in-the-1880s/yu-kil-chun-1856-1914-a-bridge-person-of-korea-to-the-west-and-the-first-korean-student-in-the-united-states/.

25. U.S. Department of State Archive, "United States Relations," https://2001-2009.state.gov/r/pa/ho/pubs/fs/90689.htm#boxer_uprising, and Fish, China Project, "End of an Era?," https://thechinaproject.com/2020/05/12/end-of-an-era-a-history-of-chinese-students-in-america/.

26. Yuasa, "Untold Story," *PSU Vanguard,* https://psuvanguard.com/the-untold-story-of-japanese-students-sponsored-by-the-u-s-military/.

27. Dye, "Japanese Students," *East-West Center,* https://asiamattersforamerica.org/articles/japanese-students-face-barriers-to-study-in-the-united-states.

28. "Pensionado Act," *DBpedia,* https://dbpedia.org/page/Pensionado_Act.

students in the US. In relation to Korea, US Cold War policies,[29] the end of World War II, the role and support of the US after the Korean War, and the Korea Miracle or "The Miracle on the Han River" contributed to the growth of Korean students in the US in this century.[30] For Indians, factors such as the rise in prestige of American education and the Immigration Act of 1965 influenced the growth of the Indian international student population.[31]

The collection of data on international students in the US began in 1915 with the first nationwide survey of foreign students, conducted by a committee on friendly relations among foreign students, which was founded by missionary statesman John R. Mott. This survey was first published in 1919.[32] In the school year 1949–1950, there were only 26,000 international students in the US, with 5,700 of them originating from three Asian countries. Three decades later, by 1980, the total number of international students had increased by more than tenfold, with over 40 percent of them coming from Asia. Four decades later, by 2020, the total enrollment of international students in the US was over one million, with seven of the top ten nations of origin being in Asia.

Hundreds of thousands of Asian international students came to the US for education during the twentieth century. A notable example is John Sung from China. A pastor's son, Sung had a strong desire to study in America and pursued this dream with the encouragement of an American lady missionary.[33] In 1920, he obtained a bachelor's degree from Ohio Wesleyan University, followed by his master's and doctorate in chemistry at Ohio State University. Sung was not only a brilliant student but also active in student life. He served as president of the International Students Association, and his leadership and popularity earned him the nickname "Ohio's most famous student."[34] In 1926, despite the lure of the academic world, he chose to pursue theological studies at Union Theological Seminary in New York City.

---

29. "Korean American Students," https://aas360koreanamericanstudents.weebly.com/history.html.
30. Seth, "Unpromising Recovery," https://www.asianstudies.org/publications/eaa/archives/an-unpromising-recovery-south-koreas-post-korean-war-economic-development-1953-1961/.
31. Rajghatta, "Indian Students," *INDUS*, http://indpaedia.com/ind/index.php/Indian_students_in_the_USA.
32. Thompson, *Unofficial Ambassadors*, 97.
33. Lyall, Flame for God, 16.
34. Lyall, 25.

Table 1: Top Ten Countries of Origin of International Students in the United States[35]

1949–50			1979–80			2019–20		
Country	Number	Share (%)	Country	Number	Share (%)	Country	Number	Share (%)
Total	26,400	100	Total	286,000	100	Total	1,075,000	100
Canada	4,400	16.5	Iran	51,000	17.9	China	373,000	34.6
Taiwan	3,600	13.8	Taiwan	18,000	6.1	India	193,000	18
India	1,400	5.1	Nigeria	16,000	5.7	South Korea	50,000	4.6
United Kingdom	800	3.1	Canada	15,000	5.3	Saudi Arabia	31,000	2.9
Mexico	800	3.1	Japan	12,000	4.3	Canada	26,000	2.4
Cuba	700	2.8	Hong Kong	10,000	3.5	Vietnam	24,000	2.2
Philippines	700	2.7	Venezuela	10,000	3.4	Taiwan	24,000	2.2
Germany	700	2.5	Saudi Arabia	10,000	3.3	Japan	18,000	1.6
Colombia	600	2.2	India	9,000	3.1	Brazil	17,000	1.6
Iran	600	2.2	Thailand	7,000	2.3	Mexico	14,000	1.3
Other Countries	12,100	46	Other Countries	129,000	45.1	Other Countries	307,000	28

Sung, who had an unquenchable desire to serve God in his home country, returned to China in 1927 and devoted himself to sharing the gospel, traveling to numerous towns and cities across China, as well as to other countries like Hong Kong, Inner Mongolia, Singapore, the Philippines, Thailand, Malaysia, and Indonesia. When Sung died in August 1944, he was considered the leading Chinese evangelist of the twentieth century, having "traveled further, spoke[n] more often, and led more Chinese people to faith than any other person."[36] The U.S. Department of State Bureau of Educational and Cultural Affairs has a comprehensive list of former international students – including those from

---

35. Israel and Batalova, "International Students," Migration Policy Institute, https://www.migrationpolicy.org/article/international-students-united-states.

36. Ireland, "Legacy of John Sung," 349.

Asia in the twentieth century – who became heads of state or held prominent government positions after returning to their home countries.[37]

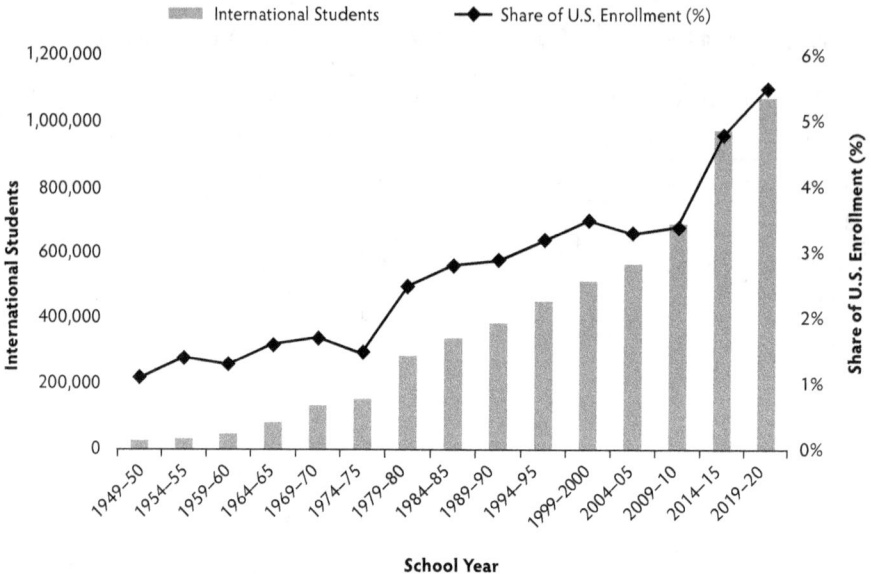

Figure 1: International students and share of total enrollment[38]

Two memorable and world-changing events drastically restricted the flow of Asian international students into the US in the twenty-first century: 11 September 2001 – the terrorist attack on US soil – and 11 March 2020 – when the WHO declared COVID-19 a global pandemic. As of the year 2000, the top five nations sending international students to the United States were from Asia: China, India, Japan, South Korea, and Taiwan. During the first two decades of the twenty-first century (2000–2020), China or India have ranked as the top two sending countries.[39] These last two decades also witnessed Asia emerging as an educational hub for international students, changing the traditional flow of Asian student diasporas and students of other nationalities.

---

37. U.S. Department of State, "Foreign Students Yesterday," https://www.csustan.edu/sites/default/files/OIE/documents/YEDTERDAYSINTERNATIONALSTUDENTS.pdf.

38. Israel and Batalova, "International Students," Migration Policy Institute, https://www.migrationpolicy.org/article/international-students-united-states.

39. Open Doors, *2023 Report*.

Report on Ministry among International Students in Asia

Numerous ISM leaders in several countries contributed to this report, notably those of the International Fellowship of Evangelical Students (IFES), ISM New Zealand, and ISM International. Several mission organizations such as Overseas Missionary Fellowship (OMF), Church Mission Society (CMS), Serving in Mission (SIM), Interserve, International Students Inc (ISI), and InterVarsity/USA-Link have staff seconded to or in partnership with national ministries for launching or enhancing the development of international student ministries. The Asia Missions Association (AMA) has contributed significantly to fostering the ISM vision in Asia through articles in its magazine *Advance* during the period 2014–2023.[40] The Lausanne Asia-Pacific ISM Leaders Forum was held twice in Singapore – in 2009, with sixty participants from fifteen nations, and again in 2015 – to connect ISM leaders and influencers, share ideas, and stimulate potential collaboration. Below are some glimpses into ISM's work in several Asian countries in the post-pandemic era.

Australia: In 2022, Australia was the second most popular destination country in the world for study abroad, with 619,371 international students.[41] During the post-pandemic recovery period, these numbers increased, with the total number of international student visa holders reaching 645,516 in August 2023 – an increase of approximately 6 percent compared to the March 2020 total of 611,077.[42] The oldest and longest-running national ISM in the Asia-Pacific sphere is the Overseas Christian Fellowship (OCF), founded in 1956 by Christian students from Singapore, Malaysia, and Hong Kong. OCF is also one of the most mature and well-organized student-led campus ministries, and it operates without any salaried staff. Currently, OCF has four hundred members at fifteen universities in six states, with over five thousand alumni influencing Asia and the world.[43] In December 2023, it will hold its sixty-fifth annual general meeting for delegates from the fifteen universities. Another highly developed ISM is FOCUS – part of the Australian Fellowship of Evangelical Students (AFES) – which began in the early 1980s and currently has eighty-nine staff across thirty-six campuses in twelve cities.[44]

---

40. Chinn, *AMA Advance Bulletin*, 2014–2023.
41. ICEF Monitor, "Surge in New Students," https://monitor.icef.com/2023/03/surge-in-new-students-has-elicos-sector-leading-australian-growth-for-2022/.
42. ICEF Monitor, "Australia's Foreign Enrolment," https://monitor.icef.com/2023/09/australias-foreign-enrolment-surpasses-pre-pandemic-benchmarks/.
43. OCF Australia, https://ocfaustralia.org/.
44. Correspondence with FOCUS and IFES leaders, June 2023.

Korea: Jeju Island – which was the site of the 2023 Korea Global Diaspora Consultation – is an education hub. Its goal is to attract more international students and become the premier educational hub of Northeast Asia,[45] competing with other Asian education hubs like China, Singapore, Malaysia, Taiwan, Japan, Hong Kong, and India. Nepal also aims to attract students from India, Pakistan, Bangladesh, and Afghanistan.[46] By February 2023, Korea had over 205,000 international students; and in June 2023, the South Korean government introduced a set of incentives designed to attract students in even greater numbers.[47] This initiative – the Study Korea 300K Project – aims to attract three hundred thousand foreign students by 2027.[48]

International Student Fellowship (ISF), founded in 1997 by Christian professors at Seoul National University, is the most developed ISM in Korea, ministering at about forty universities in nine cities and having alumni fellowships in eighteen countries.[49] SEM International (International Scientists, Engineers and Members) was founded in 1995 to minister to international students, scientists, engineers, and other foreign nationals in two cities. SEM is led by a full-time staff, as well as twenty volunteer staff and one hundred volunteers.[50] Korea may be the only country where the national church has intentionally provided support for its international students abroad through the Korean Overseas Students Abroad (KOSTA) network, which began in the US in 1986 when Korean missionaries were sent to care for Korean students in the US. KOSTA hosts annual conferences for students in a few countries. In July 2023, KOSTA USA resumed in-person events at Wheaton College.[51]

New Zealand: International Student Ministry New Zealand (ISMNZ), which grew out of the Navigators ministry over twenty years ago, ministers in seven cities.[52] Prior to forming ISMNZ as a separate ministry, the Navigators included international students in their ministry, and one of these students, Teng Yang Tan, became a Christian in the 1980s and served as the leader of

---

45. "Global Education City," https://english.jdcenter.com/business/edu/jejuen.cs.
46. Stacey, "Nepal Seeking," https://thepienews.com/news/nepal-seeking-to-become-international-education-hub/.
47. ICEF Monitor, "Korea Eases Work," https://monitor.icef.com/2023/07/korea-eases-work-and-visa-policies-in-a-bid-to-further-boost-foreign-enrolment/.
48. ICEF Monitor, "South Korea Aims," https://monitor.icef.com/2023/08/south-korea-aims-to-attract-300000-international-students-by-2027/.
49. ISF, http://isfkorea.org/about-isf-korea/.
50. SEM, http://www.semintl.org/eng/.
51. KOSTA/USA, https://www.kostausa.org/.
52. ISMNZ, https://www.ismnz.org.nz/.

ISMNZ from 2011 to 2016. In 2016, when his visa was not renewed, Teng Yang Tan returned home to Malaysia and worked with Navigators and a small catalytic group to grow the ISM.[53] In 2019, Tan delivered the plenary talk on international student ministry at the Asia Missions Association Convention in Chiang Mai, Thailand. COVID-19 significantly depleted the international student population in New Zealand, with a drop from 120,000 in 2020 to below 35,000 in 2022.[54] But there are encouraging signs of recovery, reflected in the 46,000 student visas approved by July 2023, which amounts to nearly 60 percent of pre-pandemic levels.[55]

Malaysia: In 2022, Malaysia had 170,000 international students, and its long-term goal is to increase its enrollment base to 250,000 students by 2025.[56] After six years of praying and patiently laying the groundwork for a collective impact, ISM Malaysia was officially launched in January 2023, with forty-four churches and Christian organizations sending representatives to this event.[57]

Japan: Japan had 230,000 international students in 2022 and has a ten-year plan to increase this number to 400,000 by 2033.[58] There is some ISM engagement by KGK (the Japanese IFES movement) and a few mission organizations. The Japanese Christian Fellowship Network (JCFN) has been serving Japanese returnee students for about thirty-three years. In May 2023, after a five-year gap, the JCFN finally resumed its annual global returnees conference with in-person attendance, and about 240 people participated in this conference.[59]

The Philippines: In 2019, there were 35,000 international students in the Philippines, but this number dropped to an all-time low during the COVID-19 pandemic. Currently, many students are returning to the country, primarily those in the medical field, particularly from South Asian countries. In 2022, there were 22,247 international students, an increase of 52.7 percent over 2021. The majority of these international students come from India (16,013) or China (4,462).[60] The Philippine Missions Association – in collaboration with campus

---

53. Tan, "International Students and Covid-19 Pandemic," http://ewcenter.org/?p=9239.
54. https://www.educationcounts.govt.nz/statistics/tertiary-participation.
55. ICEF Monitor, "New Zealand." https://monitor.icef.com/2023/07/new-zealand-foreign-enrolment-reaches-two-thirds-of-pre-pandemic-volumes/.
56. ICEF Monitor, "Malaysia Exceeds Target," https://monitor.icef.com/2023/02/malaysia-exceeds-target-for-new-international-student-applications-in-2022/.
57. Author's personal correspondence, June 2023.
58. Hogan, "Japan Aims High," *The PIE*, https://thepienews.com/tags/study-abroad-japan/.
59. JCFN Director's letter, June, 2023.
60. Martin, "Inbound, Outbound and TNE," *The PIE*, https://thepienews.com/philippines/?utm_campaign.

ministries, mission agencies, and churches – organized ISM training sessions last year, and InterVarsity Philippines conducts ISM staff training in Cebu, Davao, and other locations.

Taiwan: In 2019, there were 130,000 international students in Taiwan, and the government aims to increase this to 200,000.[61] ISI and SIM International have ISM staff assisting in local ministries.

Singapore: The *Business Times* reported that there were about 65,400 international students in Singapore as of April 2022, with an even larger enrollment expected for 2023.[62] Several campus ministries and some churches in Singapore have an ISM.

China: China's Ministry of Education reported a steady increase in the annual enrollment of international students, rising from 62,000 in 2001 to 492,000 in 2018, which is the last reported year. By 2018, China had achieved its goal of becoming the largest study-abroad destination in Asia by 2020.[63] The Beijing International Christian Fellowship (BICF) has an extensive ministry among international students in various locations across China. In 2021, more than one million students studying abroad returned to China, a sharp increase from the figure of 777,000 in 2020.[64] Outside China, there have been several gatherings of ISM leaders to address the needs of returnees who had become Christian while studying abroad.

Hong Kong: In 2022, Hong Kong had an enrollment of 13,376 international students. To compete with other Asian destinations, it plans to double this figure by 2024.[65] An ISM "tentmaker" reports that Hong Kong Polytechnic University has 10,500 international students and that there are at least two ISMs in the city.[66]

Thailand: In 2019, there were about twenty-five thousand international students in Thailand. The Asian Institute of Technology Christian Fellowship

---

61. Jennings, "Talent-Strapped Taiwan," *South China Morning Post*, https://www.scmp.com/economy/global-economy/article/3208748/talent-strapped-taiwan-seeks-20000-special-professionals-200000-overseas-students-amid-talent-push.

62. *Business Times*, "Foreign Enrollment in Singapore private schools picks up as borders reopen" 9 June, 2022. https://www.businesstimes.com.sg/singapore/economy-policy/foreign-enrolment-singapore-private-schools-picks-borders-reopen.

63. Qi, "Rising International Student Numbers," *University World News*, https://www.universityworldnews.com/post.php?story=20210521085934537.

64. Bing, "Overseas Students Returning Home," *China Daily*, https://www.chinadaily.com.cn/a/202209/06/WS63169212a310fd2b29e761ac.html.

65. ICEF Monitor, "Hong Kong," https://monitor.icef.com/2023/07/hong-kong-poised-to-double-intake-of-foreign-students/.

66. Author's personal correspondence, 12 July 2023.

(AITCF) has been serving international students at their school for nearly fifty years and currently has about twenty leaders and two staff members.[67] OMF and SIM have ISM staff serving in a few locations in Thailand.

India: In 2021, a total of 48,035 foreign students from 163 countries enrolled in institutions of higher education in India.[68] Emmanuel and Mercy Benjamin were a pioneering couple in ISM, having served in several Indian cities through the Union of Evangelical Students India (UESI) from 1992 to 2002. Emmanuel Benjamin became the founding director of International Students Friendship in Pune in 2002 and served in this position until June 2023, when the couple moved to England. UESI has launched ISM in a few cities in India.[69]

South Pacific Islands: The IFES Regional Secretary for the South Pacific reports that there are a few international students but no dedicated ISM staff for Fiji, Guam, New Caledonia, Papua New Guinea, Solomon Islands, and Vanuatu.[70] SIM International, which already has ISM staff in Singapore, Malaysia, the Philippines, Taiwan, Japan, and Thailand, plans to launch ISM in Indonesia, India, Hong Kong, and other Asian countries.[71]

Conclusion

Although it is still very early in this new post-pandemic era, it is evident that the emerging ISM movement in the Asia-Pacific region is recovering and progressing as greater Asia reclaims its position as a preferred destination for study abroad among diaspora students from the region and beyond.

---

67. AIT Christian Fellowship, https://aitcf.com/.
68. Murthy, "All India Survey," https://ruralindiaonline.org/en/library/resource/all-india-survey-of-higher-education-aishe-2020-21/.
69. Author's personal correspondence, 14 June 2023.
70. Author's personal correspondence, 23 June 2023.
71. Author's personal correspondence, 3 July 2023.

References

Bhandari, Rajika, and Alessia Lebefure, eds. *Asia: The Next Higher Education Superpower?* New York: Institute of International Education, 2015.

Hamrin, Carol Lee, and Stacey Bieler, eds. *Salt and Light: Lives of Faith That Shaped Modern China.* Eugene: Pickwick, 2009.

Ireland, Daryl R. "The Legacy of John Sung." *International Bulletin of Mission Research* 40 (2016): 349–57.

LaFargue, Thomas E. *China's First Hundred.* Washington: Washington State University Press, 1987.

Lyall, Leslie T. *Flame for God.* London: Overseas Missionary Fellowship, 1976.

Thompson, Mary A. *Unofficial Ambassadors.* New York: International Student Service, 1982.

Online References

AIT Christian Fellowship. https://aitcf.com/.

Bing, Kang. "Overseas Students Returning Home in Search of Better Career Prospects." *China Daily*, updated 6 September 2022. https://www.chinadaily.com.cn/a/202209/06/WS63169212a310fd2b29e761ac.html.

Center for Japanese Studies, "President Angell and the First Japanese Students." https://ii.umich.edu/cjs/history-of-cjs.html.

Chadwick, John. "When Rutgers Met Japan: The Start of an Enduring Friendship" https://sas.rutgers.edu/about/news/students/students-news-detail/a-tragic-death-and-a-fateful-journey-how-rutgers-and-japan-forged-an-enduring-connection-2.

Chinn, Leiton. *AMA Advance Bulletin*, January 2014. https://www.asiamissions.net/wp-content/uploads/2014/08/ama_42.pdf.

———. *AMA Advance Bulletin*, July 2016. https://www.asiamissions.net/international-students-a-strategic-component-of-diaspora-missions-the-great-commission/.

———. *AMA Advance Bulletin*, April 2017. https://www.asiamissions.net/ministry-report/.

———. *AMA Advance Bulletin*, January 2019. https://www.asiamissions.net/asian-missions-advances/amadvance-52-60/asian-missions-advance-62/.

———. *AMA Advance Bulletin*, Spring 2023. https://www.asiamissions.net/wp-content/uploads/2023/04/AMA79_LeitonChinn.pdf.

Columbia Global Centers. "Columbia and China in History." https://globalcenters.columbia.edu/content-beijing/columbia-and-china-history.

Duke University Library, "Charles Soong (1863–1918)." https://library.duke.edu/rubenstein/uarchives/history/articles/soong.

Dye, Dustin. "Japanese Students Face Barriers to Study in the United States." *East-West Center*, 14 May 2020. https://asiamattersforamerica.org/articles/japanese-students-face-barriers-to-study-in-the-united-states.

Fish, Eric. "End of an Era? A History of Chinese Students in America." *The China Project*, 12 May 2020. https://thechinaproject.com/2020/05/12/end-of-an-era-a-history-of-chinese-students-in-america/.

"Global Education City." Jeju Free International City Development Center. https://english.jdcenter.com/business/edu/jejuen.cs.

Graham, Elyse. "Princeton Portrait: A Samurai in a Distant Land." *Princeton Alumni Weekly*, December 2021. https://paw.princeton.edu/article/princeton-portrait-samurai-distant-land.

Hennessy, John. "Why Foreign Students Are So Important." *Stanford Magazine*, November/December 2022. https://stanfordmag.org/contents/why-foreign-students-are-so-important.

Hogan, Sophie. "79% of International Student Growth 'Should Come' from Asia by 2025." *The PIE*, 22 February 2022. https://thepienews.com/news/79-international-student-growth-come-asian-countries/.

———. "Japan Aims High with 400,000 Internationals by 2033 Ambition." *The PIE*, 23 March 2023. https://thepienews.com/study-in-japan/.

Holon Global Student Flows Project. "US International Education in 2030." *Holon IQ*, 12 April 2023. https://www.holoniq.com/notes/us-international-education-in-2030-6-charts-top-20-source-countries-and-preliminary-forecast.

ICEF Monitor. "Closer to Home: Intra-regional Mobility in Asia." 4 December, 2019. https://monitor.icef.com/2019/12/closer-to-home-intra-regional-mobility-in-asia/.

———. "Australia's Foreign Enrolment Surpasses Pre-pandemic Benchmarks." 27 September 2023. https://monitor.icef.com/2023/09/australias-foreign-enrolment-surpasses-pre-pandemic-benchmarks/.

———. "Hong Kong Poised to Double Intake of Foreign Students." 5 July 2023. https://monitor.icef.com/2023/07/hong-kong-poised-to-double-intake-of-foreign-students/.

———. "International Student Visa Holders up 98% in New Zealand since the Border Reopening." 17 May 2023. https://monitor.icef.com/2023/05/international-student-visa-holders-up-98-in-new-zealand-since-the-border-reopening/.

———. "Korea Eases Work and Visa Policies in a Bid to Further Boost Foreign Enrolment." 2 July 2023. https://monitor.icef.com/2023/07/korea-eases-work-and-visa-policies-in-a-bid-to-further-boost-foreign-enrolment/.

———. "Malaysia Exceeds Target for New International Student Applications in 2022." 1 February 2023. https://monitor.icef.com/2023/02/malaysia-exceeds-target-for-new-international-student-applications-in-2022/.

———. "New Zealand: Foreign Enrolment Approaching 60% of Pre-pandemic Volumes." 26 July 2023. https://monitor.icef.com/2023/07/new-zealand-foreign-enrolment-reaches-two-thirds-of-pre-pandemic-volumes/.

———. "South Korea Aims to Attract 300,000 International Students by 2027." 23 August 2023. https://monitor.icef.com/2023/08/south-korea-aims-to-attract-300000-international-students-by-2027/.

———. "Surge in New Students Has ELICOS Sector Leading Australian Growth for 2022." 8 March 2023. https://monitor.icef.com/2023/03/surge-in-new-students-has-elicos-sector-leading-australian-growth-for-2022/.

ISF (International Student Fellowship). http://isfkorea.org/about-isf-korea/.

ISMNZ (International Student Ministries of New Zealand). https://www.ismnz.org.nz/.

Israel, Emma, and Jeanne Batalova. "International Students in the US," *Migration Policy Institute,* 14 January 2021. https://www.migrationpolicy.org/article/international-students-united-states.

JCFN (Japanese Christian Fellowship Network). "Introduction to JCFN." https://jcfn.org/home/index.php?lang=en.

———. "Director's Letter, June, 2023." https://jcfn.org/home/index.php?option=com_content&view=article&id=1744:june-2023-directors-letter&catid=197&lang=en&Itemid=476.

Jennings, Ralph. "Talent-Strapped Taiwan Seeks 20,000 'Special' Professionals, 200,000 Overseas Students amid Talent Push." *South China Morning Post,* 2 February 2023. https://www.scmp.com/economy/global-economy/article/3208748/talent-strapped-taiwan-seeks-20000-special-professionals-200000-overseas-students-amid-talent-push.

Kim, Gun Cheol. "Yu Gil-jun (1856–1914): A Bridge-Person of Korea to the West and the First Korean Student in the United States." Korean Diaspora Project, Boston University School of Theology. https://sites.bu.edu/koreandiaspora/individuals/boston-in-the-1880s/yu-kil-chun-1856-1914-a-bridge-person-of-korea-to-the-west-and-the-first-korean-student-in-the-united-states/.

Korean American Students. https://aas360koreanamericanstudents.weebly.com/history.html.

KOSTA/USA (Korean Overseas Student Abroad). https://www.kostausa.org/.

Martin, Kim. "Inbound, Outbound and TNE: The Philippines' Commitment to Mobility." *The PIE,* 14 August 2023. https://thepienews.com/analysis/philippines/?utm_campaign.

Moore, Ray. "History of Amherst College and Japan." *Amherst College.* https://www.amherst.edu/academiclife/departments/asian/japanese_language/Amherst_Japan/node/5388.

Murthy, Sanjay K. "All India Survey of Higher Education 2020–21." New Delhi: Government of India, Ministry of Education, 2023. https://ruralindiaonline.org/en/library/resource/all-india-survey-of-higher-education-aishe-2020-21/.

Nguyen, Alicia, and Emily Jeffres. "Moung Kyaw: Colgate's First International Student." *Colgate University.* https://200.colgate.edu/looking-back/people/moung-kyaw-colgates-first-international-student.

OCF, Overseas Christian Fellowship Australia. https://ocfaustralia.org/.

Open Doors 2023 Report on Institute of International Education, https://opendoorsdata.org/.

"Pensionado Act." *DBpedia*. https://dbpedia.org/page/Pensionado_Act.

Pripas-Kapit, Sarah Rose. "Educating Women Physicians of the World: International Students of the Woman's Medical College of Pennsylvania, 1883–1911." PhD diss., University of California, 2015. https://escholarship.org/content/qt9gh5b9j1/qt9gh5b9j1_noSplash_9b8d0d9e73787d59ab1cf063070e5c93.pdf.

Qi, Jing. "Impact of Rising International Student Numbers in China." *University World News*, 22 May 2021. https://www.universityworldnews.com/post.php?story=20210521085934537.

Rajghatta, Chidanand. "Indian Students in the USA." *INDUS*, last modified 6 December 2023. http://indpaedia.com/ind/index.php/Indian_students_in_the_USA.

SEM (International Scientists, Engineers and Members). http://www.semintl.org/eng/.

Seth, Michael J. "An Unpromising Recovery: South Korea's Post-Korean War Economic Development: 1953–1961." *Association for Asian Studies*, Winter 2013. https://www.asianstudies.org/publications/eaa/archives/an-unpromising-recovery-south-koreas-post-korean-war-economic-development-1953-1961/.

Stacey, Viggo. "London Best Student City Again as Tokyo Rises." *The PIE*, 20 July 2023. https://thepienews.com/news/london-best-student-city-2024/.

———. "Nepal Seeking to Become International Education Hub." *The PIE*, 7 February 2023. https://thepienews.com/news/nepal-seeking-to-become-international-education-hub/.

Statistics and Data. "International Students in US by Country of Origin (1949–2022)." https://statisticsanddata.org/data/international-students-in-us-by-country-of-origin-1949-2022/.

U.S. Department of State: Bureau of Educational and Cultural Affairs. "Foreign Students Yesterday, World Leaders Today." https://www.csustan.edu/sites/default/files/OIE/documents/YEDTERDAYSINTERNATIONALSTUDENTS.pdf.

U.S. Department of State Archive. "United States Relations with China: Boxer Uprising to Cold War (1900–1949)." https://2001-2009.state.gov/r/pa/ho/pubs/fs/90689.htm#boxer_uprising.

Utokyo (The University of Tokyo). https://www.u-tokyo.ac.jp/en/about/history.html.

Virdhi-Dhesi, Jaipreet. "Photos of the Amazing Life of Gurubai Karmarkar." *Scroll.in*, 20 April 2014. https://scroll.in/article/661289/photos-of-the-amazing-life-of-gurubai-karmarkar-woman-doctor-in-19th-century-mumbai.

Yuasa, Karisa. "The Untold Story of Japanese Students Sponsored by the U.S. Military." *PSU Vanguard*, 18 February 2020. https://psuvanguard.com/the-untold-story-of-japanese-students-sponsored-by-the-u-s-military/.

15

Hybridity in Korean Missionary Kids: "Third Space" Pedagogy in International Schools

Grace Eun-Sun Lee and Tessa Tubbs

Introduction

In the twenty-first century, Asian countries like India, South Korea, the Philippines, Singapore, and China are continuing to send out an increasing number of missionaries.[1] Recognizing the necessity to address issues that are specific to Asian missionaries, organizations like Families in Global Transition,[2] the Shepherd's Table, and TeachBeyond are mobilizing to provide increased support. Furthermore, although the needs of missionary kids (MKs) – a diaspora in their own right – are often overlooked in missiological conversations, their experiences are an important chapter in the story of missions.

Student population trends in prominent MK international schools based in Southeast Asia reflect the global shift of Christianity from the Northern to the Southern Hemisphere. Many of these schools – such as Faith Academy in the Philippines (founded in 1957) and Grace International School in Thailand (founded in 1999) – began as educational institutions for North American missionaries. In recent years, however, the composition of the student population is changing. Asian student populations, especially Korean MKs, are increasing at a faster rate than the Western student population.[3] There is substantial

---

1. Van Reken, "Enlarging Our Tents."
2. This organization founded "TCKs in Asia" in 2019.
3. Pearce, "Internationally-National Schools," 351–72.

research on Third Culture Kids (TCKs), which has been helpful in articulating the Korean MK experience. However, the TCK or third culture language research has been primarily conducted by expats from North America focusing on North American MKs. Moreover, in postcolonial studies, the third-culture language is often associated with hierarchical structures that limit the contextualization of this terminology. To overcome these limits, we draw on Homi Bhabha's term "hybridity" as a descriptor for the mixing and mingling of cultures and experiences that MKs undergo.[4] We focus particularly on the concept of "third space," offering practical application steps for teachers to create environments facilitating third-space conversations that cultivate biblical hospitality.

Korean Missionaries and Missionary Kids

The Korean church is globally renowned for its missional fervor. From the 1980s to the 2010s, there has been an exponential increase in Korean missionaries.[5] Timothy Park asserts, "The Korean church has been a missionary church almost from the beginning."[6] This statement is significant because while the growth of Christianity does not always result in the rise and strengthening of missionary movements, the Korean church has a missionary heritage that is passed on to Korean MKs.

Many factors influence the choice of schooling. However, despite the high tuition fees, many Korean missionaries, seeking a higher quality of education, send their children to international schools. For example, Danau Tanu, who specializes in researching children of Asian diasporas, studied at an international high school in Indonesia, where 25 percent of the student body were Koreans, constituting the largest group.[7] In the international school environment, these Korean MKs are often exposed to extracurricular activities and opportunities that are not typically offered in the traditional Korean academic environment, particularly diverse cultures and upbringings that their peers in Korea would not experience. Therefore, as a result of the schooling they receive, these Korean MKs have to navigate three different cultures: (1) the home culture of the family (unless they are in a boarding school), (2) a school culture that often incorporates Western elements, and (3) their local mission field

---

4. Bhabha, *Location of Culture*, 5.
5. Ma and Ahn, *Korean Church*, xiv–xv.
6. Park, "Missionary Movement," 20.
7. Tanu, "Interdisciplinary Analysis," 26.

culture. Navigating the constant and simultaneous interactions and nuances of various cultures contributes to the hybridization that MKs experience and enables them to develop flexibility to move between different cultural contexts.

In contrast, the challenge for Western educators carrying out the Great Commission is to use the platform provided by their classroom to become intercultural disciplers. In general, Western Christianity has positively impacted Korean missions by providing economic, religious, and social resources. This gives Western teachers the advantage of being viewed positively by Korean missionary parents. In this way, Western teachers have the potential to become bridge builders for these Korean MKs, exposing them to the benefits of the world without losing or sacrificing their Korean heritage.

Teaching Korean MKs involves the challenge of navigating complexities such as being a Christian witness who is authentic, indigenous, and uncompromising without becoming Westernized. Yet it also includes the opportunity to appreciate the uniqueness of Korean Christianity without ignoring its shortcomings or discarding its cultural baggage to adopt other cultural attitudes of Christianity that are perceived as more favorable. Thus, international schools serve as a space for Western teachers to facilitate students' growth by engaging with their hybridity.

Hybridity in International Schools

From an early age, Korean MKs are immersed in global cultures that provide fertile grounds for hybridization, challenging them to grow beyond the familiar cultural understanding their parents may hold. In postcolonial theory, hybridity describes a process in which both the colonizer and the colonized are changed by each other and thus undergo a hybridization process.[8] As Elaheh Rahimi writes, "Cultural hybridity constitutes the effort to maintain a sense of balance among, values, practices and customs of two or more different cultures."[9] This cultural hybridity may sometimes be manifested in unhealthy or unhelpful ways, such as inducing MKs to abandon one or more of the cultures they navigate in favor of the other so that they can fit in. International boarding schools should encourage the Western teachers in these schools to appreciate that their students come with very different cultural understand-

---

8. See Gandhi, *Postcolonial Theory*, 131.
9. Rahimi, "Cultural Hybridity."

ings of authority and power dynamics and that this can contribute to identity upheavals and potential conflicts.[10]

Although international schools are recognizing changing trends within their student body, resources preparing teachers for the unique pedagogical challenges faced by Korean MKs remain limited. Most of these schools are still staffed mainly by Western teachers, whose training and perspective are tailored to the needs of Western MKs.[11] Thus, teachers are often not equipped to understand the unique struggles of their Asian diaspora students.[12] Ruth Van Reken, one of the leading researchers in TCK/MK, admitting that the research and resources are skewed to represent the experiences of American missionary kids, states that "we are in the 'next stage' of developing our understanding of [the challenges of diaspora children] where we acknowledge [their] diversity."[13] This next stage is necessary to prepare parents and teachers of Korean MKs to provide the best care for them.

Hybridity, along with the research surrounding it, has potential to become a valuable resource in this next stage of understanding the Asian diaspora experience. The concept of the "third space" in particular provides a language and a framework to facilitate dialogue and help adults to understand the experiences of MKs. Homi Bhabha, renowned for advancing the use of hybridity in postcolonial conversations, further conceptualizes hybridity to encompass the idea of a third space "where cultural identity must be renegotiated in ways that restructure and subvert the previous power relations between colonizers and the colonized."[14] Third space is created when people of two culturally distinct and hybrid backgrounds meet and dialogue. It is also created when "the previous power relations" are subverted. Homi Bhabha further states, "For me the importance of hybridity is not to be able to trace to original moments from which the third emerges, rather hybridity to me is the 'third space' which enables other positions to emerge."[15] When a teacher minimizes the power gap with the students and invites MKs to dialogue, it creates a "third space" thereby encouraging the development of hybridity.

---

10. Choi, "Identity Crisis," 31. Choi calls "churches . . . to pay more attention," and international boarding schools must also attend to the complexity of their students' hybridity.

11. Most MK research uses the TCK paradigm. This term, which was coined in the 1950s by sociologist Ruth Useem, describes children raised outside their parent's home culture. It focuses on American expatriate children, and most literature emphasizes a Western perspective.

12. Tanu, "Interdisciplinary Analysis," 28.

13. "TCK's of Asia," https://www.figt.org/blog/9122271.

14. Weng and Kulich, "Hybridity," 401.

15. Rutherford, "The Third Space: Interview with Homi Bhabha," 211.

In their research on third space, McKinley and colleagues acknowledge that while the third space was initially considered a zone in which transgressive acts are performed, allowing oppressed groups to develop retributive dissent,[16] the term "third space" can also become "an environment in which to negotiate learning where those present feel at ease with their own and others' cultural identities and differences."[17] If Western-trained teachers display a curiosity and willingness to learn about their students' heritage and experiences, they will be able to facilitate conversations in which a "safe" third space can emerge, enabling a sense of cultural ease and learning that helps equip their MKs to embrace hybridity and the gifts it brings.

In an international school context, the third space facilitates the exchange of ideas that lead to new possibilities, superseding the way of living of any one dominant culture. Instead of trying to understand and reflect on experiences that the teacher finds unfamiliar, teachers are free to create an environment that nurtures third-space conversations in which children of hybridity can contribute their ideas and learn from each other in a cultural exchange. This approach requires using the classroom as a space for Korean students to share their history, their rituals, and unique MK experiences that are a blend of their home and host culture so that a new understanding emerges in this "third space of enunciation."[18] By making space for their students' unique experiences and stories, teachers can encourage them to embrace their origins and accept their hybridity without elevating one cultural influence in a way that is detrimental to another.

From Hybridity toward Biblical Hospitality

The third space concept pairs well with the scriptural mandate to love our neighbors and live hospitable lives. Hospitality is not exclusive to Christian cultures; however biblical hospitality distinguishes itself in Scripture not only by generously welcoming people into one's home but by emphasizing a love for the stranger. The biblical portrayal of hospitality reveals more of God's own heart for his creation. In Greek, the word for "hospitality" is φιλο-ξενία (*philozenia*), which combines elements of the words for "brotherly love" and "stranger." This is the word the author uses in Hebrews 13:1 to instruct believers to practice hospitality, and it implies treating even strangers as brothers. It says, "remain in

---

16. McKinley et al., "Developing Intercultural Competence," 2.
17. McKinley et al., 2.
18. Bhabha, "Cultural Identity and Cultural Differences," 207.

brotherly love . . . and do not forget *philozenia*." Similarly, in Romans 12:9–13, Paul calls believers to love each other and concludes his detailed instructions with a call to "pursue hospitality" (author's translation). What better place to obey these instructions than within a diaspora community?

Hospitality is inherently a lifestyle of creating space for others, and the third space describes what can happen when hospitality is practiced. Thus, the mandate of biblical hospitality encourages third-space conversations where strangers are welcomed. This demonstrates the love of Jesus for all people and his desire for the church to "accept one another" just as he accepted them (Rom 15:7). Similarly, as those who initiate and respond to third-space conversations, MKs are then given agency to create belonging and accept others.

Korean culture greatly values hospitality, and this hospitality is experienced in unique ways. Generously sharing food is one of the key ways Koreans show hospitality.[19] One author connects the concept of "jeong" (정/情) with Korean hospitality.[20] "Jeong" is a complex concept, unique to the Korean culture, that describes a level of affection and treatment toward someone with whom you feel a personal closeness; it is an unspoken but deeply felt sense of camaraderie.[21] What characterizes "jeong" as uniquely Korean is that it is founded on collective social responsibility.[22] "Jeong" naturally lends itself to welcoming others by extending hospitality, and Korean MKs are often raised with the concept of "jeong" as part of their cultural DNA. Thus, when teachers engage in the biblical hospitality of third-space conversations with their Korean pupils, they not only help them to embrace their own culture but also demonstrate how this heritage prepares them to practice biblical hospitality.

Practical Application

Teachers at international schools can help their students to embrace hybridity and overcome identity crises by encouraging a third-space environment in their classrooms. This approach draws on the concept of biblical hospitality,

---

19. A Korean saying goes "하나만 주면 정 없어" (translated, "there is no 'jeong' if I give you only one"). "Jeong" is expressed in the generous giving or sharing of food beyond what is required.

20. Sung, "Church Leadership Journals," 89.

21. This idea requires accepting someone into your inner circle by lowering your guard or walls. "Jeong" is different from romantic affection because it can be offered regardless of status or background, between a boss and a worker, between friends, or between married couples.

22. Koreans say "U-ri" (우리) our mom rather than my mom. One Korean mother will treat her child's friends with motherly affection.

facilitating dialogues where there is mutual sharing of unique experiences and where all voices are heard and welcomed. We highlight below two practical approaches that teachers can adopt to create such a third-space environment.

Biblical Truth and Awareness of Cultural Lenses

Jeff and Karyn Kamphausen, teachers at Grace Academy in Thailand, said, "All of [our MKs] have cultural baggage, but when we can come back to biblical things, it goes beyond cultures we are in."[23] The Kamphausens believe that when MKs struggle with hybridity and identity, the solution is to focus on grounding them biblically and helping them to take ownership of their faith. This will equip them to navigate the stormy waters they will encounter when they leave the protective environment of international schools. While the Bible provides guidance and truth for anyone, people's cultural backgrounds and worldviews affect their interpretation of Scripture.

Teachers may not always be aware of the assumptions inherent in their own cultural experiences and those that their students hold when approaching Scripture. Korean theologian and pastor Moonjang Lee states that while Western Christians helped to bring Christianity to the world, unfortunately, they have also imposed on other cultures "certain habits and beliefs that are now considered normative in Christianity but do not necessarily line up with the biblical narrative."[24] By practicing awareness and cultivating curiosity about the differences in their international students, teachers can foster a hospitable environment that creates a "third space" for conversations between students hybridities. The use of phrases such as "I wonder . . ." or "I notice . . ." allows teachers to comment without shutting down the conversation. If teachers immediately respond to questions or observations, offering answers or explanations, they miss opportunities for spiritual growth through in-depth discussions that are necessary for the evaluation of assumptions and worldviews. Without awareness of their own cultural assumptions, teachers can miss opportunities for conversational hospitality, especially in situations where worldviews clash.

Being grounded in biblical truth requires teachers to be aware of the cultural lens through which they interpret and apply the word. Since no one is exempt from the influence of culture, it is important that teachers grow in awareness of how their own North American cultural understanding shapes

---

23. The Kamphausens interviewed by Tessa Sydnor on 6 January 2023.
24. Johnson, "Korean Christianity," 75.

their interpretation of the Bible and understand in what ways this is different from the biblical context of the ancient Near East. By modeling cultural self-awareness, teachers can help Korean MKs to understand that their own hybrid experience of Korean culture and the local host culture impacts the way they read and engage with Scripture.

Using Pedagogy That Encourages Discussion

In a traditional Korean classroom, the teacher has the highest authority, and the pedagogy is primarily lecture-based with minimal discussion. Rote memorization is emphasized, often to the detriment of critical thinking and creativity. The Socratic method of teaching is an alternative pedagogical strategy that moves away from lecturing and didactic teaching. Instead, this approach involves asking students open-ended questions that encourage discussion and the exchange of ideas.[25] This method can be helpful for students from Korean backgrounds because it helps them to find their own voice, rather than conforming to the group mentality that is often expected in Korean classrooms. Teachers can explore other pedagogical methods such as techniques used by the Montessori system, which aims to nurture and develop ideas already growing in the student.[26] By learning what interests their students and allowing this to shape and steer classroom conversations, teachers create an environment that promotes the development of well-rounded students.

Conclusion

As Korean MKs follow their parents to the mission field and engage with their classmates in international school contexts, they are exposed to many different cultures. This mingling of cultures creates cultural hybridity that can be difficult for them to fully understand or articulate. Therefore, teachers play a crucial role in helping these students to thrive in their hybridized world. Just as foreign missionaries helped Korean church leaders to realize their missionary responsibility, Western teachers working in international schools can help their students to recognize the missional potential of their diverse hybrid experiences. Implementing pedagogical approaches that encourage third-space conversations in the classroom will empower Korean MKs to embrace their

---

25. Conor, "Socratic Method," https://tilt.colostate.edu/the-socratic-method/.

26. "Montessori Education," *American Montessori Society*, https://amshq.org/About-Montessori/What-Is-Montessori.

unique identities – which encompass speech, actions, and experiences. By understanding and embracing the students' own culture, teachers can use concepts like "jeong" to help MKs adopt their hybridity as a means of accepting others, looking beyond appearance and stereotypes. In this way, Korean MKs can be helped to understand that their life stories, empowered by the Holy Spirit, can be "missional gifts" of hospitality to the world, following the example of Christ Jesus himself.

References

Bhabha, Homi K. "Cultural Diversity and Cultural Differences" in *The Post Colonial Studies Reader*, eds. Bill Ashcroft, Gareth Griffiths, and Helen Tiffin. New York: Routledge, 1990: 206–9.

———. *The Location of Culture*. London; New York: Routledge, 1994.

Choi, Sungho. "Identity Crisis for the Diaspora Community." In *Korean Diaspora and Christian Mission*. Edited by S. Hun Kim and Wonsuk Ma. Oxford: Regnum Books, 2011: 25–34.

Conor, Peter. "The Socratic Method: Fostering Critical Thinking." *The Institute for Learning and Teaching, Colorado State University*. Accessed 17 November 2023. https://tilt.colostate.edu/the-socratic-method/.

Crossman, Tanya. *Misunderstood: The Impact of Growing Up Overseas in the 21st Century*. UK: Summertime, 2016.

Gandhi, Leela. *Postcolonial Theory: A Critical Introduction*. New York: Columbia University Press, 1998.

Han, Chulho. "Mission Korea: The Contribution of Global Youth Mobilization." *Korean Diaspora and Christian Mission*. Edited by S. Hun Kim and Wonsuk Ma. Oxford: Regnum Books, 2011: 164–70.

Johnson, Todd. "Korean Christianity in the Context of Global Christianity." In *Korean Church, God's Mission, Global Christianity*, edited by Wonsuk Ma and Kyo Seong Ahn, 71–84. Oxford: Regnum Books, 2015.

Kim, Hun S., and Wonsuk Ma. Introduction to *Korean Diaspora and Christian Mission*, edited by S. Hun Kim and Wonsuk Ma, 1–7. Oxford: Regnum Books, 2011.

Kim, Kirsteen. "The Significance for Mission Studies of Korean World Mission." In *Korean Church, God's Mission, Global Christianity*, edited by Wonsuk Ma and Kyo Seong Ahn, 48–56. Oxford: Regnum Books, 2015.

Ma, Wonsuk, and Kyo Seong Ahn. Preface to *Korean Church, God's Mission, Global Christianity*, edited by Wonsuk Ma and Kyo Seong Ahn, xvii–xx. Oxford: Regnum Books, 2015.

McKinley, J., K. Dunworth, T. Grimshaw, and J. Iwaniec. "Developing Intercultural Competence in a 'Comfortable' Third Space: Postgraduate Studies in the UK." *Language and Intercultural Communication* 19 (November 2018): 9–22.

Mohizin, Vahitha. "Hybridity and Third Space." YouTube video, 1 July 2021. https://www.youtube.com/watch?v=t6tH6mkmYIA.

Park, Timothy K. "The Missionary Movement of the Korean Church: A Non-Western Church Mission Model." In *Korean Church, God's Mission, Global Christianity*, edited by Wonsuk Ma and Kyo Seong Ahn, 19–31. Oxford: Regnum Books, 2015.

Pearce, Sarah. "Internationally-National Schools: A Critical Review of This Developing Sector and the Frameworks That Define International Schools." *Research in Comparative and International Education* 18, no. 3 (September 2023): 351–72.

Pollock, David C., Ruth E. Van Reken, and Michael V. Pollock. *Third Culture Kids: Growing Up among Worlds*. 3rd ed. Boston: Nicholas Brealey, 2017.

Rahimi, Elaheh. "Cultural Hybridity and Its Implications and Status in Intercultural Competence." *International Conference on Narrative and Language Studies*, May 2018. https://www.researchgate.net/publication/327120730_Cultural_Hybridity_and_Its_Implication_Status_in_Intercultural_Competence.

Rambo, Elizabeth L. "Third-Culture Kid Identity Paradigms in the *Buffy the Vampire Slayer* Episode 'Lies My Parents Told Me.'" *Slayage: The Journal of Whedon Studies* 16.1 [47], (2018): 1–16.

Rutherford, Jonathan. "The Third Space: Interview with Homi Bhabha" *Identity: Community, Culture, Difference*. London: Lawrence and Wishart, 1990: 207–21.

Scholle, Charles. "Understanding the Socratic Method of Teaching." *Abraham Lincoln University*, 10 February 2020. https://www.alu.edu/alublog/understanding-the-socratic-method-of-teaching/.

Sung, Grace Hyejung Kim. "Church Leadership Journals of Korean American Christian Women." PhD diss., Cook School of Intercultural Studies, Biola University, 2023.

Tanu, Danau. "Toward an Interdisciplinary Analysis of the Diversity of 'Third Culture Kids.'" In *Migration, Diversity, and Education: Beyond Third Culture Kids*, edited by Saija Benjamin and Fred Dervin, 13–34. London: Palgrave Macmillan, 2016.

Tavangar, Homa Sabet. *Growing Up Global: Raising Children to Be At Home in the World*. New York: Ballantine Books, 2009.

"TCKs of Asia on Privilege and Diversity." *Families in Global Transition*, 24 July 2020. https://www.figt.org/blog/9122271.

"The Uniquely Korean Concept of Jeong." *Knowing Korea*. Accessed 12 July 2023. https://www.knowingkorea.org/contents/view/204/The-uniquely-Korean-concept-of-Jeong.

Van Reken, Ruth, and KT. "Enlarging Our Tents: How Covid Exposed Unrecognized Wellness Needs in Missions." Handout distributed at Mental Health and Missions Conference, 17–20 November 2022.

Weng, Liping, and Steve J. Kulich. "Hybridity." In *The SAGE Encyclopedia of Intercultural Competence*. Edited by Janet M. Bennett. Thousand Oaks: SAGE, 2015.

"What Is Montessori Education?" *American Montessori Society*. Accessed 17 November 2023. https://amshq.org/About-Montessori/What-Is-Montessori.

16

Intentional Mission to Internal Migrants in India

J. N. Manokaran

Introduction

Migration is currently a hot topic, debated in public forums, academia, and the media. While global migration entails crossing national borders and continents, there is also migration taking place over shorter distances within national boundaries – sometimes within the same cultural context and other times, beyond. India, the world's most populous country, which has a vast land area, has a significant movement of people within its borders. A vast country like India has both, migrants within the local vicinity, as well as those who cross boundaries of state, language and culture.

Internal Migrants in India

According to the 2011 Census, there were 450 million internal migrants in India. The majority (62 percent) of these migrants moved within the same district, 26 percent moved within the same state, while 12 percent moved to other states.[1] There are more migrants who move within the country as it is cheaper, affordable, requires no documentation like a visa and no problems with foreign currency exchange. The internal migrant flows were almost four times greater than international migrant flows.[2]

---

1. De, "Internal Migration," https://blogs.worldbank.org/peoplemove/internal-migration-india-grows-inter-state-movements-remain-low.

2. Kumar and Bhagat, *Migrants*, 2.

Challenges Faced by Internal Migrants

To survive in India, internal migrants must overcome many challenges. Although effective governance requires accurate and relevant information, according to Shreehari Paliath, there is no reliable information or data about internal migration. During the COVID-19 lockdown, around 11.4 million migrant workers returned home to India, resulting in at least 971 non-COVID deaths, including ninety-six workers who died on trains.[3] Tracing internal migration is a complex process because it involves many kinds of migration: low-skilled and high-skilled labor migration, seasonal and circular migration, and migration caused by factors such as ethnic conflicts, civil wars, and environmental crises.[4] Migrants in cities are often excluded from the political decision-making and governing process for three reasons.

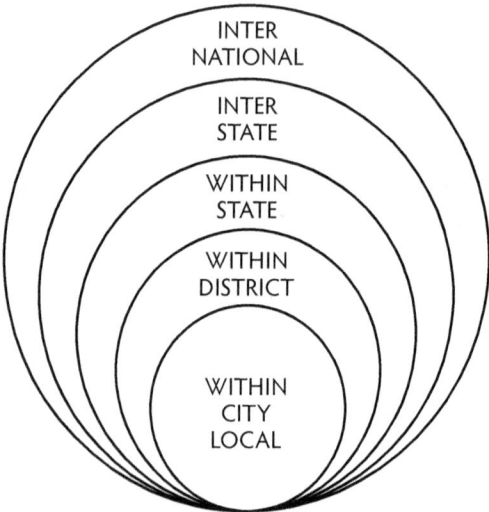

Figure 1: Types of Migration

First, migrants whose focus is returning to their native places may not want to get involved *in* the political process. Second, the bureaucratic hurdles involved in obtaining the necessary documents may discourage migrants from participating in the electoral process. Third, anti-migrant sentiments are often

---

3. Paliath, "Year after Covid-19," https://scroll.in/article/990527/a-year-after-covid-19-lockdown-india-still-doesnt-have-reliable-data-or-policy-on-migrant-workers.
4. Kumar and Bhagat, *Migrants*, 61.

prevalent among the native population.⁵ Deepak Sharma writes that migrants are attracted to cities because of employment opportunities.⁶ However, the jobs available to these migrants are often "3D jobs": dirty, difficult, and dangerous.⁷ Short-term migration during the harvest season – for example, working as farm laborers in Punjab – is usually driven by poverty. In contrast, better jobs may be available for long-term migrants, and their migration may even become permanent.⁸ Some seasonal migrants come from regions that produce winter garments that are sold in other parts of the country. However, migrants from Northeast India, especially from the seven sister states, are unique because they are tribal people, with Mongolic features and distinct languages. They initially came as government employees but later found employment in private companies through referrals and job melas (job fairs).⁹ Recently, riots, killing, and violence between different ethnic groups in Manipur caused thousands to migrate out of Manipur in May and June 2023. Migrants who are often poor and come from the lower strata of society and are therefore not respected, protected or treated well by those in authority.

Push and Pull Factors in Migration

Factors driving migration can be categorized into push and pull factors. In India, significant factors driving migration are based on socioeconomic and political dominance. As in most other parts of the world, violence is a key "push" factor influencing internal migration in India. The caste system, oppression, and caste conflicts are other factors that compel people to move from rural to urban areas. Migration is a key survival strategy employed by households in rural villages.¹⁰

> While people continue to get displaced from their land in the villages, or to leave it "voluntarily" as agriculture, forestry, fisheries, and handicrafts are rendered difficult survival propositions, they try their hand at other occupations in the village itself (without any assistance from the state) or migrate to the cities or other rural areas that need cheap labor. Such cheap, exploited labor

---

5. Gaikwad and Nellis, "Overcoming the Political Exclusion of Migrants," 1133.
6. Mishra, *Internal Migration*, 7.
7. Manokaran, *Christ and Migrants*, 22.
8. Mishra, *Internal Migration*, 14.
9. Mishra, 77.
10. Mishra, 181.

is the secret behind the successful sweatshops which contribute significantly to Indian exports.[11]

Natural disasters also cause people to migrate. For example, there were ninety-six cyclones in Odisha's coastal region between 1891 and 2021. While the frequency of cyclones along the Odisha coast has now decreased, their intensity has increased.[12] Other disasters such as floods, landslides, earthquakes, tsunamis, drought, and famine also cause migration. A section of the city of Mumbai called Kamatipura was established by distressed migrants. It was named for the Kamati tribe of artisans and laborers who came to Bombay from Andhra Pradesh in the late 1800s, to escape famine.[13]

According to Darpan Singh, lack of industrial development pushes people to move, seeking jobs

> as farm laborers, construction and sanitation workers, hawkers, watchmen, dhobis, rickshaw pullers, auto-rickshaw drivers, and now lift attendants. Along with populous states like Uttar Pradesh, Bihar had a surplus labor force for industrially developing Maharashtra, Gujarat, Tamil Nadu, and Karnataka or agriculturally progressing Punjab and Haryana. Before that, Kolkata was a strong pull for job-seekers.[14]

Migration can have positive results such as better agricultural productivity and the creation of jobs in the industrial and service sectors. However, wrong priorities and flawed government policies have led people to migrate.[15]

The pull factors that drive migration include education, awareness, mass media, social media, and the experiences of others. Migrants are attracted by economic opportunities and the chance to fulfill their aspirations.[16] Cities provide opportunities for earning money which is tangible and thus attractive. "In Bihar, migration has provided a route to 'work with dignity and freedom.'"[17] Since the rigid caste structure that shackles the lower castes is often not operative in the regions people migrate to, they find this an empowering experience.

---

11. Shrivastava and Kothari, *Churning the Earth*, 169.
12. Kumar, "India's Eastern Shore," https://scroll.in/article/1017277/along-indias-eastern-shore-coastal-erosion-is-forcing-people-to-abandon-their-homes.
13. Faleiro, *Beautiful Thing*, 92.
14. Singh, "Biharis."
15. Shrivastava and Kothari, *Churning the Earth*, 191.
16. Mishra, *Internal Migration*, 1.
17. Mishra, 210.

This freedom may also become addictive.[18] One of the dance girls who migrated to Mumbai said, "I make money and money gives me something my mother never had. *Azaadi*. Freedom."[19] Migrants in cities have a lot of freedom that they did not have before. When they are humiliated or treated unfairly by the dominant caste employers, they either escape or find another employment.[20]

Cities attract migrants because of the many livelihood opportunities available there. Aparna Bhattacharya calls trains from West Bengal to Tamil Nadu "The Migrant Train." Although many laborers were killed after a major train accident, the migration did not stop. Since they had no other options, these people prioritized livelihood over life.[21] "The urban poor are largely the overflow of the rural poor who had migrated to urban areas of alternative employment and livelihood, laborers who do a variety of casual jobs and the self-employed who sell a variety of things on roadsides and are engaged in various activities."[22]

Migration is inextricably linked to the modern world and modern life.[23] The talents and skills that may not be valued in a person's own village or town may be appreciated in another place. For example, a talented singer who has been limited to entertaining people in a single village may enjoy great success in the film industry. Educated youth from villages also migrate. White-collar migration patterns reflect "occupational movements" rather than "community movements."[24] In other words, individuals or nuclear families migrate because of jobs or business opportunities.

Strategic Migration

Migration may sometimes be a social reengineering process in rural areas. There are two categories of migration from rural areas. First, those from upper castes may choose to migrate as an outward-looking strategy to avoid the loss of status and prestige. For example, Brahmins may systemically sell everything they have in the village over a few weeks or months before making the final

---

18. Mishra, 60.
19. Faleiro, *Beautiful Thing*, 33.
20. Kumar and Bhagat, *Migrants*, 183.
21. Bhattacharya, "Migrant Train."
22. Gathia and Gathia, *Christianity's Contribution*, 484–85.
23. Mishra, *Internal Migration*, 218.
24. Jayaraman, *Who Me, Poor?*, 163.

break of migrating.[25] Second, those from lower castes may view migration as an inward-looking strategy that helps them to improve their earnings and buy more land, build houses, or invest in businesses such as dairy farming. These migrants plan to return to their villages with capital, skills, and experience.[26] For example, Rekha Baai and family, who migrated to Pune, earn approximately INR 4,000 a day. They now own land and a multistory house, and plan to return to their village upon retirement.[27]

Migrants' Struggles in the Host Culture

Migrants face many stressful challenges. Apart from emotional and social distress, they also face external challenges. Swati Shikha writes, "Failed by the governments, systems, and policies, abandoned by rights and protections, exposed to dangers and punishment – the reality of migrants from their point of origin to the transit and destination is inhuman, dangerous, and sordid."[28] They may face cultural barriers such as differences in language and food. When migrants succeed in areas where the native population have failed, this may give rise to hatred, violence, subjugation, and displacement. There may also be efforts to protect the elite from having to compete with migrants. Public opinion is often hostile toward poor migrants[29] – for example, the "Sons of Soil" concept blames migrants for taking local jobs from the sons of the soil. There is also anti-migrant violence over the sharing of resources.[30] In the paranoid middle-class narrative, slums are dens of crime and squalor which threatens both social peace and public health.[31] "Migrants are often competing with locals and with rapid advancements for their wages."[32] Employers often perceive migrants as hard workers, compared to locals whom they view as lazy or as people who demand, as a right, too many privileges. This results in a strained relationship between the host community and migrants. Exclusion of and discrimination against migrants may take place through political and

---

25. Kumar and Bhagat, *Migrants*, 180.
26. Kumar and Bhagat, 181.
27. Interview with Rekha on 20 July 2023.
28. Shikha, "Hope on Iron Rails," 14.
29. Mishra, *Internal Migration*, 35–37.
30. Kumar and Bhagat, *Migrants*, 54.
31. Shrivastava and Kothari, *Churning the Earth*, 8.
32. Jayaraman, *Who Me, Poor?*, 94.

administrative processes, market mechanisms, or socioeconomic processes.[33] For instance, three migrants in Bangalore, after being denied their wages, walked and hitchhiked one thousand kilometers over seven days to reach their home in Odisha.[34]

The living conditions for poor migrants are pitiful. "The majority of labor migrants live in fenced-in and guarded worksites, with conditions similar to those of labor camps. Many of them live under tarpaulin roofs with poor amenities."[35] Most migrants end up in slums. Without the right information for the poor, labor contractors control the migrants. The network middlemen exploit the hapless migrant laborers, who have no legal remedy. Even white-collar migrants face housing issues and are often disadvantaged.[36] However, if they continue living in the city over a long period, these migrants may be able to obtain bank loans to buy houses or apartments.

While male migration is usually considered a sacrifice that brings pride to the family, female migration is regarded as a basic duty.[37] Female migrants are neither recognized nor rewarded either by their families or the government. Women migrants are homemakers and caregivers in the family.[38] Women migrate for three key reasons: first, for the sake of family, to uplift family members; second, to work as housemaids or in similar jobs in the informal sector; and in third, market-driven migration when educated women move to get employment in the market industry.[39] "There are compounded layers of vulnerabilities for women migrant workers, especially with the absence of childcare facilities, decent housing, and sanitation at work sites in destination regions."[40] Two-thirds of migrant women workers reported that their minor children also migrated with them.[41] An estimated 63 million Indian children are migrants, according to the 2011 Census. While the government runs central schools for central government employees and defense personnel, none is done for the poor migrants' children.[42]

---

33. Kumar and Bhagat, *Migrants*, 42.
34. *Deccan Chronicle*, "Migrant workers denied pay . . . ."
35. Kumar and Bhagat, *Migrants*, 91.
36. Jayaraman, *Who Me, Poor?*, 31.
37. Mishra, *Internal Migration*, 50.
38. Kumar and Bhagat, *Migrants*, 39.
39. Kumar and Bhagat, 139.
40. Banerjee, "Revisiting Lockdown," 18.
41. Kumar and Bhagat, *Migrants*, 43.
42. Bashir, "How Education remains out of reach for India's Invisible Migrant Children."

Without the necessary documents, migrants find it difficult to find employment or places to stay. "Many migrants also lack proof of identity and residence in the city. This turns out to be the biggest barrier to their inclusion."[43] This often leads to their exploitation by shrewd employers and, sometimes, even the police. The poor are double disadvantaged; first marginalized and second illegalized.[44] They are subjected to multiple precarities, vulnerabilities, and exploitation.[45] While most states do not extend an enthusiastic welcome to migrants, the state of Kerala is an exception. "Kerala was the only state to address the migrant laborers as guest workers and all the actions taken by the government were inclusive of them."[46]

Unintended Good

There are certain good things that have happened for migrants and their families. When men migrate to cities, women must take on family responsibilities. Indirectly, women were empowered as men lost control and relied on wives and thus a small change in the patriarchal family set-up has happened.[47]

Migrants from various states such as Kerala, Tamil Nadu, Andhra, Karnataka, Punjab, Maharashtra, Gujarat, and Delhi send remittances back home, which also helps in the development of those states. "Migration contributes to the economic development of Bihar, it is a common livelihood strategy of the rural households, and the remittances sent by migrant workers support their families back home."[48] Poverty alleviation, which should be a priority of the government, is often taken care of by migrants themselves. Migrants face a TINA factor: There Is No Alternative. "Despite being abandoned by the cities during the lockdown, migrants who had returned to their native villages trickled back to cities in search of work as rural material conditions are dependent on urban remittances."[49]

---

43. Kumar and Bhagat, 42.
44. Sadana, *Metronama*, 39.
45. Datta, "Cost of Poverty," 27.
46. Shahina, "Migrant Crisis," 31.
47. Arya, "Women Lead."
48. Mishra, *Internal Migration*, 205.
49. Datta, "Cost of Poverty," 27.

Missional Challenges and Missiological Questions
Direction of Migration

Why do so many people from unengaged and unreached geographical regions and people groups flock toward South India? Economic, social, political, and climate change are not the only visible or obvious reasons for migration. Should not the church think, reflect, and ask the Lord for wisdom on how to respond to migration? In South India, with its long history of Christianity dating back to the apostle Thomas and the tremendous work done by missionaries during the eighteenth to the twentieth centuries, people's quality of life is significantly better than in other parts of India. The educational and medical missions pioneered by missionaries created the modern society that we see today in South India. People are better educated and healthier; the rule of law is respected; and there is good governance, peace, social justice, and economic development. The "pull" factor of a better life draws millions of people from the least reached, least engaged regions and people groups in India. It seems like since the church is not sending enough missionaries to these people, so God is sending these people to these "unsending" churches to hear the gospel.

Centripetal or Centrifugal Missions

The apostle Paul declares that he boasts in the cross and preaches Christ crucified. Ultimately, mission is centripetal – the crucified Christ draws people to himself. In the first twelve chapters of the Acts of Apostles, beginning with the day of Pentecost, the mission is centripetal. However, from chapter thirteen onward, the mission becomes centrifugal, with the church in Antioch sending out Paul and Barnabas to begin the work of evangelizing the whole world, starting with the Roman Empire.

Mission Movements and Migrant Movements

The direction of internal missionary movements was mostly from south to north and also from northeast to north. Although these centrifugal missionary movements spread to many interior regions of the country, there are still many parts of India that have not been reached. Today, God seems to be sending people from the most unreached regions of the country to South India. In Solomon's time, people from other nations came seeking wisdom rather than the God of Solomon. Likewise, many of these migrants are attracted to the economically, socially, and politically prosperous South India for employment, educational, or business opportunities, all of which have been shaped by the efforts of missionaries and the church. The crucial question is this: Will these migrants recognize the root cause behind all these blessings and embrace the truth of the gospel?

Paradigm Shifts in Mission Contexts

In the southern states of India, the church has, to some degree, acted as a centrifugal force with its missionary efforts to the rest of India. However, as changes in the global economy since the 1990s led to changes in the direction of migration and a new pattern of migration, the church failed to adapt to this paradigm shift. Failing to understand the necessity and importance of reaching out to migrants, the churches were caught unprepared.

Great Commission Orphans

The mission involves both being a city on the hill and going out as sheep among the wolves with the innocence of doves and the wisdom of serpents.[50] Several parachurch agencies in South India have valiantly attempted to reach the unreached. Yet those same agencies and local churches seem to have a blind spot when it comes to reaching migrants in their own backyard because of differences in the cultures, attitudes, worldviews, and beliefs of host culture churches and migrants. Unlike the churches in Northeast India, the home churches of these migrants in South India do not seem to know how to minister to or disciple their own members. As a result, these migrants become "Great Commission Orphans" (neglected people).

Being Something and Going Somewhere

In the contemporary world, migrants represent a new mission frontier. This necessitates developing mission strategies to reach diverse migrant groups around the world. "Understanding the pressing needs of people is important in mission. Missiologists call them felt needs. When a person's need is met there is an opportunity for him or her to discern the greater needs of forgiveness of sins and reconciliation with the Lord."[51] What do migrants dream about? "They dream of nothing but employment. Education, dignity, and safety are

---

50. Matthew 5:14; 10:16.
51. Manokaran, *Christ and Transformational Missions*, 16.

luxuries – unthinkable concepts to them."[52] To minister effectively among migrants, it is important to contextualize the gospel in a way that takes into consideration these aspirations.[53]

Responsibilities of Pastors and Local Churches

The local church's attitude toward migrants should be different from that of society at large and be shaped by a biblical worldview and biblical principles. First, since God is concerned about migrants, pastors, local churches, and individual believers should also be concerned about them, and they must actively seek them out since they may not always be immediately visible. Second, finding a man or woman of peace among migrants can lead to important breakthroughs, and the whole congregation must actively look for such opportunities. Third, words alone are not enough but must be accompanied by love, care, and concern. Migrants should not be viewed merely as targets for evangelism but, rather, as people created in the image of God, blinded by Satan, and living like sheep without a shepherd. Since such people are outside the fold, these shepherds should "bring them in." For example, a migrant from Delhi came to know the Lord as she worked in Kerala. A colleague had helped her to become a follower of Christ. However, when she went to the local church seeking baptism, she was not welcomed. This new believer could have been not only a member of this church but also a woman of peace who brought many more people to the Lord.

Here are some helpful methods and tools for engaging with migrants:

1. Building friendships: It is essential to know where migrants gather based on their language, age, and economic status. Such places could include malls, markets, eateries, and public places such as beaches or parks. Meeting migrants at such places and developing friendships is essential.

2. Holistic mission: Migrants have many needs. When lockdown was implemented in India, migrants were in disarray. In an article in *Christianity Today*, Christina Martin reports how a group of young Christians – led by Rahul George and others – created a WhatsApp

---

52. Shikha, "Hope on Iron Rails," 11.
53. Manokaran, *Christ, Culture and Communication*, 185–92.

group for volunteers who then started helping the migrants, touching the lives of thousands.[54]

3. Language affinity: Migrants love their mother tongue and cherish literature in their own language. Providing them with New Testaments, books, and songs – perhaps through audio or video links – in their native language will often please them and may serve as conversation starters that lead to sharing the gospel.

Conclusion

Ministry to migrants should be intentional. The Lord commanded the disciples to "look at the fields" (John 4:35). They were spiritually blind. They did not see the harvest. Today, the global church as well as every local church should actively perceive the challenge of reaching migrants in every corner of the world. Like an eagle with its 340-degree vision, the church should adopt a 360-degree vision to reach out to all people, including migrants. "Migration – whether it is internal or international – is almost always undertaken in hope."[55] Only the church could offer true hope through the gospel of the Lord Jesus Christ.

---

54. Martin, "I Was Sick."
55. Shrivastava and Kothari, *Churning the Earth*, 176.

References

Arya, Divya. "Women Lead Indian Families as Men Migrate." *BBC News*, 2 June 2023. https://www.bbc.com/news/world-asia-india-65751270.

Auerbach, Adam Michael, and Tariq Thachil. *Migrants and Machine Politics: How India's Urban Poor Seek Representation and Responsiveness*. Princeton: Princeton University Press, 2023.

Banerjee, Arindam. "Revisiting Lockdown." *Outlook*, 11 April 2023. https://www.outlookindia.com/national/revisiting-lockdown-magazine-274801.

Bashir, Sajitha. "How Education Remains Out of Reach for India's Invisible Migrant Children." *Scroll.in*, 11 February 2023. https://scroll.in/article/1041923/how-education-remains-out-of-reach-for-indias-invisible-migrant-children.

Bhattacharya, Aparna. "A Migrant Train, the Coromandel Express Had Been a Ticket to Livelihood for Bengal's Poorest." *The Wire*, 5 June 2023. https://thewire.in/labour/coromandel-express-bengal-migrants-labour-problem.

Datta, Amrita. "The Cost of Poverty." *Outlook*, 11 April 2023.

De, Supriyo. "Internal Migration in India Grows, but Inter-state Movements Remain Low." World Bank blogs, 18 December 2019. https://blogs.worldbank.org/peoplemove/internal-migration-india-grows-inter-state-movements-remain-low.

Deccan Chronicle, 5 April 2023. "Migrant workers denied pay, walk, hitch hike 1000 km in 7 days to return Odisha." https://www.deccanchronicle.com/nation/current-affairs/050423/migrant-workers-denied-pay-walk-hitch-hike-1000-km-in-7-days-to-ret.html.

Faleiro, Sonia. *Beautiful Thing: Inside the Secret World of Bombay's Dance Bars*. New Delhi: Hamish Hamilton, 2010.

Gaikwad, Nikhar, and Gareth Nellis. "Overcoming the Political Exclusion of Migrants: Theory and Experimental Evidence from India." *American Political Science Review* 115, no. 4 (2021): 1129–46.

Gathia, Joseph A. and Sanjay V. Gathia. *Christianity's Contribution in Shaping of Modern India*. Delhi: Anugya Books, 2023.

Jacob, Jikku Varghese. "NRI Remittance Share: Maharashtra Pips Kerala, US Now Top India Remitter." *ONmanorama*, 18 July 2022. https://www.onmanorama.com/news/business/2022/07/18/nri-remittance-share-india.html.

Jayaraman, Gayatri. *Who Me, Poor? How India's Youth Are Living in Urban Poverty to Make it Big*. New Delhi: Bloomsbury, 2017.

Kumar, Ashwani, and R. B. Bhagat, eds. *Migrants, Mobility, and Citizenship in India*. New York; London: Routledge, 2022.

Kumar, Manish. "Along India's Eastern Shore, Coastal Erosion Is Forcing People to Abandon Their Homes." *Scroll.in*, 14 February 2022. https://scroll.in/article/1017277/along-indias-eastern-shore-coastal-erosion-is-forcing-people-to-abandon-their-homes.

Manokaran, J. N. *Christ and Migrants: Biblical Understanding of Migration Missional Response to Migration*. Hyderabad: GS Books, 2017.

———. *Christ and Transformational Missions*. Chennai: Mission Educational Books, 2007.

———. *Christ, Culture and Communication*. Bangalore: Omega Book World, 2022.

Martin, Christina. "I Was Sick and You Gave Me a WhatsApp Group." *Christianity Today*, 2 July 2021. https://www.christianitytoday.com/news/2021/july/india-christians-covid-whatsapp-love-your-neighbor-network.html.

Miller, Sam. *Migrants: The Story of Us All*. London: Abacus, 2023.

Mishra, Deepak K., ed. *Internal Migration in Contemporary India*. New Delhi: SAGE, 2016.

Paliath, Shreehari. "A Year after Covid-19 Lockdown, India Still Doesn't Have Reliable Data or Policy on Migrant Workers." *Scroll.in*, 26 March 2021. https://scroll.in/article/990527/a-year-after-covid-19-lockdown-india-still-doesnt-have-reliable-data-or-policy-on-migrant-workers.

Sadana, Rashmi. *Metronama: Scenes from the Delhi Metro*. New Delhi: Lotus Collection, 2022.

Shahina, K. K. "Migrant Crisis in Kerala." *Outlook*, 30 March 2023. https://www.outlookindia.com/national/the-guest-worker-crisis-magazine-274725.

Shikha, Swati. "Darbhanga To Delhi: A Train Journey With Migrant Workers." *Outlook*, 31 March 2023. https://www.outlookindia.com/national/hope-on-iron-rails-magazine-274799.

Shrivastava, Aseem, and Ashish Kothari. *Churning the Earth: The Making of Global India*. New Delhi: Viking, 2012.

Singh, Darpan. "Why So Many Biharis Still Work as Labourers in Tamil Nadu, Punjab, and Other States." *India Today*, 7 March 2023.

17

Holistic Mission with People Affected by Forced Migration and Human Trafficking

Christa Foster Crawford

Millions of people worldwide are affected by sexual abuse and exploitation, various forms of sexual and gender-based violence, modern slavery, forced labor, and a host of other horrors, and some of those people are in our congregations. Do we see them hurting? Do they see us responding? We can never end human trafficking and other forms of exploitation – at least not without God and not without God's people playing their part. These issues matter deeply to God. How do these issues shape our understanding of the role of church in mission and to what extent do they impact our theology and practice? When we acknowledge the extent to which these issues affect and harm people within our churches and the communities we serve, we must admit that the church and missions is due for a radical overhaul.

Perhaps we have already realized that we must do something. But what? And how? Let us consider what we can learn from Scripture and from experts about how we can better see, hear, and respond to those affected by exploitation, especially within the context of diaspora and forced migration.

A Different Kind of Diaspora

When we think about diaspora, we must distinguish between voluntary migrants – those who have left their homes by choice to start a new life in another place – and involuntary migrants – those who are forcibly displaced from their homes. Voluntary migration involves community: there is a farewell by friends and family, goodbyes are said, plans are made for meeting again, and resources and arrangements are in place for safe travel. When these migrants reach their destination, there is celebration: a new home in a new community but with ongoing ties to the old community of origin. However, these elements are absent in involuntary migration, which is full of uncertainties and dangers, sometimes even the possibility of death.

The experiences of people who are forced to migrate or become victims of human trafficking are often very different. Some who initially migrate voluntarily may later fall prey to trafficking. The hallmarks of involuntary migration and human trafficking are force, fear, exploitation, and isolation. Whether fleeing war, famine, disaster, injustice, or other dangers, it is not by choice that forced migrants find themselves in a foreign country. This involuntary diaspora is a displaced community: a fractured group of people who were not able to say goodbye, whose travel is perilous and uncertain, and whose final destination is often unknown or permanently unreachable due to migration and asylum laws. Many never have the opportunity to return home again, and the fate of friends and family left behind remains unknown.

But what opportunities for God's kingdom would exist in the midst of their displacement if we responded? Similarly, it is not by choice that people who are trafficked for labor or sexual exploitation find themselves in a foreign country. This involuntary diaspora results in ruptured community: vulnerable children or adults are ripped apart from their own people and families by force or lured away by false promises. They did not willingly choose to leave, their destination is determined for them, and their journey is as frightening and as dangerous as the exploitation that awaits them when they finally arrive at their destination. Dreams of returning home are a luxury while the struggle to survive even another day is a constant nightmare.

But what opportunities for God's kingdom would exist in the midst of their displacement if we responded? Thankfully, despite the rising incidence of forced migration and human trafficking, the global response to these issues has been encouraging. The global community – from UN agencies to faith-based organizations – has taken steps to care for the needs of forced migrants at many stages of their journey – internal displacement, refugee camps, third-party resettlement, and repatriation. Other organizations, including governments and NGOs, also help trafficked and exploited people to find freedom through effective prevention, safe intervention, holistic recovery programs, and sustainable reintegration initiatives, with Christian organizations often leading the way. *But is this enough? And what more can – and should – be done by the church as part of the mission of Christ on earth?*

Exploitation of the Forcibly Displaced: A Challenge and an Opportunity

Although voluntary migrants know that success is not guaranteed, from origin to destination, they hope for freedom and opportunity, and support from a caring community. Their migration offers the hope of improvement for themselves, the families they left behind, and the generations to come. By contrast, people who are forced to migrate or who are trafficked into exploitation experience fear and harm before, during, and after their displacement. They are isolated from those who could help them and abused by many along the way. Their migration guarantees that their life not only goes from bad to worse but also poses an ongoing threat to their families and to future generations.

Most services for displaced people focus on short- to medium-term individual relief, with little being done to safeguard sending communities and ensure the long-term flourishing of all parties involved. Responses rarely address the complex, systemic, and multidisciplinary causes of harm or the damaging effects on all areas of life. Despite the best efforts of all those trying to help the displaced persons, full recovery from the trauma is rare. This is in contrast to the biblical narratives of Joseph and Esther, who also experienced some form of trafficking and forced migration. However, instead of remaining vulnerable and exploited, they each experienced abundance in their new communities and used their newfound resources to bless their communities of origin.

What lessons can Esther and Joseph teach us as members of Christ's body – the church – and as those who are the hands and feet in God's mission to all of creation? What difference would it make if we viewed forced migrants and victims of trafficking as diaspora people? How can we not just seek to protect them from harm but also empower them to become agents of transformation in their new communities, providers of hope to their old communities, and prophetic witnesses of God's goodness to the entire world? What difference would it make if we viewed forced migrants and victims of trafficking as diaspora people empowered by God and assisted by the church to enjoy greater freedom and flourishing for themselves and to become agents of these blessings to others?

Joseph and Esther: Turning Exploitation into Freedom

Both Joseph and Esther were survivors of forced migration and trafficking, but their displacement and exploitation did not mark the end of their story but only a turning point that would change the narrative for the better – for themselves, their families, and their people. What was meant for evil, God meant for good (Gen 50:20).

What lessons do the diaspora experiences of Joseph and Esther offer on transforming the evils of forced and exploitative migration into opportunities for church and mission to restore individuals, rebuild communities, and advance the unfolding realization of God's good kingdom? Many of us think of Joseph and Esther as successful diaspora stories but forget the element of force and exploitation present in these narratives. For example, Joseph was sold into slavery by his brothers. Slavery seemed like a better option than murder to his brothers.[1] Even today, cultural and financial pressures from family, community leaders, or religious leaders, combined with the lack of truly viable options, pushes people into forced, dangerous, and exploitative labor – for example, the children who harvest the chocolate we eat or the minerals used in our phones, the men who construct our cities or catch our seafood, the women who manufacture our textiles or care for our children and homes, and entire families who grow the food for our tables or the cotton for our clothes. These scenarios do not just happen in some distant place "over there" but in every country on earth. These push factors are fueled by macro-level economics, legal, and political forces that condone our demand for these products at the expense of depriving vulnerable people of viable options for safer migration or nonexploitative work.[2]

Joseph also experienced sexual harassment after his enslavement. It is not surprising that people who are exploited for labor are often vulnerable to sexual harassment and harm. Someone who is confined in a private home as a domestic worker or trapped at sea on a fishing boat is unable to resist if the person in power sexually violates them; in addition, because they are also isolated, they cannot seek help when such violations take place. Sexual abuse and exploitation are about power. Therefore, people of any gender can be sexually abused and exploited, including boys and men – and because of social norms

---

1. Indeed, Judah suggested that enslavement was a better option for Joseph than the one the other brothers offered – namely, death.

2. All of us, including those in the church, may contribute to such demand. We must remember that throughout Scripture, the prophets confronted the people of God, rather than the world, for behaving in ways that satisfied cultural and religious standards while violating God's commands to act justly and care for the vulnerable among them.

and stigma, such people may not readily admit that this happened to them, and they may not be believed even if they do seek help.

But sexual abuse and imprisonment was not the end of Joseph's story. Ultimately, despite all that he suffered, Joseph was used by God to save his family and home community, who had themselves become climate refugees who had been forced to migrate due to famine. God does not will that anyone be enslaved or abused, but he somehow turned Joseph's exploitation-diaspora position into an opportunity for him to flourish individually and to help his family also to flourish by providing for them in their need. Joseph's experience of exploitation – beginning from his position as a mere slave to that of Pharaoh's adviser – shows how God can and does use what the enemy meant for evil and turn it into good to fulfill God's own good purposes.

Esther was recruited for sexual service.[3] Child marriage, forced marriage, forced surrogacy, forced prostitution and pornography, commercial sexual exploitation of children, and other evolving forms of sexual and reproductive exploitation continue to abound today, amplified by the internet and other technology that makes it easier both to harm others and to access the fruit of that harm. Ultimately, Esther's family and indeed her people, who were oppressed and in exile, experienced blessing because of the reversal of the harm she endured.

Just as Mordecai knew that Esther's marriage to this king would mean a better life for her and her family, today's families who lack other options due to factors such as climate change, forced relocation, war, human rights abuses, and lack of legal rights and protections, may encourage, facilitate, or simply turn a blind eye to exploitation – sexual or otherwise – of their own daughters and sons. Sometimes, like Esther, this exploitation comes in the form of cultural practices such as arranged marriages and betrothing of minors for future marriage. Practices that may otherwise be neutral become corrupt when vulnerability is combined with harmful gendered beliefs – for example, the low worth of girls, the high value of men's sexual pleasure, the "protection" of a girl's virginity, the "promotion" of men's virility, the exclusion of those who do not fit the norms, and the common but corrosive temptations of consumerism and greed.[4]

---

3. Although this incident is sometimes portrayed as a "beauty contest" for marriage to a king, this was no fairytale, regardless of its happy ending.

4. Harmful beliefs and outcomes can exist in our theology and practice, especially when we fail to critically examine whether things that we consider part of Christianity are actually contrary to the principles and values of Christ's kingdom.

But being trafficked for child marriage was not the end of Esther's story. Ultimately, Esther was able to save the Jewish diaspora exiled in Persia. God does not want anyone to experience sexual harm or exploitation, but he turned Esther's exploited state into an opportunity for her to help her people by changing the heart of the king. Though it was not by consent that Esther was in the palace, truly she was in that place "for such a time as this" (Esth 4:14).

What can we learn from the stories of Joseph and Esther about opportunities for God's kingdom amid modern-day displaced and exploited diasporas? What helped Joseph and Esther not merely to survive but also to thrive and even become agents of transformation to others? How can we shift our perspective from one that seeks merely to reduce or remedy harm to one that actively pursues opportunities for flourishing? What implications does this have for ministry by professional responders – such as refugee and anti-trafficking organizations – and by mission agencies, local churches, and individual Christians within their everyday communities?

The Integral Role of the Church and Missions in Addressing Human Trafficking

Throughout the Old and New Testaments, responding to injustice lies at the core of God's call to his people. This is fundamental to the nature of God's kingdom and central to Jesus's own mandate and the mandate he gave his followers. Addressing exploitation is integral to the identity and mission of the church; it is also one way in which the church fulfills its role as a witness of God in the world. Quite simply, exploitation cannot and will not end unless the people of God fulfill their God-given role in Christ's kingdom on earth.

So, what have the church and the people of God been doing to address exploitation? Human trafficking and sexual exploitation are not new, as we see from Scripture. For thousands of years, Moses and others worked to liberate people from exploitation and lead them into God's freedom and shalom. Christians have been influential in ending – but, sadly, also in promoting – cultural and legal practices such as the sale of human beings as chattel during the transatlantic slave trade. They have also been involved in alleviating various forms of exploitation both through individual efforts and by influencing policymakers. A good example of this is Amy Carmichael, who worked tirelessly to rescue temple prostitutes in India.

As we enter the third decade of the modern anti-trafficking efforts, Christians have played a leading role focusing primarily on combating the exploitation that takes place overseas. The first to respond were "regular" missionaries who encountered human trafficking and labor exploitation in the daily lives of the people they served. By the early 2000s, with the rise of the internet and the creative efforts of people like Gary Haugen – founder of International Justice Mission – everyday Christians locally and overseas have become involved in anti-trafficking efforts.

But a calling without an equipping is not enough. Despite increasing awareness of human trafficking, the quality and strategic focus of our response has suffered due to the lack of an integrated and well-resourced spiritual, theological, missional, practical, and professional response. Instead, over the last two decades or more, the responses resemble a patchwork of initiatives by parachurch organizations and short-term church mission teams working overseas. These initiatives have been, to a large extent, focused on the short-term, as well as poorly coordinated, duplicative, and lacking relevance, resulting in high attrition rates and disturbingly low levels of personal thriving and faith retention among workers. While this might have been acceptable at the start of an emerging social movement, it is an ineffective and unsustainable way to move forward as representatives of Christ in pursuing his call.

Thankfully, in recent years, having observed injustices abroad, Christians have begun to recognize and respond to exploitation in their own backyards, finally calling out situations that they had earlier failed to acknowledge as being exploitation. Such responses have come from Christians working as skilled professionals in traditional social service roles such as social workers and prosecutors. Domestic parachurch ministries are also growing, employing trained professionals who work within legal and regulatory frameworks that foster the well-being of both those who serve and those who are served.

Both at home and abroad, churches are also helping people in their congregation, and this is especially true of churches in the majority world and churches in communities that have vulnerable populations in their congregations. But there is certainly more that the church and missions can and should be doing to see, care about, and respond to exploitation. This raises some fundamental questions that we must ask and begin to answer together: How is the church essential to addressing exploitation, and how is addressing exploitation essential to being the church? The same questions also apply to missions. Answering these questions requires us to *reframe* how we understand the problem of exploitation – both in Scripture and in our daily lives – and gives us the opportunity to reshape how we might respond based on the wisdom of

Scripture and the advice of experts.[5] Answering these questions also requires us to *re-form* our theology to recognize that shalom, freedom, and holistic flourishing are part of Christ's present and coming kingdom and, therefore, must be part of the teaching and practice of church and mission. We must also be willing to examine ways in which our theology might be supporting ideas that feed the root causes of exploitation or unintentionally encouraging practices that fuel abuse and exploitation.[6]

Finally, answering these questions requires us to reexamine our own spiritual formation – and get rid of the things in our own lives that represent the abuse, control, and exploitation that lie at the heart of more obvious commercial forms of exploitation – and reimagine discipleship so that the roots and fruit of exploitation can finally be brought to an end.[7] God's people have always been on the move – both individually and as communities. Often, this movement has involved exploitation: Abram "pimping" his wife to two rulers on their way to Canaan, Moses's cohorts being held in horrific slavery in Egypt, and generations of God-followers living in exile and abuse under empire after empire from Babylon to Rome. When the prophets of God told God's people to care for the alien, the widow, and the poor, this was no empty platitude but a response to their lived reality. Jesus and his parents sought refuge in Egypt when, as predicted by the prophet, his life was under threat from the moment of his birth (Matt 2:13–15). This was not a metaphorical issue but literally a matter of life and death for both Jesus and the people of the time – a visceral, lived experience that serves as a clarion call to us today as well.

Will we hear the call?

Will we respond?

Will we see those in need in our own backyards and also around the world?

Will the church follow God's call and Jesus's plea to do justice, to rescue the oppressed, and to set the captives free? How will they do this?

---

5. For example, in what ways might we, even without realizing it, consider some people more "worthy" of protection while justifying poor treatment of others such as immigrants, "fallen women," or anyone else whom we view as "other" rather than as fellow humans created in the image of God?

6. For example, in what ways do our teachings on biblical sexual ethics unintentionally contribute to making women, children, and youth more vulnerable to abuse in their own homes? How might our teachings discourage them from seeking help in the church or isolate them from family and community, thereby making them more vulnerable to traffickers?

7. For example, how often do we emphasize sexual sins or other "sensational" sins that we ourselves do not struggle with, while ignoring the greed and selfishness that all humans experience or justifying the manipulation and control that "good" Christian leaders engage in?

A Roadmap for Excellence in Holistic Christian Response

In responding to this call to address the issues of exploitation, it is essential that the church and mission do not just do *something* but do *the right thing*. What is the "right" response to exploitation, and how can the church and missions best respond? How do we ensure that we do not do more harm than good? How can we go beyond good intentions to responses that are truly excellent, effective, and ethical? Answering all these questions is obviously beyond the scope of this chapter, but there are a number of resources available to help those who desire to learn more.[8]

In this section, we explore three important considerations for Christians seeking to improve their response to exploitation: (1) a better understanding of the problem and how addressing root causes is a critical role of the church and Christian missions; (2) a better understanding of the need for a holistic Christian response and how individuals, churches, and mission can partner with others; and (3) a better understanding of how to begin integrating and responding to the exploited in the life and mission of the church.

Church and Mission Must Address Root Causes

The first area that must be addressed is the issue of why the problem of exploitation exists. There are many complex, interrelated, and interdisciplinary causes – as illustrated in the stories of Esther and Joseph and summarized in Figure 1 below. Human trafficking, forced migration, and related forms of exploitation are the fruit of root issues that people in the church are already experiencing and the church and missions are (hopefully) already addressing. These issues include values, identity, and behavior related to gender, culture, economics, policy, and more.

The body of Christ is called to respond to those root causes, and if they are not doing so, then they are not being the church. Our church and missions have failed in discipleship if they do not call and equip people to change negative beliefs about the value of people, especially women, if they do not confront issues of power and greed present in every person, and if they do not become a community that is challenged and changed by the gospel to be different from prevailing norms.

Instead of preventing exploitation, the church often contributes to it unknowingly. A church or mission that lack holistic impact and deep cogni-

---

8. See Freedom Resource International, www.freedomresource.org; Chab Dai Global Learning Community www.chabdai.org/glc; and http://gmmiles.co.uk.

tive, emotional, and behavioral change is *not* a church or mission at all. It is just an empty, clanging gong. The good news is that the church and missions do not have to do something new or specialized to address exploitation. The church simply needs to do what God has already called and equipped it for.

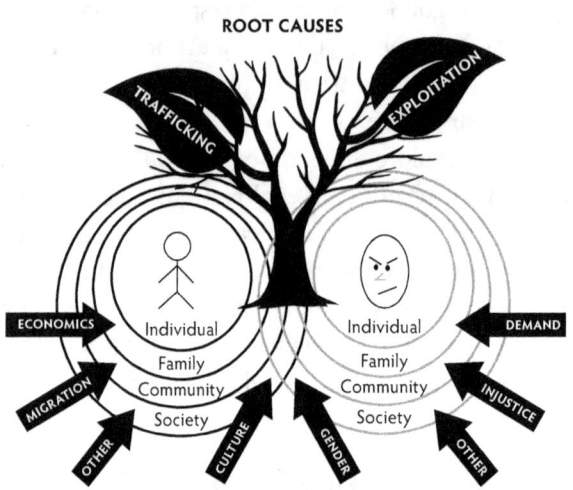

Figure 1: Trafficking Supply and Demand

Church and Mission Must Respond Holistically and Collaboratively

The church is called to help bring about God's kingdom of shalom, freedom, and flourishing. Therefore, the church and mission must be ready to address all areas of a person's life. In order to end exploitation and ensure the freedom and flourishing that Jesus promises, the church needs a holistic Christian response. As illustrated in Figure 1 below, this response must be comprehensive (addressing micro and macro levels on both the supply and demand side) and holistic (addressing all parts of human flourishing) across the entire trafficking spectrum (before, during, and after exploitation occurs) through a variety of responses involving all sectors of society (mental and physical health care, enforcement of laws, reform of laws and policies affecting migration and other key issues, economic development of individuals, families, and overall societies, and much, much more). A key reason the church is essential to effective response is that it is, by nature, a body made up of many different parts. In every congregation, there are people who could be encouraged and supported to consider how their gifts and vocations can be used to help advance the kingdom of God.

Mind	Body	Spirit
"Emotional/Cognitive Effects"	"Physical Effects"	"Spiritual Effects"

include:
Cognitive Impairment
Attachment Ruptures
Trauma
Dissociation
Anxiety
Depression
Poor Self-Concept
Sexual Dysfunction
Shame
Helplessness
Stockholm Syndrome
Resignation/Denial/
Disbelief

include:
Physical Injury
Traumatic Brain Injury
Sexual and
Reproductive Health
General Health and
Nutrition
Impaired
Development
Violence/Abuse/
Torture
Self-Harm
Substance Abuse
Psychosomatic
Disorders

include:
Distorted Image of
God
Damaged View
of Scripture and
Christianity
Destroyed Sense of
Self-Value and Worth
Broken Sexuality
Alienation
Loss of Trust
Despair and
Disillusionment
Spiritual Oppression
Impact of Sin

Figure 2: Effects of Sexual Exploitation

No single organization or individual can accomplish all this alone. These diagrams, though simple, demonstrate that actually addressing all these interrelated areas is extremely complex. We must partner with others, specializing in our own areas of strength and expertise while recognizing the areas in which others are more suited, always growing in our knowledge of the problem and keeping up-to-date with responses that are proven effective (evidence-based) and ethical (do not cause harm, even unintentionally).

Ensuring that our responses are ethical, evidence-based, and collaborative is the only way that the problem of exploitation can ever be mitigated. This requires coordination and equipping of all those involved in responding to exploitation. Unfortunately, many people prefer to fund only "direct services." But if those services are not effective or ethical, then this only perpetuates the cycle. Therefore, one quick and easy step that church and mission can take to address exploitation is to support the vital work of organizations that help connect and resource the entire movement.[9]

---

9. See previous footnote for some organizations and individuals who are engaged in this vital work.

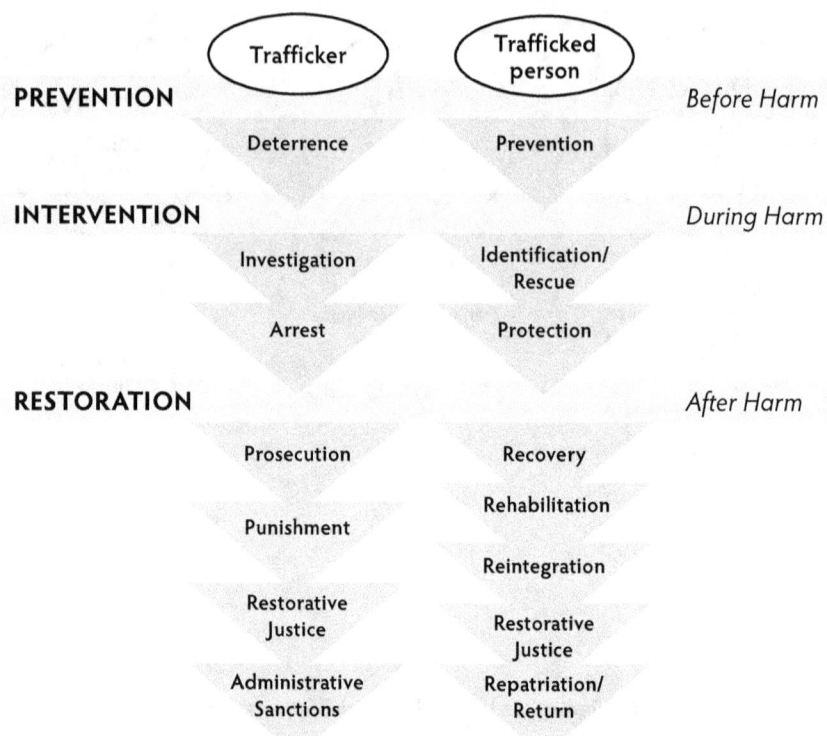

Figure 3: Trafficking Spectrum

Ending Exploitation as a Gospel and Discipleship Issue

The roots of power, greed, and control are present in every human being. Therefore, addressing root causes requires that we first look within our own selves. Church and mission must ensure that teaching, discipleship, and other aspects of spiritual formation look *within* to ensure that we are not feeding the roots of exploitation even if we are not directly engaged in it. For example, rather than merely instructing people to avoid pornography as a personal sin of lust, the church should raise awareness about the ways in which the pornography industry exploits those involved in its production and disciple people to take positive action in all their viewing, purchasing, and other related decisions to ensure that they are advancing God's kingdom instead of inadvertently fueling exploitation.

The solutions to exploitation lie within all of us, as a body, as we seek to grow together in Christlikeness. Church and mission can encourage a Christianity that, like Jesus, seeks "to proclaim good news to the poor ... to proclaim freedom for the prisoners" (Luke 4:18b). The church must intentionally begin to discover how best to provide theological and practical answers to the problems of forced migration, human trafficking, and other forms of exploitation. One practical way to begin is to listen to and learn from the voices and experiences of those of diverse ages, genders, and nationalities about what exploitation looks like in their context and what is needed to provide effective and ethical responses to it.

Here are some questions to consider:

- What experience do you have with exploitation? How have you or those you know been affected personally?
- How have you participated in exploitation – directly or indirectly, intentionally or unintentionally?
- How have you responded to exploitation? How do you wish others would respond to it? What more needs to be done? What can we do, both collectively and individually?
- What are some barriers to responding? How can we address these barriers?
- What more must we learn or know before responding? From whom can we learn? How can we learn from those who have experienced exploitation firsthand?
- How safe is our church or mission for people who have been exploited? How can we be safer, more welcoming, and more trauma-informed?
- How can we better integrate these issues into our regular church and mission? How can we normalize discussing these difficult issues?
- How can we better recognize attitudes, worldviews, and behaviors – including those that have a "Christian gloss" – that feed exploitation? How can we cultivate more Christlike attitudes, worldviews, and behaviors?
- How can we more faithfully follow the teachings of Scripture about how to treat others, including our global and local "neighbors" who are different from ourselves? How can we know them better and listen well to them?
- How can we become better at seeing Scripture through the lens of people who have been marginalized?

- How might our "correct" theology be causing unintentional harm in practice (for example, messages that communicate that women should stay with their abusers)?
- How can we help pastors, missionaries, professionals, and lay people to learn more about these issues? How can we help congregations and communities to allow their leaders to respond positively to these issues?
- How does our current theology and practices address human exploitation? How can we do better?

None of these questions are simple, and exploring these issues will take time. But as the church integrates this way of thinking and doing and being into how it does church and mission, it is participating in the process of becoming more like Christ and bringing about Christ's kingdom. And doing so will help to drastically reduce exploitation in the lives of Christians and non-Christians alike.

Freedom and Flourishing despite Displacement and Exploitation

The Bible begins with a garden and ends with a city. From Genesis to Revelation, the people of God are on the move. In the Bible's opening scenes, God plants a couple in fertile land, where they enjoy the goodness that comes from full knowledge of God, themselves, and each other. They experienced *shalom*. Thereafter, there is an ongoing series of displacements: exile from the garden, fleeing from cities of harm, narrow escapes from deep waters, wandering across deserts, and so on. But amid all this chaotic movement, there is the consistent voice and call of God: "Come home" and "Return to me and be restored."

In the movie *Sleepless in Seattle*, the main character says, "It was like coming home . . . only to no home I'd ever known." We, too, have a true home that we have never known before. From the fertile garden in Genesis to the holy city in Revelation, God is calling all of us home to a better place, where shalom is no longer shattered but is fully and wholly restored. We are all people on the move, called by God to help others find a true home and to care for their needs along the way – just like Abraham, who was sent out from the home of his father to become the father of all nations; just like Jesus, who chose to leave the home of the Father to make a home here with us and bring all of us into the family of God; and just like Esther and Joseph, who did not choose to leave their homes but did choose to allow God to transform their experiences of exploitation into channels of freedom for themselves and their people.

We, too, can and must help make the journey home safer for those who are being trafficked, forced, and exploited along the way. May God's full kingdom come and God's true will be done here in this realm of forced displacement and exploitation just as it is in the realm of God's reign. And may we – as Christ's church and his witnesses to all the peoples of the earth – be faithful in seeing and caring for people of the exploited diaspora until, together, we all reach our true home.

References

Miles, Glenn, and Christa Foster Crawford, eds. *Finding Our Way through the Traffick: Navigating the Complexities of Christian Response to Sexual Exploitation and Trafficking*. Oxford: Regnum Books, 2017.

———. *Stepping Out of the Traffick: Pausing for Theological Reflection on Christian Response to Sexual Exploitation and Trafficking*. Oxford: Regnum Books, 2024.

———. *Stopping the Traffick: A Christian Response to Sexual Exploitation and Trafficking*. Oxford: Regnum Books, 2014.

18

Climate Migration: Mission in the Face of Two Global Crises

Jasmine Kwong and Sam George

Introduction

Whether we like to admit it or not, two major global realities – migration and climate change – are converging and likely to cause unthinkable and catastrophic consequences that will have ripple effects across the planet. Climate upheaval alone is predicted to produce more migrants globally over the next thirty years than all other factors that contributed to migration over the last three hundred years. The convergence of these crises will undoubtedly alter our world, impacting everyone and leading to the creation of a "supercrisis."

Millions of people will be forced to relocate to more hospitable regions of the planet due to the dramatic changes brought about by climate change. Migration is one of humanity's most ancient survival strategies in the face of livelihood threats caused by climate-related factors, economic disruption, social unrest, and political conflicts. All around the world, record numbers of people are being displaced by the increased frequency of fires, droughts, floods, storms, volcanoes, sinking cities and islands, the devastation of farmlands, dwindling food supplies, rising sea levels, erratic weather patterns, and dwindling biodiversity. In the decades ahead, almost everyone on the planet will be impacted by this looming demographic shift – either as people who are being displaced or as part of communities or countries that receive displaced people.

This large-scale population transfer will present both unforeseen challenges and new opportunities for the global church as a result of the new dispersion of Christians and diaspora missions among new global neighbors. It may also create new levels of consciousness about environmental stewardship among Christians worldwide. In this chapter, we unpack climate change-induced global migration, explore possible Christian responses in the face of climate change, consider the importance of creation care for the global church, and explore new mission contexts in the light of this emerging reality.

Migration and Climate

Climate migration is:

> the movement of a person or groups of persons who predominantly for reasons of sudden or progressive change in the environment due to climate change, are obliged to leave their habitual place of residence, or choose to do so, either temporarily or permanently, within a state or across an international border.[1]

Sometimes referred to as the "Crisis of the Century" or "Environmental Migration," climate change threatens to upend global societies and is expected to result in unprecedented levels of human displacement. Historically, environmental upheavals have been a major driver of migration, resulting in what some refer to as "climate refugees." Still others may relocate to new places as economic migrants, international students, or asylum seekers, falling under other categories of displaced persons.

The International Organization for Migration (IOM) – an agency of the United Nations – has projected that there could be as many as 1 billion environmental migrants within the next thirty years. More recent estimates indicate that this figure might be over 1.2 billion by 2050 and 1.4 billion by 2060. In 2021, the World Bank reported that climate change is a key driver of displacement and estimated that by 2050, there would be as many as 86 million climate migrants in sub-Saharan Africa, 19 million in North Africa, 40 million in South Asia, 49 million in East Asia and the Pacific, 17 million in Latin America, and 5 million in Eastern Europe and Central Asia – a total of 216 million globally.[2] The warnings given by climate activists are even more alarming. For example, Gaia Vince predicts that 3.5 billion people will be impacted by climate change

---

1. For various terms, definitions, and data, see United Nations, "Environmental Migration," https://www.migrationdataportal.org/themes/environmental_migration_and_statistics; International Organization for Migration, "Environmental Migration," https://environmental-migration.iom.int/environmental-migration; and "State of the Global Climate," https://wmo.int/files/provisional-state-of-global-climate-2023.

2. See World Bank's Groundswell Report.

over the next fifty years.³ Regardless of the exact figure, it is evident that climate migrants will increase significantly in the future.

Global climate change will trigger more internal and international displacements in the coming decades than ever before. For instance, in 2022, more than a million Somalis were displaced due to drought, while another million people from Bangladesh were displaced due to cyclones. Several million from the coastal and rural Caribbean island nations have migrated to cities, to countries in the north, and to other parts of the world due to rising temperatures and violent storms. In Southeast Asia, increasingly unpredictable rainfall and typhoons have made farming difficult. In Mexico, food insecurity is driving millions to migrate to nearby cities and neighboring nations. Across the world, increased carbon emissions, water shortages, declining crop productivity, and rising sea levels will drive millions to relocate to other parts of the globe. Although the impacts of climate change are widespread and climate migration occurs globally, the largest climate-driven migration in the future is expected to occur out of the most populous regions of Asia and Africa.⁴ Unlike other groups such as refugees, these climate migrants who flee their homelands are not entitled to protection under any international law. While national governments and local laws are responsible for all internal migrants, many are not in an economic position to do so and do not feel obligated to protect those crossing borders volitionally even when such migrants are unwelcome in their destination host countries. Since these migrants are not technically refugees or regular migrants, there is no legal consensus on how to classify or categorize them.

In contrast to the starkly huge prediction of mass migration worldwide, the majority of migration resulting from natural disasters is transient rather than permanent and occurs within countries rather than across borders. The likelihood of such migration depends on factors such as the degree of damage caused by the disaster, the likelihood of future occurrences, and prevention and mitigation measures taken by local governments such as erecting sea walls or offering compensation. Individual factors such as motivation to migrate and access to resources, legal pathways, finances, social networks, and transportation also impact the decision to migrate. Most climate migrants tend to return to their homes within a year. Nevertheless, human migration on an

---

3. Vince, *Nomad Century*, xi; see also, Thunberg, *Climate Book*.

4. Huang, "Climate Migration 101," https://www.migrationpolicy.org/article/climate-migration-101-explainer.

unprecedented scale continues to dominate news reports, political debates, economic plans, and public discourse.

Climate change is a threat multiplier that exacerbates other crises facing humanity. It intensifies conflicts over resources, labor force, supremacy of nations, and geopolitical order. As large regions of the Global South become uninhabitable for the growing population in these areas, the more livable northern region will struggle with demographic decline, workforce shortage, and an impoverished elderly population. For every one-degree rise in temperature, it is estimated that about a billion people will be driven to relocate from places that have been their homes for hundreds of years. The poor and vulnerable suffer the most from climate change, and most of them move to the nearest city or within their own countries. However, even the most advanced nations are not immune from this. For example, according to the United States Census data, 3.2 million adults were displaced or evacuated due to natural disasters in 2022, and of these, more than half a million had not returned to the US by the beginning of 2023. Since 1980, the US has sustained around 258 weather and climate disasters, with the overall damage amounting to more than US$1 billion and cumulative costs exceeding US$1.75 trillion. In 2022, the US experienced eighteen weather-related disasters costing at least a billion dollars.[5] After adjusting for inflation, the aggregate and average costs of these disasters over time are even higher.

Additionally, underdeveloped nations that are vulnerable to climate change rely heavily on remittances from their global diaspora. In some instances, these migrants may not want to invest any more in their ancestral homeland but may, instead, encourage more of their relatives to migrate abroad in order to survive. The global warming trends may open up new and shorter shipping routes over the Arctic Circle – tragically, polluting the region – and establish a major transportation corridor between Asia, Europe, and North America as an alternative to the Suez Canal. The frozen regions of Siberia, the Arctic, and Antarctica will become more livable, which may result in the establishment of permanent settlements for people who have been displaced from uninhabitable parts of the planet.

---

5. NOAA blog, https://www.climate.gov/news-features/blogs/beyond-data/2022-us-billion-dollar-weather-and-climate-disasters-historical.

Christians and Climate Change

Both human beings and the natural world are increasingly affected by the intensifying climate crisis. Forced migration due to climate change is one of the stark realities we face today. This crisis presents a real challenge to the global church: How should Christians respond to the climate crisis? In order to respond well, we must first understand why the Christian perspective is important in the global response to the crisis.

First, for Christians, our relationship with the natural world is not limited to responding to a crisis; rather, it begins with responding to our Creator. Made in God's image, we are designed for relationship with God and with his creation, a relationship that is grounded in love and compassion. Contrary to the common view that the earth and its resources are merely for human consumption and exploitation, the biblical view is that humans must help God's creation to flourish. This means that we must not idly sit by while natural resources are depleted and human communities are displaced. Instead, we must demonstrate a loving relationship with our Creator by our active stewardship of his creation.

Second, Christians are called to steward God's creation, knowing that "the earth is the LORD's and everything in it" (Ps 24:1). We are called to steward creation under God, and just as the Lord reigns with justice and righteousness (Ps 97:1–2), our stewardship must also reflect these qualities. This stewardship involves becoming aware of current issues – such as forced migration due to climate change – and recognizing where relationships within God's creation have been broken. Among the most vulnerable and deeply impacted communities are those affected by climate change – coastal communities, the urban poor, small-scale farmers, and fisherfolk. However, the actions of Christians must extend beyond merely defending such communities to reflecting the lordship of Christ over all creation. Although we cannot fix all that is unjust and broken in our world, we are called to strive for shalom – wholeness in our relationship with God and with his creation. The goal of Christ-followers must be to bring shalom wherever and however we can, while clinging to our hope in Christ, who will one day bring full restoration to all creation.

Third, creation care is a gospel issue. Our Christian witness is at stake because how we relate to God's creation is an indicator of how we relate to our Creator God. Marina Silva, Brazil's former Minister of Environment, from the Amazon region, shared this powerful statement at the Lausanne Younger Leaders Gathering: "It is greatly inconsistent to say that we love the Creator while we destroy his creation."[6]

---

6. Silva, "Broken Vase," https://lausanne.org/content/broken-vase-restored.

How we respond to issues affecting God's creation greatly impacts our Christian witness. For instance, some of the most vulnerable communities affected by the climate crisis live in regions where it is particularly difficult and challenging for the gospel of Jesus Christ to take root. Our physical and spiritual lives are deeply intertwined. There is no doubt that addressing the climate crisis is necessary within the global church. Much of the world is already awakening to the reality and urgency of this crisis. At the recent COP28 in Dubai, the agreement to transition away from fossil fuels marks a significant step.[7] However, such commitments at the international level are not enough. Actions at the individual and civil society level are equally important. The global church should play a key role in the global effort to address climate issues since our motivation goes beyond merely responding to an emergency. As the Jamaica Call to Action of the Lausanne Movement states, "We [Christians] would care for creation even if it were not in crisis."[8]

God cares not only about our vertical relationship with him but also about our horizontal relationships with other people and the rest of creation. Therefore, Christians today should practice welcome, hospitality, and generosity as part of what it means to care for God's creation. Our homes and churches should be places of refuge for those in need. Speaking out against injustices and advocating for the poor and vulnerable should be common practice for those committed to following Jesus.

Creation Care as a Discipleship and Stewardship Issue

For Christians, creation issues are both urgent and important. The current climate crisis demands urgent attention. But even more important, Christians have a biblical mandate to care for God's creation. Since both humanity and the natural world are part of God's creation, responding to climate issues is inextricably linked to our relationship with our Creator and his creation.

This is why the Christian response to climate migration issues presents a significant opportunity for the global church. A commitment to God's creation – which includes the most vulnerable human populations as well as wildlife – is not just about "saving the planet" or tackling the climate crisis; rather, it is about faithfully integrating our love for God and care for his creation into

---

7. United Nations, "COP28," https://unfccc.int/news/cop28-agreement-signals-beginning-of-the-end-of-the-fossil-fuel-era.

8. "Creation Care," *Lausanne-WEA Creation Care Network*, https://lausanne.org/content/statement/creation-care-call-to-action.

our daily lives. Our Christian faith goes beyond a personal relationship with Jesus to *how* we live for Jesus in this world alongside the rest of God's creation. In order for these issues to take deeper root in our lives, we must embrace the biblical foundation for creation care. What does the Bible say about God and God's creation? How do we understand God's biblical story, which includes both salvation and restoration, in the light of *all* of God's creation?

Urgent action is needed to address the climate crisis, but our actions should be linked to the renewal of our hearts and minds in Christ toward God and his creation. This transformation is not about quick, one-time action; rather, it is a lifelong commitment to faithfulness and obedience in Christ. Engagement with God's creation is part of our lifelong journey of following Jesus, who is Lord of all creation. In order for the global church to care well for creation, it is of utmost importance that Christians also lament with creation. Christian discipleship includes addressing issues of the heart. Our outward actions toward creation may lack integrity if we do not also hear the cries of creation and grieve with those who are suffering. So, as part of caring for creation, the global church may need to repent of our contribution or our apathy toward the suffering of creation. We can also incorporate lament as part of our Christian worship.

In caring for creation, the global church must humbly learn with and from those who are already actively caring for creation. For example, the global church has much to learn from today's younger generation, many of whom do not need to be convinced about the urgency of these issues as they see how failure to respond to the climate crisis will impact their future and the planet. We need to listen to younger voices, including those of Christians, who speak truth about our actions in the light of Christ's teachings. Vanessa Nakate, a young Ugandan Christian and UNICEF Goodwill Ambassador, is one such leader, who often speaks about engaging in the climate crisis while focusing unwaveringly on Jesus.[9] At COP28, Nakate shared,

> For me, activism is beyond a passion: it feels like a responsibility from God to speak for those who may not be able to speak for themselves, to be able to heal those who are broken-hearted, to be able to heal those who have lost their loved ones as a result of climate change, and be able to bring justice to those who have lost their lives and those who are seeing terrible impacts right now . . .

---

9. Nakate, "Humanity's Shared Lifeboat," https://www.theguardian.com/commentisfree/2023/dec/12/cop-28-humanity-leaders-activists-dubai-fossil-fuel-phase-out-adaptation?ref=upstract.com.

So, I see our response should be a response of grace, of love, to continue to do the work we are doing.[10]

What would change in the global church if more of us rise up, like Nakate, not only engaging in thoughtful action but doing so with clear, Christ-centered motivation? What deeper integration will we experience if we better understand that the climate crisis is both an ecological and a spiritual issue? Our influence can move beyond isolated action and blossom into a coordinated effort as the collective body of Christ, faithfully endeavoring to help God's human and nonhuman creation to flourish. The global church has an opportunity to lead by example, but we must first recover care for God's creation as a core value in our own lives. After all, this is our Father's world.

Climate Migrant Mission

The climate migrant crisis is both an amazing opportunity and an enormous challenge for the global church. As climate migrants become our new neighbors and colleagues, how should Christians across the globe respond to this emerging reality? First and foremost, we must educate ourselves about the harsh realities faced by climate migrants. Since it is not easy for those who have not been directly affected by this issue to fully comprehend the far-reaching repercussions of this crisis, this is best done by meeting people who have been directly affected by this issue or visiting places impacted by climate change.

Every church and mission agency must develop a climate and migration task force to explore how they could be part of the solution in these growing crises. In most Christian communities, awareness of climate change or mission in the wake of climate migration is nonexistent or remains in its infancy. Recently, however, as the ramifications of climate change have become more evident, greater attention has been paid to this issue. In approaching this issue, we must refrain from geopolitical debates on how various nations have contributed to the crisis or what they have failed to do to address it. Nor should we adopt a narrow and secular view of climate change. Instead, we must anchor our theology in the mission of God and a hopeful vision of earthly restoration under God's eternal reign.

The global church must initiate (if it has not already done so) and multiply efforts to help vulnerable people to adapt to climate-related changes and

---

10. Ware, "Ugandan Climate Activist," *Church Times*, https://www.churchtimes.co.uk/articles/2023/15-december/news/world/ugandan-climate-activist-speaks-of-faith-that-sustains-her.

develop resilience to the resultant shocks and disruptions. The church must be involved in both preventive action in the form of educating Christians to be better stewards of the created order and corrective action to undo the harmful effects of human activities that contribute to climate change. They must also advocate for climate-informed lifestyle choices for all Christians and pursue evangelistic opportunities arising out of this crisis. These matters are integral to discipleship for all Christ-followers and must include economic and operational commitments by the church.

Migration is an inevitable reality of history. All of us are either migrants or descendants of migrants. Our lives have been and are being shaped by migration of some sort.[11] From a historical perspective, our national identities and all geopolitical borders are an anomaly. The story of Christianity has been greatly shaped by migrations of various kinds and the Bible is a product of migrations. All cross-cultural displacement holds tremendous potential for diffusion of the gospel when Christians everywhere realize the potential and embrace migrants, whatever be the cause of their displacements. Such a view of climate-induced migration does not undermine the importance of responsible creation care and stewardship of the environment to mitigate its effect but, rather, offers a more proactive and restorative approach to dealing with the situation and its consequences.

Conclusion

Migration and climate change are inextricably interlinked, and this nexus will inevitably catapult these issues into deeper levels of crises. As the effects of climate change become more frequent and severe, compounded by socioeconomic, demographic, and geopolitical problems, there will be a surge in global human migration. Just as is the case with other migrants, climate migration includes both Christians who need to be welcomed into our faith communities and non-Christians who need to be reached compassionately and holistically.

---

11. "People on the Move," https://lausanne.org/occasional-paper/lausanne-occasional-paper-people-on-the-move.

References

"Creation Care and the Gospel: Jamaica Call to Action." *Lausanne/WEA Creation Care Network*, 2012. https://lausanne.org/content/statement/creation-care-call-to-action.

Huang, Lawrence. "Climate Migration 101: An Explainer." *Migration Policy Institute*, 16 November 2023. https://www.migrationpolicy.org/article/climate-migration-101-explainer.

International Organization for Migration. "Environmental Migration." *Environmental Migration Portal*, 2023. https://environmentalmigration.iom.int/environmental-migration.

Nakate, Vanessa. "Humanity's Shared Lifeboat Is Sinking." *The Guardian*, 12 December 2023. https://www.theguardian.com/commentisfree/2023/dec/12/cop-28-humanity-leaders-activists-dubai-fossil-fuel-phase-out-adaptation?ref=upstract.com.

"People on the Move." Lausanne Occasional Paper No. 70. *Lausanne Movement*, 2023. https://lausanne.org/occasional-paper/lausanne-occasional-paper-people-on-the-move.

"Provisional State of the Global Climate 2023." *World Meteorological Organization*, 30 November 2023. https://wmo.int/files/provisional-state-of-global-climate-2023.

Silva, Marina. "A Broken Vase Restored." *Lausanne Movement*, 2016. https://lausanne.org/content/broken-vase-restored.

Smith, Adam B. "2022 U.S. Billion-Dollar Weather and Climate Disasters in Historical Context." NOAA blog, 10 January 2023. https://www.climate.gov/news-features/blogs/beyond-data/2022-us-billion-dollar-weather-and-climate-disasters-historical.

Thunberg, Greta. *The Climate Book: The Fact and the Solutions*. New York: Penguin, 2023.

United Nations. "COP28 Agreement Signals 'Beginning of the End' of the Fossil Fuel Era." *United Nations Climate Change*, 13 December 2023. https://unfccc.int/news/cop28-agreement-signals-beginning-of-the-end-of-the-fossil-fuel-era.

———. "Environmental Migration." *Migration Data Portal*, last updated 5 June 2024. https://www.migrationdataportal.org/themes/environmental_migration_and_statistics.

Vince, Gaia. *Nomad Century: How Climate Migration Will Reshape Our World*. New York: Flatiron Books, 2023.

Ware, Joe. "Ugandan Climate Activist Speaks of Faith That Sustains Her." *Church Times*, 15 December 2023. https://www.churchtimes.co.uk/articles/2023/15-december/news/world/ugandan-climate-activist-speaks-of-faith-that-sustains-her.

World Bank. "Groundswell Part 2: Acting on Internal Climate Migration." https://openknowledge.worldbank.org/entities/publication/2c9150df-52c3-58ed-9075-d78ea56c3267. Accessed 27 December 2023.

Section C

19

A Diasporic Pastoral Letter: Background and Greetings of 1 Peter 1:1–2

Elizabeth Mburu

Introduction

The Kiswahili proverb, *Iwapo nia, njia hupatikana* ("Where there is hope, there is a way") is an apt reflection of the message of 1 Peter. For Peter, the believer's hope can only be found in Christ, and this is what gives one the strength to endure suffering.[1] Peter was an eyewitness of Christ during his life, ministry, death, and resurrection. He betrayed Jesus at a crucial moment but was later reinstated (John 18:17, 25, 26; 21:15–19). For Peter, "These experiences had convinced him that while believers are foreigners and strangers in a hostile environment, there is an eternal home to be enjoyed once this brief life is over."[2]

Background
The World behind the Text: Historical Context

Author: The author identifies himself as Peter, an apostle of Jesus Christ (1:1). His original name was Simon, but in John 1:42 Jesus gives him the Aramaic name Cephas (meaning "rock"), of which Peter is the Greek translation. He is also the author of 2 Peter (2 Pet 1:1). His secretary was Sylvanus (Silas). Peter was the son of Jonas and brother to Andrew. He was a part of the innermost

---

1. Muriithi, "1 Peter," 1543.
2. Muriithi, 1543.

circle of twelve disciples, one of the three closest to Jesus. He was an eyewitness to the life, ministry, death, and resurrection of Jesus. He was present at the transfiguration (Matt 17). He denied Christ during the events leading up to the crucifixion but was restored after the resurrection (1 Cor 15:5). He was the key speaker on the day of Pentecost (Acts 2) and God's instrument to open the way of salvation to Samaritans (Acts 8) and Gentiles (Acts 10–11). Paul publicly rebuked him for hypocritically withdrawing from fellowship with Gentile believers (Gal). He was martyred during Nero's reign around AD 63–64.

According to tradition, when Peter was condemned to death, he asked to be crucified on an inverted cross. He believed that his denial of Jesus made him unworthy to die the same way as Jesus had. Archaeological evidence reveals a second-century memorial to Peter's martyrdom that had been erected in Rome.[3] However, this is only a tradition, and we see no evidence for the truth or falsehood of this claim in the Bible. The internal evidence and early church tradition (e.g. Polycarp, Papias, Clement of Alexandria, Irenaeus and Eusebius) attribute authorship to Peter. Modern doubts about authorship can therefore be countered.[4]

Recipients: The recipients of 1 Peter are not a specific group of believers. Peter refers to them as "exiles scattered throughout the provinces" – the regions of Pontus, Galatia, Cappadocia, Asia, and Bithynia (1 Pet 1:1c), most of which are in modern-day Turkey. This was therefore a general letter that would have been circulated among a large number of churches consisting of mainly gentile readers (1:14, 18; 2:9–10, 25; 3:6; 4:3–4). A gentile readership is supported by Peter's description of their former way of life, including idolatry and pagan practices (1:18; 4:3–4). Peter applies categories generally restricted to Jews to this gentile audience. However, the recipients also included some Jewish believers (1:1).

Place of Writing: The references to persecution suggest that Peter wrote from Rome, with Babylon (5:13) being used symbolically as a code name for the city (cf. Rev 14:8; 17:9–10). Rome was the heart of the empire in Peter's day, much as Babylon was in the past. As Watson points out with regard to the persecution of Christians throughout the empire, "Emperor worship became popular in the first century A.D., and its claims for the divinity of the emperor were antithetical to Christianity's claim that Jesus was Lord."[5] It was during

---

3. Keener, *IVP Bible Background Commentary*, 684.

4. See general introductions such as Elwell and Yarbrough, *Encountering the New Testament*, 362–63; Carson and Moo, *Introduction to the New Testament*, 642–43.

5. Watson, "Roman Empire," 977.

Nero's reign that Peter (and Paul) lost his life. Nero was known for his cruelty (it is said he used Christians as live burning torches for his garden parties) and he blamed Christians for the burning of Rome in AD 64. As Keener points out "it would be appropriate for Peter to send advance warning of that situation to believers in Asia minor, the stronghold of emperor worship."[6]

Date: 1 Peter was probably written around AD 62–63. Peter's familiarity with Paul's letters from prison (such as Colossians and Ephesians) makes this the most likely date. It appears to have been written in two sections, with 1:1–4:6 written when the persecution was not as severe as it appears to be in 4:7–5:14.[7]

Purpose: The tone of this letter is highly pastoral. Peter wrote to encourage and comfort believers in diaspora as they faced persecution and hardship. He emphasized that such perseverance, which would reveal the grace of Christ in their lives (5:12), is only a result of God's power.

The World of the Text: Literary Context

Genre: 1 Peter is a letter that was written according to the Hellenistic letter-writing conventions of the first century. As a circular letter, it was intended for distribution beyond one church. It is generally referred to as one of the general epistles. Letters are occasional in that the writer intends to address specific issues. When reading one must try and determine the purpose and not treat it like a theological handbook that addresses every situation a believer might face.

Style: There is a strong resemblance between this letter and the Gospel of Mark. It is generally held that Peter provided much of the material in this Gospel since Mark was not an apostle. The similarity extends to words attributed to Peter (cf. 1 Pet 1:20 and Acts 2:23; 1 Pet 2:7–8 and Acts 4:10–11; 1 Pet 1:7 and Acts 10:34). The literary style is excellent, with a sophisticated use of the Greek language and metaphors. (This is one of the reasons why some scholars doubt Petrine authorship.) Peter's inclusion of Old Testament concepts, vocabulary, allusions, specific references, and quotations shows his heavy dependence on the Old Testament.

Structure: 1 Peter is divided into five main parts, including the greeting (1 Pet 1:1–2) and the closing (5:12–14). In 1:3–2:3 he expounds the implications of salvation in Christ and rebirth by the Holy Spirit. Following this, 2:4–10 explains how this impacts the identity of believers as God's chosen people.

---

6. Keener, *IVP Bible Background Commentary*, 685.
7. Keener, 684.

From 2:11 to 3:7 Peter writes about the believers' responsibility to Christ, as aliens and strangers in the midst of hostility. This is explained in terms of submission to authorities in government, the workplace, and the home. Before he closes, Peter addresses submission in the context of the church in 3:8–5:11.

The World in Front of the Text: Contexts

Theological context: The fact that Peter is a practical theologian is revealed through the letter as he relates his theology to the everyday lives of believers.

The identity of believers: It has already been noted above that Peter has a high dependence on the OT. This can be seen also in how he describes believers in language that reflects that of OT Israel. For Peter, believers are exiles and foreigners, whose identity is as temporary residents of, as well as witnesses to, this world. The implication is that they are to live holy lives – a posture that runs counter to the ideals and morals of society.

Persecution and perseverance: Peter addresses the suffering of believers (every chapter refers to suffering) in the context of the imminent second coming of Christ. For Peter, suffering must be understood in the perspective of the temporary nature of the believer's life in this world, the hope presented by Christ's own example of enduring suffering, Christ's resurrection, and the believers' future inheritance. Although the suffering may not necessarily come to an end, if his readers are able to adopt this perspective, they will be able to endure it with a positive attitude.

The Trinity: Peter also presents God as a Triune being who is holy and to be imitated. The assurance and hope that believers possess derives from the fact that God has predestined them. Jesus Christ is the substitutionary sin offering that was given by God's will. His suffering and death are an example for future believers who live in their own contexts of suffering. Moreover, his death is a model for how believers are to die to sin daily, and his resurrection is power for how they are to live. Believers are sanctified through the Holy Spirit and he is the one who empowers the preaching of the gospel to the unbelieving world.

The church: Peter also provides a theology of the church. While there is continuity in that it is the inheritor of the blessings promised to Israel, there is also discontinuity and newness because it is built on the foundation of Christ himself. The purpose of the church is to offer worship to God and to be a witness to the world.

Twenty-First-Century Global Diasporas

Before looking at the twenty-first century, we should understand how apostle Peter uses the Greek term διασπορά (diaspora), which is usually translated as scattered or dispersed. It is a transliteration of the Greek term and is found in the New Testament, the Greek Old Testament (the Septuagint), and extra-biblical literature produced during the biblical period. The verb form of this word is found only three times in the New Testament in 1 Peter 1:1, John 7:35, and James 1:1. It generally refers to Jews who lived outside Palestine.[8] It is thus the technical name for all the nations outside of Palestine where Jewish people came to live. This is the sense used in James 1:1, where it refers to Jews scattered across the Roman Empire.

The earliest Jewish dispersion was the deportations by the Assyrians in 722 BC and the Babylonians in 597 BC. According to Santos, there appear to be two main reasons for the Jewish diaspora. The first was forced deportation as a result of conquests by the Assyrian, Babylonian, and Roman (specifically, Pompey) Empires. These were meant to reveal "God's severe judgment through scattering, thus emphasizing pain and curse."[9] They would have experienced ridicule and derision from their enemies as a result of this kind of exile (cf. Ps 79:4, 10). The second was voluntary migration. Unlike the forced deportations, this would not have involved any sense of "curse or shame, but a sense of optimism and restoration of dignity and pride."[10]

Jews later spread throughout the Roman Empire to Egypt, Asia Minor, Greece, and Italy. Since the original Jewish dispersion, the term *diaspora* has been used to include any religious or racial minority living in the territory of another religious or political society. In the NT, it "is also associated with exile, in reference to Israel's subjugation to the nations (particularly Rome), which only Messiah Jesus can remedy."[11] The book of Acts in particular shows the reality of diasporic Jews in the first century.[12] Peter applies this term literally but also uses it figuratively for believers who live as foreigners and exiles on earth but who belong to heaven.

---

8. Keener, 687.
9. Santos, "*Diaspora* in the New Testament," 9.
10. Santos, 9.
11. Trebilco and Evans, "Diaspora Judaism," 294.
12. Santos, "*Diaspora* in the New Testament," 9.

Relevance to Diaspora in the Twenty-First Century
Cultural expectations and Christian values

The entire letter reveals that Peter was writing to people who had given their allegiance to Jesus (3:15). As a result, their departure from Judaism and paganism was being questioned and they were being treated with hostility (2:12; 3:16). Romans viewed Christians as antisocial (like Jews), atheistic (for rejecting the gods), cannibalistic (a misunderstanding of the Eucharist), and incestuous (for their statements of love toward "brothers and sisters").[13] Because they refused to join in religious and social activities of pagan worship (4:3-4), these believers received sharp criticism from unbelievers, some of whom lived in the same households as they did (2:18; 3:1). In the Roman Empire, such rejection of these socially acceptable pagan practices was interpreted negatively, particularly where civic life was concerned. Peter's christological repurposing of the Greco-Roman household code is most likely addressing this (2:13-3:7; 2:11-12; 3:8-12). He encouraged his readers to live within societal and cultural constraints while never deviating from their Christocentric focus (3:15). This meant that those living in diaspora must learn to adapt to their, often hostile, new environments without compromising their Christian faith.

Diaspora and Christian mission

The Jewish diaspora was a precursor to the Christian mission. The mode of evangelization by the early missionaries provided "a valuable vehicle for the proclamation of the gospel" and the synagogues that Jewish communities had built provided the first point of contact and effectively "served as a precursor for a strategic and viable venue for Christian mission to the dispersed Jews."[14] None of this would have been possible without God's sovereign direction.

The persecution and martyrdom that God allowed many Christian Jews to experience and that resulted in their dispersion, served as a catalyst that launched the gospel into Judea, Samaria, and the ends of the earth (Acts 1:8; 8; 11:19-20). As Santos points out in his brief survey of *diapeirō* and *diaspora* passages in the New Testament, "Despite the persecution of Jewish Christians, God in his sovereignty catalyzed the spread of the gospel and the expansion of God's kingdom in Christian mission."[15] In the same way, those who have been forced out of their countries for political, social, economic, ecological

---

13. Keener, *IVP Bible Background Commentary*, 685.
14. Santos, "*Diaspora* in the New Testament," 14.
15. Santos, 14.

or other reasons, should see this as an opportunity for mission in their host countries. As in the early church, God's sovereignty undergirds these negative circumstances.

Commentary on 1 Peter 1:1–2: Greetings

Greetings are an essential part of any society. Sicily Mbura Muriithi points out that in African cultures, greetings are extensive, including inquiries into the well-being of those greeted, as well as their families and community. This is because "greetings are rooted in the belief that individuals are intimately connected with their communities."[16] This sense of community is what we see in Peter's opening words.

The opening two verses form the salutation and thanksgiving part of the letter. The salutation is in the typical fashion of Hellenistic first-century letters. It includes the name of the sender, the recipients, and an expression of good wishes. Peter introduces himself as "an apostle of Jesus Christ," meaning one who has received a special commission from God (1:1a). This identification also serves to emphasize his credentials and his authority to address his readers in the diverse situations that they find themselves.

He next identifies his recipients as "exiles scattered throughout the provinces" (1:1b). As noted above, the term diaspora (and the verb form used here) was applied to those Jews who lived outside Palestine. However, Peter repurposes this Jewish term and uses it for the Christian population in diaspora, including Jews and Gentiles.

He also describes them as *parepidēmois* (foreigners or exiles) located in the regions of Pontus, Galatia, Cappadocia, Asia, and Bithynia, which is modern day Turkey (1:1c). This Greek term is rare in the New Testament, occurring only here, in 1 Peter 2:11 and in Hebrews 11:13, where it refers to the children of Abraham (LXX Gen 23:24; LXX Ps 38:13; 39:12 ET). The synonym *paroikos* appears in 1 Peter 1:17 and Acts 7:6 with a similar sense. This is a word that encompasses both foreign nationality and temporary residence. Peter's purpose in using this word is to help them remember that although they may be physically dislocated from their homeland, of greater importance is that they are temporary residents on earth.

Peter then jumps straight into a reminder of their identity with regard to the world and to God. Why is this? It is because, "Scattered exiles often feel

---

16. Muriithi, "1 Peter," 1544.

isolated and insignificant."[17] He therefore begins by reminding them that they are God's elect, and chosen by him (1:1a, 2a). The term "elect" is a common self-designation in Judaism. It refers to Israel, the nation God chose through Abraham. Peter also repurposes this term and uses it for his Christian readers. As Marshall rightly notes, "at the outset of the letter Peter fastens on the theme he will develop in the letter as a whole – the situation of Christians in an environment to which they do not belong and from which they may well expect an unsympathetic reaction."[18]

God's election and choice is not based on human merit. While we cannot be certain how this foreknowledge operates, what is clear is that all three persons of the Trinity are active in this choice. The Father foreknows the believers; the Holy Spirit is at work in them, sanctifying them so that they can achieve God's purpose; and this purpose is "to be obedient to Jesus Christ and sprinkled with his blood" (1:2b). The reference to blood hearkens back to the OT sacrifices and, coupled as it is with obedience, it is reminiscent of covenantal language (Exod 24:7–8).

In light of this, the introductory part of the letter ends with an appropriate prayer for "grace and peace . . . in abundance" (1:2c). In the midst of their difficult lives, Peter's well wishes for his readers assures them that their relationship with God, as his elect, is secure. In the midst of the hostility directed against them as they live out their lives in diaspora, God will bestow his blessings upon them – not only in the future, but also in the present as well.

Conclusion

Peter writes to a people in diaspora that are experiencing great tribulation. In the midst of their suffering, he urges them to persevere in hope in the face of their trials, trials that will prove the genuineness of their faith. There are many Christians in the world who live as foreigners in foreign countries. They may be there voluntarily or involuntarily. The situation of Peter's readers in Asia Minor might not be identical to theirs, but the encouragement and comfort that Peter provides is still relevant today.

Peter urges his readers to adopt the attitude of Christ who suffered unjustly and was abused and mistreated beyond description (2:21–23). This attitude, which promotes spiritual growth and sanctification, should be sought after above all else. This letter speaks vividly to believers in diaspora who are suf-

---

17. Muriithi, 1544.
18. Marshall, *1 Peter*, 30.

fering war, famine, disease, economic hardship, political marginalization, religious persecution, and who may be doubting the presence of God in the midst of their suffering. No matter what they are experiencing, whether severe or mild, they are called to persevere by following the example of Jesus Christ and to live in the hope that heaven is their true home and that one day, God will take them there.

References

Carson, D. A., and Douglas J. Moo. *An Introduction to the New Testament*. Grand Rapids: Zondervan, 2005.

Elwell, Walter A., and Robert W. Yarbrough. *Encountering the New Testament: A Historical and Theological Survey*. Grand Rapids: Baker Academic, 2005.

Keener, Craig. *The IVP Bible Background Commentary*. 2nd ed. Downers Grove: InterVarsity Press, 2014.

Marshall, I. Howard. *1 Peter*. The IVP New Testament Commentary Series. Edited by Grant R. Osborne. Downers Grove: InterVarsity Press, 1991.

Muriithi, Sicily Mbura. "1 Peter." In *Africa Bible Commentary*, edited by Tokunboh Adeyemo, 1543–51. Carlisle: HippoBooks; Grand Rapids: Zondervan, 2006.

Santos, Narry F. "*Diaspora* in the New Testament and Its Impact on Christian Mission." *Torch Trinity Journal* 13, no. 1 (2010): 3–18.

Trebilco, Paul R., and Craig A. Evans. "Diaspora Judaism." In *Dictionary of New Testament Background*, edited by Craig A. Evans and Stanley E. Porter, 281–96. Downers Grove: InterVarsity Press, 2000.

Watson, Duane F. "Roman Empire." In *Dictionary of New Testament Background*, edited by Craig A. Evans and Stanley E. Porter, 974–78. Downers Grove: InterVarsity Press, 2000.

20

New Family of God: Rediscovering Diaspora Identity in 1 Peter 1:3–2:10

Narry F. Santos

Diaspora experience in the context of twenty-first-century global Christianity can mean a struggle of identity for those scattered. With the increase in migration across the world comes a corresponding increase in opposition to such migration. In 2022 "around five million more people moved to affluent countries . . . than left them, as COVID-era travel restrictions eased."[1] Such record immigration to affluent countries is igniting bigger backlashes globally, putting pressure on governments to tighten policies to stem the migration wave. With increasing frequency, the displaced are blamed for spikes in crime and higher housing costs. The message here is clear: global migrants are facing more pushback.

Polls in affluent countries show a jump in opposition to immigration, including places that have been the most welcoming to newcomers. According to a poll by Léger, a research company based in Montreal, roughly half of Canadians think the government's new target of about a "half-million immigrants a year is too many in a country of 40 million, while three-quarters worry the plan will result in excessive demand for housing and health and social services."[2] According to a March 2023 poll in the UK by Public First, nearly half of the

---

1. Fairless, "Immigration Backlashes."
2. Fairless.

people surveyed think legal migration is too high in the UK.[3] According to Gallup polls, the "Americans' satisfaction with the level of immigration into the U.S. declined to 28 percent in February, the lowest reading in a decade, from 34 percent a year earlier."[4] The message here is clear: host nations are becoming less welcoming to legal immigrants.

Attitudes to illegal immigrants are also growing harsher, especially in view of the record levels of illegal entries across the Mediterranean into Europe and from Mexico to the US. Voters in wealthy nations express concern for how illegal immigration tends to weigh on wages and social-welfare systems. In the mid 2010s to 2025 in the US, there continues to be a tough stance on border security and immigration policy. In Europe, efforts are expanding to build more new barriers on land and sea to decrease illegal migration. The message here is clear: host nations are treating illegal migrants with increasing harshness.

In addition, refugees and asylum seekers, driven by climate-related disasters, conflicts, and economic woes, are increasing in record numbers. According to the UNHCR, there were 108.4 million forcibly displaced individuals – one in seventy-four people worldwide – at the end of 2022 (up nineteen million compared to 2021). About 52 percent of refugees and other people in need of international protection came from just three countries: Syria (6.5 million), Ukraine (5.7 million), and Afghanistan (5.7 million). At the same time, there were 2.6 million new asylum claims in 2022.[5] Despite this upward trend in forced displacement, response plans and budgets for the displaced remain severely underfunded. The right to asylum is also under threat in some places, making it difficult to provide protection to those who need it the most. The message here is clear: there is less help for those who need more help.

When we combine these clear messages for those displaced or in diaspora – global migrants getting more pushback; legal immigrants becoming less welcomed; illegal migrants being treated increasingly harshly; forcibly displaced people having less available help – we can see how diaspora experience in the context of twenty-first-century global Christianity can mean a struggle for the identity of those scattered. Whether as immigrants, migrants, refugees, asylum seekers, or international students, diaspora identity is complex and can be complicated as one person can have multiple of these and move in and out these identities during their sojourn. Migration is an enigma for

---

3. Public First, "Public First Poll for UUK," https://www.publicfirst.co.uk/wp-content/uploads/2023/03/PF_UUK.pdf.

4. Fairless.

5. Gottbrath, "Record 110 Million People."

many affluent nations because though they do not like migrants, immigration is needed for ongoing economic growth due to their plummeting birth rates.[6]

One way to understand the plight of the diaspora during their sojourn is to use sociological language to view them as a minority group. Louis Wirth defines a minority group this way: "any group of people, who, because of their physical or cultural characteristics, are singled out from the others in the society in which they live for differentiated and unequal treatment and who therefore regard themselves as objects of collective discrimination."[7] As a social minority group, the discriminated diaspora holds a position of subordination, as opposed to the position of dominance by the social majority.

In the social context of early Christianity, specifically during the time of the recipients in Peter's first letter, we see the diaspora in Asia Minor (modern-day Turkey) described as "exiles, scattered throughout the provinces of Pontus, Galatia, Cappadocia, Asia and Bithynia"[8] (1:1) and the "sojourners and exiles" (2:11) according to their "time as foreigners" (1:17). Even in their first-century context, the *parepidêmos* (or the temporary residents in a location, rendered "exiles" in the NIV) and the *paroikos* (noncitizen residents in a location, rendered "sojourners" in the NIV) can be considered as a social minority, recipients of discrimination, and socially located at the level of subordination. Scot McKnight describes the scattered people in 1 Peter this way: "Those who occupied these social locations stood firmly on a special rung on Rome's social ladder: below citizens and above slaves and foreigners."[9]

Moreover, the four criteria for identifying the marginalized, in the social context of early Christianity seen in the New Testament, can be applied to the audience of 1 Peter. First, this underrated diaspora group could have exhibited minority attributes. They could have lacked social self-autonomy, freedom, and wholeness, showing attributes of marginality and minority status. Second, this diaspora group could have displayed comprehensive sociopolitical power deficiency – being excluded from resources of political and socioeconomic power. Third, this diaspora group could have been exposed to involuntary and habitual stereotyping, stigmatizing, and name-calling. They could have regularly received collective judgments and disparaging labeling related to

---

6. Kight, "Record Migration."

7. Wirth, "Problem of Minority," 347.

8. The "exiles" here are persecuted Christians who were forced to leave their homes and live as strangers in a new place. See Jobes, *1 Peter*, 32–33. Cf. Pienaar, *Called to Suffer*; Reese, *1 Peter*.

9. McKnight, "Aliens and Exiles," 381. Cf. Horrell, "Aliens and Strangers?," 176; McKnight, *1 Peter*, 1996.

shame (e.g. being called primitive, weak, immoral, and second-class in intelligence). Given the honor-shame culture of the first-century Mediterranean world under the Roman Empire, shaming was a common public strategy for social control, used in order to pressure the minority group to conform to conventional values and standards of conduct approved by the social majority.[10] In this context, stigmatizing could become more dangerous if the social minority group appropriates the stigmas against them and then internalizes them into their self-perception, that is believing what others say about them. Fourth, the diaspora group could have been pressured to bear the collective burden of subordination and discrimination. This relentless branding of the minority's subordination could have damaged the people's self-worth as the concepts of minority and discrimination would have been synonymous to structural and interpersonal powerlessness.[11]

In the case of the diaspora in 1 Peter, the aliens and exiles became targets and victims of verbal abuse intended to shame and discredit these believing sojourners, whom Dennis Edwards describes as disinherited people whose backs were against the wall.[12] Here is a sampling of the hostility and hatred from their neighbors: (1) "among the pagans that, though they accuse you of doing wrong" (2:12a); (2) "by doing good you should silence the ignorant talk of foolish people" (2:15b); (3) "Do not repay evil with evil or insult with insult" (3:9a); (4) "so that those who speak maliciously against your good behavior in Christ may be ashamed of their slander" (3:16); (5) "and they heap abuse on you" (4:4b); and (6) "If you are insulted because of the name of Christ, you are blessed" (4:14a). Valentina Pagliai refers to these insults or impoliteness as aggressions or attacks against the face, with the face representing our emotionally sensitive concept of self.[13] It was also possible that the verbal abuse, slander, and false accusation against the Christian sojourners could have been coupled with or have escalated to physical abuse, as may be implied in these verses: (1) "not only to those who are good and considerate, but also to those who are harsh" (2:18b); (2) "For it is commendable if someone bears up under the pain of unjust suffering" (2:19a); and (3) "Who is going to harm you if you are eager to do good?" (3:13).

---

10. For more details on honor and shame in 1 Peter, see Campbell, *Honor, Shame, and the Rhetoric of 1 Peter*.

11. For more, see Berg, "Four Criteria," 6–27.

12. Edwards, "Jesus and the Disinherited," 257.

13. Pagliai, "Performing Disputes," 65. Cf. Pilch, "Insults and Face Work."

Given such physical and verbal abuses, the underrated minority status of the believers during their dispersion, and the relentless affront to their worth by unbelievers in Asia Minor, how can they rediscover their new identity in Christ? I see Peter address this crucial question in 1 Peter 1:3–2:10. In this passage, Peter was "formulating their new identity"[14] in Christ as the precious family of God. If they could understand, appreciate, and live out the reality of their new identity in God's new household (or *oikos*), then they could rise above the hostility, hatred, and hurt that their enemies inflict upon them. In other words, the new communal social reality that counteracts the demoralizing impact of their position as social minority is their new distinctive communal identity as the church. John Elliot uses the language of honor for this new identity as God's family, "The paramount locus of honor in society, the family (*oikos*), becomes here the honor basis of the community as the household of God."[15] In 1 Peter, the expressions *oikos pneumatikos* (spiritual household) in 2:5 and *oikos tou theou* (household of God) in 4:17 are descriptors for the believers' new identity as God's family.

As part of God's new family, the *parepidêmos* (or visiting strangers) and the *paroikos* (or resident aliens) have found their *oikos* (family or household). But without their spiritual household and the household of God, the visiting strangers would remain displaced in their new place or residence in Asia Minor where they live as strangers. In fact, without their spiritual household, the resident aliens would feel alienated despite their long stay in Asia Minor. Without their spiritual household, both sojourners and exiles would remain to be strangers, without roots, without a home. Paul Hines describes this rootlessness and homelessness this way, "To be homeless is to be a stranger, and to be a stranger meant that one was denied the ability to socially identify with those around."[16] But with the new family of God, the sense of strangeness with the status of isolation and inferiority goes away, instead giving way to a new home and a new sense of belonging. In other words, from having no home, they could now move to a new home – the family of God.

Peter explained the corporate and communal nature of this new family of God with these words: "But you are a chosen people, royal priesthood, a holy nation, God's special possession" (2:9a). Note that those who are chosen are all the people of God, those who are priests under one King are all the people of

---

14. Punt, "Mapping Human Dignity," 630.

15. Elliot, "Disgraced Yet Graced," 173. For Elliot's other reflections on 1 Peter and the family of God, see *A Home for the Homeless* and *1 Peter*.

16. Himes, *Foreknowledge*, 51.

God, those who were the holy that comprise God's nation are all the people of God, and those who are valued as a special possession (or God's own people, or the people of God's possession) are all the people of God. What makes the family of God united, amid their uniqueness and diversity, is that all of them are precious in God's sight, taking away the stigma of isolation and inferiority, of subordination and strangeness, of marginalization and minority status.

God's new family members are also described as recipients of ascribed honor; recipients of new birth into a living hope in light of God's mercy (1:3); recipients of "an inheritance that can never perish, spoil or fade" (1:4); recipients of God's shielding power through faith (1:5); recipients of proven and genuine faith that is "of greater worth than gold" (1:7a); and recipients of "inexpressible and glorious joy" (1:8b). Such images of ascribed honor were all given to the precious diaspora believers by God, who is the "ultimate conferrer and arbiter of honor and shame."[17] As a result of God's acts of grace to those in diaspora, the sojourning and exiled believers are taken from a position of shame and disgrace in the eyes of a shaming society to a position of honor and preciousness in the eyes of the most honorable God.

Aside from the communal nature of belonging and the precious and gracious acts of God in honoring the Christians in diaspora, God's new family in Christ also underwent an identity shift, a divine reversal of status, or what James Scott calls a "symbolic inversion."[18] The identity of the members of God's new family shifted from darkness into God's wonderful light (2:9), from not being a people to being God's people (2:10a), from not receiving mercy to receiving mercy (2:10b), from living in ignorance to living as obedient children (1:14), from living a life of emptiness (1:18b) to living a life of hopefulness[19] (1:3b), from simply having to suffer grief in all kinds of trials to also greatly rejoicing (1:6), and from being scattered, strangers, and lost (1:1a; 2:11a, 25a) to being gathered together in Christ (2:25b).

As a result of such identity reversal, the ones who trust in God despite the shaming culture of their day "will never be put to shame" (2:6c). The words "will never be put to shame" are literally rendered as a double negative, expressing this intense thought: those who trust in God will never ever (no not ever) be shamed. God's act of honoring his new family creates a new identity for them that takes away any shame through belonging to God and his family in

---

17. Elliot, "Disgraced Yet Graced," 173.
18. Scott, 1990, 166–82.
19. Achtemeier, *1 Peter*, 65.

Christ. Because of their new identity in Christ though his death, resurrection, and ascension (1:18–21), they will never ever (no not ever) be put to shame.

In summary, a crucial image in 1 Peter for rediscovering diaspora identity for the believers in Asia Minor is kinship. These believers were able to rediscover their new identity as God's new family ("a people belonging to God") who had a new birth, a living hope, a permanent inheritance, shielded, saved, and secure in God (1:3–5), recipients of mercy (2:10), living stones in a spiritual household (2:5), a chosen people, a royal priesthood, a holy nation (2:9) – though they briefly had to suffer in the hands of a hostile and hateful world (1:6). As obedient children, the diaspora communities could live differently with holy[20] lives in a strange land (1:13–17, 22; 2:1–3), love one another deeply from the heart (1:22b), stop conforming to their evil desires (1:14b), rid themselves of all malice and all deceit (2:1), crave the pure spiritual milk of God's word (2:1a), and set their hope fully toward a final home with sure salvation as exiles, because of the death, resurrection, and ascension of Jesus Christ (1:18–21). In other words, the image of diaspora as God's new family did not only bring a new identity for God's precious people but also a new way of thinking and a new way of living in a hostile and hateful social environment.

Such honorable living became possible amid hostile conditions because of the practice of following the example or footsteps of Jesus called *imitatio Christi*,[21] or the attempt to live and act as Christ acted and lived. Just as Christ is the living Stone (2:4a), his followers are God's living stones (2:5a). Just as Christ is "chosen and precious" to God (2:4b), his followers are "God's elect" (1:1a) and "chosen according to the foreknowledge of God the Father" (1:2a). Just as Christ is the "chosen and precious cornerstone" (2:6a), his followers "are being built into a spiritual house" (2:5a). Just as Christ suffered for them, his followers could also suffer for him. As Thomas à Kempis wrote, "Without the way, there is no going; without the truth, there is no knowing; without the life, there is no living."[22]

In conclusion, as we have seen in the diaspora experience of the recipients of Peter's first letter in the first century, the diaspora experience of twenty-first-century global Christians does not have to be a struggle for the identity of those scattered. Despite the increase in opposition to the growing global migra-

---

20. Jennifer Strawbridge sees holiness as the imitation of God's embrace and self-sacrificial movement toward the other in *The First Letter of Peter: A Global Commentary*.

21. For more information on *imitatio Christi*, see Capes, "Imitatio Christi," 1–19.

22. *The Imitation of Christ*, written by Thomas à Kempis, was a Christian devotional book. It was first penned in Medieval Latin as *De Imitatione Christi*.

tion, those scattered can rediscover a renewed diaspora identity by rethinking the dynamic image of the family of God. The family of God image gives the sojourners and exiles a dynamic tension; just as the early church in diaspora faced rejection by society and yet were chosen and made precious by God, so the contemporary church in diaspora can also have a double consciousness of being vulnerable, scattered, and troubled, yet strengthened, gathered, and encouraged by God in the midst of their sojourn, because of Christ, who is in solidarity with those who are identified with his family and yet are suffering and are scattered in his name.

Shively Smith states, "Diaspora condition is created, controlled, and remedied by God, which has implications for the social situation and movements of God's people. The movements of diaspora people, therefore, are never without purpose, direction, or aim."[23] The twofold purpose, direction, and aim of the family of God in diaspora is: (1) for them to declare the praises of him who called them out of darkness into his marvelous light (2:9b); and (2) for them to give praise to the God and Father of our Lord Jesus Christ (1:3a). In this way, the people in diaspora can taste and see daily that the God of the diaspora is good (despite their suffering), so that many more can also taste and see this same God on the move and be part of this new family that can never ever (no not ever) be put to shame.

References

Achtemeier, Paul J. *1 Peter*. Hermeneia. Minneapolis: Fortress, 1996.

Berg, Inhee Cho. "Four Criteria for Identifying the Socially Marginal in the Social Context of Early Christianity Reflected in the New Testament." *Acta Theologica* 40, no. 1 (2020): 6–27.

Campbell, Barth L. *Honor, Shame, and the Rhetoric of 1 Peter*. Society of Biblical Literature Dissertation Series 160. Atlanta: Scholars Press, 1998.

Capes, David B. "Imitatio Christi and the Gospel Genre." *Bulletin for Biblical Research* 13, no. 1 (2003): 1–19.

Edwards, Dennis R. "Jesus and the Disinherited and 1 Peter." *Journal for the Study of the Historical Jesus* 17, no. 3 (2019): 256–70.

Elliot, John H. "The Church as Counterculture: A Home for the Homeless and a Sanctuary for Refugees." *Currents in Theology and Mission* 25, no. 3 (1998): 176–85.

———. "Disgraced Yet Graced: The Gospel according to 1 Peter in the Key of Honor and Shame." *Biblical Theology Bulletin* 25, no. 4 (1995): 166–78.

---

23. Smith, *Strangers to Family*, 26.

———. *A Home for the Homeless: A Social-Scientific Criticism of 1 Peter, Its Situation and Strategy*. Eugene: Wipf & Stock, 1990.

———. *1 Peter*. Anchor Bible 37B. New Haven: Yale University Press, 2000.

Fairless, Tom. "Immigration Backlashes Spread Around the World." *The Wall Street Journal*, 8 July 2023. https://www.wsj.com/articles/immigration-backlashes-spread-around-the-world-142124bc.

Gottbrath, Laurin–Whitney. "Record 110 Million People Forcibly Displaced Worldwide, UN Says." *Axios: World*, 13 June 2023. https://www.axios.com/2023/06/14/displaced-people-record.

Himes, Paul A. *Foreknowledge and Social Identity in 1 Peter*. Eugene: Pickwick, 2014.

Horrell, David G. "Aliens and Strangers? The Socioeconomic Location of the Addresses of 1 Peter." In *Engaging Economics: New Testament Scenarios and Early Christian Reception*, edited by Bruce W. Longnecker and Kelly D. Liebengood, 176–202. Grand Rapids: Eerdmans, 2009.

Jobes, Karen H. *1 Peter*. Baker Exegetical Commentary on the New Testament. Grand Rapids: Baker Academic, 2005.

Kight, Stef W. "Record Migration Sparks Backlash in Wealthy Nations." *Axios: Politics & Policy*, 16 July 2023. https://www.axios.com/2023/07/16/record-migration-backlash-us-europe.

McKnight, Scot. "Aliens and Exiles: Social Location and Christian Vocation." *Word & World* 24, no. 4 (2004): 378–86.

———. *1 Peter*. NIV Application Commentary. Grand Rapids: Zondervan, 1996.

Pagliai, Valentina. "Performing Disputes." *Journal of Linguistic Anthropology* 20, no. 1 (2010): 63–71.

Pienaar, Frans-Johan. *Called to Suffer: The Necessity of Suffering in Christian Formation in First Peter*. Eugene: Wipf & Stock, 2022.

Pilch, John J. "Insults and Face Work in the Bible." *HTS Teologiese Studies/Theological Studies* 70, no. 1 (2014): 1–8.

Punt, Jeremy. "Mapping Human Dignity in the New Testament: Concerns, Considerations and Concepts." *Scripture* 105 (2010): 621–35.

Reese, Ruth Anne. *1 Peter*. New Cambridge Bible Commentary. Cambridge: Cambridge University Press, 2022.

Scott, James C. *Domination and the Arts of Resistance*. New Haven: Yale University Press, 1990.

Smith, Shively T. J. *Strangers to Family: Diaspora and 1 Peter's Invention of God's Household*. Waco: Baylor University Press, 2016.

Strawbridge, Jennifer. *The First Letter of Peter: A Global Commentary*. London: SCM Press, 2020.

Wirth, Louis. "The Problem of Minority Groups." In *The Science of Man in the World Crisis*, edited by R. Linton, 347–72. New York: Appleton, 1945.

21

Connecting with the World (1 Peter 2:11–4:11)

Yoon Hee Kim

Introduction

The passage of 1 Peter 2:11 to 4:11 forms a nice literary unit; 2:11 begins with "Dear friends" (*Agapetoi*) and 4:11 ends with a doxology; the repetition of "Dear friends" in 4:12 indicates the beginning of another literary unit. The context of the passage is that during Peter's time God's people were under persecution and suffering. By reflecting on the persecution and suffering in our current lives, we may be better able to understand Peter's audience.

In 2:11 Peter calls his audience foreigners and exiles. In a way, we are also resident aliens and a diaspora in this world. Here, the apostle Peter is addressing how then we should live as those living in a foreign land (not in heaven yet) as diaspora. While there are many points of importance in this long passage, I would like to focus on three.

Honorable Conduct among the Gentiles (1 Peter 2:11–3:7)

On this subject, I would like to emphasize four sub-points. First, be mindful of social holiness. The apostle Peter suggests a way of living before a watching world which I call social holiness. Gentiles (in our terms nonbelievers) need to see our good deeds and glorify God when they are converted.

In how many countries are people turning to the Lord because of the good conduct of the Christians? In Korea, the church and Christians generally do not have a good image these days. Nonbelievers criticize Christians for their selfish ways, for only focusing on their own success in life. We also have a case where a church elder became the president of our country, and he ended up in prison. You can imagine people's cynical outlook at the incident.

Peter addresses our roles in the different societal structures we belong to. The key word here is the word "submit" (*hupotasso*):

1. To citizens (under Emperor Nero), submit (*hupotasso*, 2:13) to every authority instituted among men (2:13–17).
2. To slaves, submit (*hupotasso*, 2:18) to your masters (2:18–25).
3. To wives, submit (*hupotasso*, 3:1) to your husbands (nonbelievers in mind) (3:1–7). Although it is only one verse, Peter is considerate in instructing not only the wives but the husbands as well, to ensure it is a mutually shared responsibility. Otherwise, it could have felt a little unfair to the wives.

The groups of people addressed here (citizens, slaves, wives) are not in power in the structure of society (rather they are minorities) but Peter thinks they still can be powerful if they choose to live a "winning lifestyle" as Peter suggests instead of a "losing lifestyle."

Second, for Peter, the basic motivation for submission should stem from a "fear of God."

1. For citizens, they do submit to authority because they fear (*phobeomai*) God (2:17).
2. Slaves submit to their masters with all respect (*phobos*, fear, 2:18). They do this because they are conscious of God.
3. When husbands see the purity (*phobos*, fear, 3:2) of their wives' lives, they may be won over by the behavior of their wives. Here again the wives' voluntary motivation is because they fear God. Here *phobos* implies fear of God. We submit because we have a reverential fear of God. That is the basic motivation for our submission.

Third, how do they, then, accomplish social holiness? How do we apply this in our lives?

1. As citizens, by doing good (*agathopoieo*, 2:15) we silence the ignorant talk of foolish men.
2. As slaves, if you suffer for doing good (*agathopoieo*, 2:20) and you endure it, it is commendable before God.

3. As wives, if you do what is right (*agathopoieo*, 3:6), they join the holy women of the past, like Sarah. Doing good is a true barometer for whether one has joined a life of faith.

Of course, there are also the inner qualities to consider as stated in 3:3–4: "beauty should not come from outward adornment . . . rather, it should be that of your inner self." These qualities should be reflected publicly in whatever we do by doing good. "Doing good" reminds us of Jeremiah 29:7, "Seek the peace and prosperity of the city to which I have carried you into exile. Pray to the LORD for it, because if it prospers, you too will prosper." As citizens of society, we also reap the benefits of doing good by keeping our conduct honorable.

Fourth, why do we have to do this? What benefit do we gain from doing good? Many reasons are listed throughout the passage.

1. By watching our good deeds, Gentiles may be converted and glorify God. It can be evangelism through our lifestyle (2:12).
2. It is for the Lord's sake (2:13).
3. By doing good, we can silence (muzzle) the ignorant talk of foolish men (2:15).
4. We are doing it because it is a calling from God, "To this you are called" (2:21).
5. It is a way of fearing God (2:17).
6. It is the way of living as servants of God (2:16). Ironically, Peter calls us to live as free men, and yet, also calls us to live as "servants of God." One commentator notes: "The notion of being both free and slaves of God expresses one of the great paradoxes of human life, as Philo also has noted: 'For in truth he who has God alone for his leader, he alone is free.'"[1]
7. Wives might win over their husbands (3:1).
8. For wives, their hope is in God (3:5).
9. For husbands, their prayers will not be hindered (3:7).
10. Above all, there is a strong christological basis (2:21–25). Peter provides his message with a christological foundation. Peter is saturated by Christ and what Christ has done. Christ is all around Peter, admirable. Christ is the supreme example of one who suffered unjustly.

---

1. Reese, *1 Peter*, 144.

We must follow in his steps.[2] In these verses, there are four relative clauses that portray Christ's suffering as a model: (1) Christ who did not commit sin; (2) Christ who did not retaliate; (3) Christ who bore our sins; (4) Christ by whose wounds we are healed. Therefore, we need to step out courageously as true witnesses of God through our good works. These deeds act as visible manifestations of our expression of faith in following in the footsteps of Christ.

Learn to Communicate with the World (1 Peter 3:8–22)

We tend to talk to the world with our language of doctrine and theology, which the world does not care for and does not understand. Peter teaches us the ways in which we can connect with the world (3:13–22). First, we should prepare our attitude: "Finally, all of you, be like-minded, be sympathetic, love one another, be compassionate and humble. Do not repay evil with evil or insult with insult. On the contrary, repay evil with blessings, because to this you were called so that you may inherit a blessing" (3:8–9). Nonetheless, we are not going to be exempt from suffering, even when we do the right things (3:17). Another preparation of our attitude is stated as, "Do not be startled even if we suffer for what is right, do not be frightened for doing good" (3:14). It is what is expected of living as aliens and strangers in this world. This should be our attitude. It is a missional action.

Second, with prepared attitudes, communication opportunities will come. As Peter states in 3:15, "But in your hearts revere Christ as Lord. Always be prepared to give an answer to everyone who asks you to give the reason for the hope that you have. But do this with gentleness and respect." The reason for the hope that we have – a hope that is shared among believers – is the belief in the gospel of Jesus Christ. Christians should be able respectfully to defend their hope in Christ. When we truly seek to do what is right, that very hope separates and alienates us from nonbelievers and invites the kind of conflict that Peter describes. As Goppelt puts it, "Faith does not close doors to relationships with other people out of either fear or hate. In turns, rather in openness to others just as it turns to God."[3] The opportunity to communicate is an evangelistic moment. We need to learn to address the questions from nonbelievers in ways that are meaningful to them.

---

2. Jobes, *1 Peter*, 196.

3. Jobes, 231.

These days, BTS (Bangtan Boys is a South Korean boy band) seems to win more young people's hearts than anyone else. Many young people confess that they find comfort in their songs, for example in their song "Answer: Love Myself" (some of the lyrics are as follows, "You've shown me I have reasons I should love myself. I'm learning how to love myself"). Because of BTS, many young people are finding ways to have better self-esteem. BTS researched the hearts and needs of young people and used the power of lyrics to address those needs and in turn, give them hope. BTS has found the secret to inspiring young people in ways modern churches and the Christian community are not able to.

Third, how should we treat these communication opportunities? With gentleness and respect (3:15). Gentleness is toward man and respect (*phobos*) is toward God. When we fear God, we can treat nonbelievers with gentleness. If we are impatient, maybe we lack fear in God as well. Fourth, a clear conscience will make the world ashamed of their slander. Are we making a world where they are ashamed of their slander or are we ashamed of our unclear conscience before the world? There has been a steep decline in church attendance among the MZ generation in Korea.[4] A study found that 50 percent of young people between the ages of nineteen and thirty-four have left the church in the past five years. This is the official figure from research done by the government.[5] The Korea Church Research Center surveyed Christian young adults on the reasons for their dissatisfaction with the church: (1) church leaders' authoritative attitude (34.9 percent); (2) the church's seemingly slow approach to keeping pace with the progress of society and the ever-evolving world (31.4 percent); (3) superficial relationships among church members that lack love and genuineness (25.6 percent); (4) dissonance between the words and actions of church leaders (23.3 percent).

While not all young people are necessarily disowning the Christian faith, many have left the church institution. Another way we can understand one of the reasons stated above is that the MZ generation is uninspired by the church leaders and people. MZ generation Christians ask us, how are Christians any different from nonbelievers?

We are not communicating well with the young people in the church, and even less with young nonbelievers. But the question here is, do we even know enough about their struggles? Are we addressing their needs? Are we

---

4. Generation MZ refers to pairing of two groups – Millennials (born 1981–1995) and Generation Z (born 1996–2005).

5. Lee Yeon-woo, "Tired of outdated practices, church-related scandals, some quit going to church," in *Korean Times*, 1 September 2022.

providing them with hope and inspiration? Again, Peter lays down a strong christological foundation for us (3:18–22). The central message of 3:18–22 is on the personal, exemplary, righteous suffering of Jesus Christ, his mission, and his eventual glorification.[6]

Virtuous Living in a Morally Bankrupt World (1 Peter 4:1–11)

Living as diasporic people should not be about living by worldly standards but about focusing on how to transform society. We must depend on God and commit to lead victorious lives in this world. Why? So that God may be praised through Jesus Christ (4:11).

Peter again, lays out a christological foundation for us. Christ suffered in his body and was done with sin: emphasis on suffering! We are encouraged to follow in his footsteps and endure times of suffering to be done with past sins. As a result, we will not follow evil human desires but rather follow the will of God (4:1–2).

Suffering is inevitable for the followers of Christ because Christ suffered. However, in 2022 a study from Lifeway Research on churches in the United States found that comfort (67 percent), control or security (56 percent), and money (55 percent) have a significant influence on Christians. Suffering is not on that list. In other words, Christians in general do not like suffering at all. Who would? Yet that is why we are not influential. We are not victorious because we are not willing to suffer! Ironically, this is the only way to live a winning life, that is, sacrifice and suffering, then it will move people's hearts.

As 1 Peter 4:11 says, "if anyone speaks, they should do so as one who speaks the very words of God. If anyone serves, they should do so with the strength God provides, so that in all things God may be praised through Jesus Christ." This is the way we bear witness to Christ to our spouse, our children, our nonbelieving friends, our village, our society, our country, and our world.

Steve Jobs once said:

> We have to be really clear about what we want them to know about us. Our customers want to know who Apple is and what is it that we stand for. What we are about isn't making boxes (computers) and getting people to do their jobs. Apple at the core, its core value is that we believe that people with passion can change the world to be better. And those people who are crazy enough that they

---

6. Forbes and Lim, *1 Peter*, 103.

think they can change the world are the ones who actually do. We got to let people know who Apple is and why it's still relevant in this world.[7]

I would like to borrow Steve Jobs words and apply it to Christians: We have to be really clear about what we want them to know about us. People want to know who we are and what is it that we stand for. Who we are at the core, our core value is that we believe that people with passion for Christ can lead people to the saving knowledge of Jesus Christ and can change the world to be better. And those people who are crazy enough that they think they can change the world through Christ are the ones who actually do. We've got to let people know who we are and why we are still relevant in this world. I hope we all can be crazy enough to go out and help change the world.

References

Elliot, John H. *A Home for the Homeless: A Social-Scientific Criticism of 1 Peter, Its Situation and Strategy*. Minneapolis: Fortress Press, 1990.

Forbes, Greg W., and Jason Jit-Fong Lim. *1 Peter*. Asia Bible Commentary. Singapore: Asia Theological Association, 2006.

Gallo, Carmine. "Steve Jobs: People with Passion can change the world" in *Forbes*, 22 March 2011. https://www.forbes.com/sites/carminegallo/2011/01/17/steve-jobs-people-with-passion-can-change-the-world/.

Jobes, Karen. *1 Peter*. Baker Exegetical Commentary of the New Testament. Grand Rapids: Baker Academics, 2005.

Reese, Ruth Anne. *1 Peter*. New Cambridge Bible Commentary. Cambridge: Cambridge University Press, 2022.

Smith, Shively T. J. *Strangers to Family: Diaspora and 1 Peter's Invention of God's Household*. Waco: Baylor University Press, 2016.

Yeon-woo, Lee. "Tired of outdated practices, church-related scandals, some quit going to church." *Korea Times*, 1 September 2022. https://www.koreatimes.co.kr/www/nation/2024/11/113_335381.html.

---

7. Quoted in an article in *Forbes*, 22 March 2011, Carmine Gallo, "Steve Jobs: People with passion change the world."

22

Power Structures within the Diaspora Community in 1 Peter

Samson L. Uytanlet

One important characteristic of 1 Peter is that this letter, although short, is rich in quotations and paraphrases from the Old Testament, including subtle allusions to the OT stories. In alluding to the OT, Peter did not just take random stories or passages from the OT, but particularly those that talk about sojourners from the OT. He focused on how the Lord worked in their lives and used the messages that the Lord *originally* spoke to the OT sojourners to address the believers in diaspora.

Peter spoke about OT sojourners in a way as if his contemporaries and these OT sojourners are just one group, and that God's message to the OT sojourners is the exact same message God is saying to them. The exhortations in the first four chapters of 1 Peter are related to how the believers ought to relate to everyone, including both believers and nonbelievers.

Sojourning of Believers in Relation to Both Believers and Nonbelievers

In 1 Peter 1, when Peter talks to his contemporaries, he refers to them as those on whom Christ's blood was sprinkled (1:2), recalling Exodus 24:8 wherein a community that came out of Egypt was also sprinkled with blood as they entered a covenant with God to become his people. This is the same community that received the injunction, "Be holy" (Lev 11). This is the same message Peter says to his contemporaries (1 Pet 1:16). In the same way that the Exodus community was still journeying toward their destination (the promised land) when they were called to be holy, the diasporans must also pursue holiness while they journey through their present life.

Then in 1 Peter 2:6–10, Peter cites a series of quotations from stories of Israelites prior to the exile. Passages from Isaiah 43:20–21 (quoted together with a passage from Exodus 19:6) about being the chosen race whose purpose was to declare God's praise, and a passage from Hosea 2:1 that reminds them that they are now the people of God. The passages from Isaiah and Exodus were first addressed to the Israelites who were appointed to be light to the nations (see also Isa 42:6; 49:6), but we can see from OT history that they were not able to fulfill this role. Other New Testament writers point out that what Israel failed to do, to be "light to the Gentiles," Jesus (Luke 2:32) and Paul (Acts 13:47) fulfilled. Now Peter is reminding them of their new identity; and because they have a new identity, they also have a role in the proclamation of God's message.

In 1 Peter 2:13–3:7, Peter discusses the household using stories from Abraham's life to explore honoring others and proper submission. The instruction to the slaves to be submissive to their masters, even to the unjust (2:18) recalls Sarah's harsh treatment of Hagar, and how God protected and blessed Hagar and Ishmael (Gen 21:8–21). The instruction to husbands and wives also reminds us of the time when Abraham lied about Sarah to protect himself even if it would place Sarah in danger (Gen 20). Sarah was known for her beauty (Gen 12:11), which might be the reason why Abimelech wanted to marry her. This explains Peter's discussion about a woman's beauty (1 Pet 3:3). Moreover, Sarah submitted to her husband despite his being inconsiderate, and this explains Peter's instruction to wives about submission (3:1). When Abimelech took Sarah to be his wife, there is no record that Abraham prayed, but Abimelech temporarily suffered the consequences of this wrong. When Abraham admitted his fault, it was then that he was able to pray for Abimelech (Gen 20:17–18). This explains why Peter linked the husbands' prayer to being considerate toward their wives (1 Pet 3:7).

Within 1 Peter 3:8–4:11, Peter talks about how to deal with sufferings using the story of David while he was running away from Saul and he pretended to be insane (1 Sam 21:10–15). With the quotation from Psalm 34:12–16 in 1 Peter 3:10–12, Peter admonishes the believers to persevere in suffering. Interestingly, in the Greek OT, Psalm 34:4 was rendered, "I sought the Lord, and he answered me and delivered me from all my *sojourning*." This makes Psalm 34 an even more appropriate text to use to encourage the diasporans who go through suffering. Finally, in 1 Peter 4:12–19, there are allusions to Psalms 89 and 106 about the transitory nature of life, but then he quotes from Malachi 3:1–5 to warn the believers of God's "fiery judgments." Peter talks about the "fiery trials" that believers may go through sometime (1 Pet 4:12), but they can always be assured of God's presence.

To summarize the first four chapters of 1 Peter, Peter spoke about OT sojourners in a way as if his contemporaries and those OT sojourners are just one group; and that God's message to the OT sojourners is the exact same message God is saying to them.[1]

OT Sojourner	Message
Exodus community	Be holy
Pre-exilic community	Declare God's praises
Abraham	Be submissive
David	Do not repay evil for evil
Unknown psalmists	Life is transitory; God vindicates

Sojourning of Believers within the Community of Believers

Peter now addressed the diaspora Christians/church, focusing on the two groups of people within the congregation: the leaders (which he addressed as elders) and the members (which he addressed as the younger ones).

Another observation we can make is that when he used the examples of OT sojourners, it has something to do with the power structures at work. In relation to the nonbelievers, the believers take the role of the "powerless" people. So, they must conduct themselves properly, submit to proper authorities, and endure suffering. This power dynamic changes once they are within the community of believers because some of their members will assume some kind of power within the community. There are elders who would assume leadership roles, and there are "younger" ones (not necessarily in terms of age) who do not assume the leadership role of the elders. Peter addressed both groups.

In this section, Peter gives some instructions to the "elders" about serving willingly and even about finances, and to the "younger ones" about the reality of the spiritual battle and the necessity to persevere in sufferings. But Peter also discusses the issue of power within the community. The exhortation can be summarized this way: those who are accorded power should not abuse it, and those who are not in power should not usurp it.

---

1. For a fuller discussion on this, see Uytanlet and Uytanlet, *Manual for Sojourners*.

Elders (1 Peter 5:1–4)

Peter gave these instructions to the elders: (1) to exercise oversight voluntarily (which has to do with their attitude); (2) to serve not for financial gain; and (3) to not domineer. I would like to focus only on the third one by focusing on the word "domineer" (*katakurieuō*). That we should be servants like our Lord is not difficult to understand cognitively. What servanthood "looks like" may be a bit difficult to define. Does servanthood mean that we should be cleaning toilets or serving tables or washing dishes? Or do we just obey what we are told to do? These may all be evidence of servanthood, and church leaders who are willing to do even menial tasks are indeed commendable if they do them with pure intentions. But before we jump to the application, it may be good to go back to what the text says.

Aside from 1 Peter 5, the other instances in the NT the word *katakurieuō* is used are Matthew 20:25 and Mark 10:42. But these two passages are not really helpful in understanding the nuances of the word, because they are all talking about the same thing. This requires us to look at other instances in the NT or even in the Greek OT where the word *katakurieuō* is used.[2]

1. Israel conquering (*katakurieuō*) the land, suggesting that they have rendered the original inhabitants powerless (Num 32:22, 29); or one nation exercising dominion (*katakurieuō*) over another (Dan 11:39; cf. Ps 10:5 [9:26, LXX]).

2. The Messiah subduing (*katakurieuō*) all his enemies, rendering them powerless by being made his footstool (Ps 110:2 [109:2, LXX]).

3. A lion catching (*katakurieuō*) his prey, rendering it powerless before devouring it (Ps 10:9 [9:31, LXX]).

4. Sin having dominion (*katakurieuō*) over humans (Ps 119:133 [118:133, LXX]; cf. 19:13 [18:14, LXX]), rendering them powerless so that would commit sin.

5. Death overpowering (*katakurieuō*) humans (Ps 49:11 [48:15, LXX]), rendering them powerless to live beyond the day of death's visit.

6. Adam ruling (*katakurieuō*) over God's creation (Gen 1:28; 9:1; Ps 72:8 [71:8, LXX]).

---

2. A similar discussion in Uytanlet, "Pastoral Leadership," 25–26.

7. God exercising authority (*katakurieuō*) over a wayward son, rendering him powerless to continue in his wrong ways by making him obey (Jer 3:14).

8. A demon-possessed man overpowering (*katakurieuō*) other humans (Acts 19:16), rendering them powerless to control him.

Except for point 6, all other passages suggest that the one who *katakurieuō* another renders the latter powerless. This concept, it seems, informs us as to what Jesus was telling his disciples, namely, his followers should not be rendering others powerless by their manner of leadership. If this is correct, to rephrase Jesus's command, those in leadership should be empowering others.

Jesus exemplified this by sending his disciples out, giving them authority to preach and heal (e.g. Matt 10; Luke 9–10), empowering them by giving them an opportunity to do as he did. No wonder Paul said that the main role of church leaders is to equip God's people for the work of service, empowering them to serve and not monopolizing the service to produce a personality-centered or pastor-centered congregation (Eph 4:11–13). Having said this, one may conclude that true leadership is one that empowers others to serve.

Now we are ready for the application part. "Lording-it-over" someone is not really about being bossy or being a slave driver, although these may be expressions of it too. Pastors "lord-it-over" their congregation if they do not equip them to serve, hence monopolizing the ministry and producing a personality-centered congregation. Senior pastors "lord-it-over" their associates if they do not allow them to thrive by limiting their opportunities. Leaders "lord-it-over" their peers when their personal ambitions govern their activities to the point that they are ready to put others down to get ahead of the rest. Pride, insecurity, and selfishness are at the root of all this. This is the way the world works, but Jesus's warning is clear, "it should not be this way among you . . ."

In addition to these, leaders "lord-it-over" their members by abusing their power over their members, instead of using their power to serve and protect the flock. There is a reason why in the recent years there is an increasing number of books about narcissistic leaders, spiritual abuse, bully pulpit, and abuse of power within Christian communities: because this is a serious and persistent problem even among those who claim to be followers of Jesus. This is the elephant in the room that we prefer to ignore, perhaps out of courtesy or for fear of offending our colleagues. The danger is when this type of narcissistic tendency among church leaders becomes normalized to the point that we do not consider it as a problem anymore.

In an interview about his recent work "Bully Pulpit," Michael Kruger was asked if there were more discussions about abuses in Christian leadership in the United States because there is an increasing number of incidents or because people are just more aware of the problem.[3] He responded by saying that it does not matter whether there are increasing cases or increasing awareness, the fact that it is still a problem, we must therefore address it.

Our tendency is to train ourselves how to act properly, that we have mastered the externals, but oftentimes the narcissism is covert. I am not a trained counselor or psychiatrist, so I am not qualified to make a diagnosis on anyone, but there are signs that we should not just ignore. It seems that the biggest problem among Christian leaders is not the inability to handle funds, or sex (although many have fallen), but the biggest problem is still pride and a desire for power, or the inability to handle power once we have it.

Power is like perfume, a little of it may make us "smell good." When we wear it, we will notice more people will flock around us, whether with good motives or for selfish gains. Power, like perfume, can attract both the right people and the wrong people around us. That is why we really need to ask God for wisdom to discern. Power is like perfume, when we wear too much of it, the people around us may get suffocated. When we overuse our power, our coworkers around us suffer. They may do so silently or out of fear of suffering consequences should they complain or speak up. Power is like perfume, once we begin ingesting it, we only poison ourselves. When we begin to embody the power of the office temporarily given to us, and our temporary office becomes our identity, we eventually destroy ourselves. No wonder Scripture emphatically reminds leaders to make sure not to abuse the power they have.

The Younger Ones (1 Peter 5:5–11)

Instructions about power is not only given to the elders but also to the "younger" ones. They are called "younger" not necessarily in terms of their age but in terms of their role in the community. In the OT, the members of a community who are given some leadership roles are the older ones, so it is not surprising that leadership is associated with age. But there are examples in the NT, like Timothy, who assume leadership roles despite being young (1 Tim 4:12).

Once again, while there are several instructions given to members, our focus will be on the issue of power. The "younger ones" are instructed to be

---

3. The Gospel Coalition, "How to Confront Spiritual Abuse," https://www.youtube.com/watch?v=STzYvDhKLm4. See especially 8:30–10:25 within the video.

submissive to their leaders as an expression of humility (1 Pet 5:5). But humility is also expressed by waiting for the Lord's exaltation (5:6). This suggests that the "younger ones" need not try to usurp the authority of the elders. The instruction is followed by a warning that the devil prowls like a roaring lion seeking someone to devour (5:8). In the discussion above about domineering (*katakurieuō*), one of the passages briefly discussed is Psalm 10:9, which talks about a lion "lording-it-over" their prey, rendering them powerless before devouring them. The "younger ones" may not be rendered powerless by an abusive leader, but by usurping power they are being devoured by the devil (in a metaphorical sense), being made powerless to do his cause and cause chaos within the community.

Summary

To conclude, leaders should not abuse their power, and members should not usurp it. If there is one thing that causes the Christian community to be chaotic, it is having leaders who abuse their power and ambitious members who want to gain power. No wonder Peter closes this section with this statement, "To [God] be the dominion forever and ever. Amen" (1 Pet 5:11). Power belongs to God alone; not to the elders or anyone within the community.

The command to be subject to their leaders, the exhortation to be humble, and the reminder that God alone holds all dominion made it clear that gaining power is not the primary purpose of a sojourning believer. The ideal community is to have people in power who are not abusing it, but empowering others; and to have people who are not in power not usurping it but waiting for the Lord to exalt them. This is one important principle that followers of Jesus must remember as they continue in their sojourning.

References

The Gospel Coalition. "How to Confront Spiritual Abuse." *Gospelbound*, interview with Michael Kruger, 22 November 2022, https://www.youtube.com/watch?v=STzYvDhKLm4.

Uytanlet, Samson L. *The Multidimensional Pastor: The Many Faces of Pastoral Ministry*. Eugene: Wipf & Stock, 2020.

———. "Pastoral Leadership as a Ministry of Empowerment." *BSOP in Focus* 84 (2014): 1–2.

Uytanlet, Samson L., and Juliet Lee Uytanlet. *Manual for Sojourners: A Study on Peter's Use of Scripture and Its Relevance Today*. Eugene: Wipf & Stock, 2023.

Conclusion

Bulus Galadima

Asia is an enigma! It has been the most populous continent for over half a century, home to 4.5 billion of the 7.6 billion people on earth. That is nearly two-thirds (60 percent) of the world's population. There is a drop from 1980 through 2015 when Asia's population was at 65 percent of the world. Though it is the largest continent covering 30 percent of earth's land, it is also the most densely populated. Its people will inevitably be very transient. They are indeed everywhere, and their influence is felt globally. There is no region or country in the world devoid of Asian presence. Their presence is felt in all spheres of life from the serious to the mundane, from religion to business. There is nowhere in the world where you will not find a Chinatown and Chinese and Indian food, with Japanese, Korean, and Thai food gaining ascendancy.

Nearly fifty years ago even in a remote small town in Nigeria, there were South Asians. At my secondary school in Northern Nigeria, the mathematics, chemistry, physics, and biology teachers were Indians and Pakistanis. Their influence was present in education, business, health, and entertainment. Some of the supermarkets in the major cities were owned by Indians. The major forms of entertainment then; cinemas showed Indian and Chinese movies. On many occasions, the movies were in Hindi or Chinese without translations. The music in Indian movies influenced Hausa (a major ethnic group in Africa), spurning a new genre of music used in Kannywood – a branch of Nollywood.[1]

Asia has global influence in its religions. It is home to most of the major religions of the world like Hinduism, Buddhism, Jainism, Sikhism, Judaism, Christianity, and Islam. Even as a child, I knew that the religions of Asia differed from ours in Nigeria. There were articles in the newspaper and stories about people getting mystical powers from Indian religions. The West also has been influenced by Eastern forms of spiritualities in the form of meditation. As an undergraduate student in Nigeria, I first heard about Korean Christianity and was intrigued by its history, spirituality, and dedication to prayer. I longed

---

1. Nollywood is the Nigerian movie industry. Kannywood refers to the movies coming from Kano, the major city of Northern Nigeria.

for such spirituality. Later in graduate school in the US, I met Korean Christians, and after my graduation in my denomination and seminary in Nigeria in the 1990s I got to know them and do ministry with them. They enriched our Christian life in Nigeria. One Korean missionary family in Nigeria built a prayer retreat center outside of Jos, Nigeria.

The influence of Asia continues to grow around the world. At the consultation, and in this book, we had scholars and practitioners examining Asians in diaspora from different perspectives, present papers and discuss the implications of different issues for Christian missions in Asia with the participants. Prior to this consultation, I was aware of the big picture in Asia. However, the consultation and the chapters in this volume expanded my horizon and deepened my knowledge by painting a more nuanced picture of Asia than I knew existed. They exposed me to the impact of policies on the lives of people on the move locally, regionally, and globally. They showed not only what the church can and should do locally but also what Christians can do from far away in collaboration with local believers. The history of Jeju Island, the venue of the consultation, revealed that one person in a position of power can use their influence to pass a policy that will have a long-lasting impact on hundreds of thousands of people and many generations. Today the population of the Island is about 350,000 and increased by half a percent last year.[2] Thousands of people on the move have found refuge on this Island due to the no-visa policy of the Island. Several thriving churches exist on the Island today trying to reach all of these diaspora peoples and tourists on the Island.

China is currently facing a population decline due to the one-child policy decades ago as well as other Asian nations like Japan, Singapore, and South Korea. This has serious implications for the labor force of these countries as was explained in one paper. South Korea is revising its current policies of migrant workers to address this issue. The church needs to consider participating in such social issues that on the surface have no religious implications. Also, Christians in government and policymakers could be encouraged to consider how to pursue policies that will ensure the welfare of migrants and ward off violations of their rights as is suggested in Chapter 9. Policy advocacy for such purpose can be a form of mission along with holistic and integral care of these migrants. WiThee Mission International is an example of an innovative Christian response resulting in the training and sending of migrants in Korea as missionaries all over the world.

---

2. See Macrotrends, "Jeju, South Korea Metro Area Population 1950–2024," https://www.macrotrends.net/global-metrics/cities/21735/jeju/population.

This book is as theological as it is practical. A unique feature of the consultation and this book is that the diaspora discussion was engaged against the backdrop of the exposition of the first Petrine epistle addressed to Christians in diaspora. Several of the papers examined the Asian diaspora from a theological perspective analyzing the experiences of Asians and explored what this means for Christian citizenship and Christian hospitality (as described in chapters 5 and 6 respectively).

The last three chapters of this book introduced new vistas in diaspora missions. With the increase in conflicts and global warming, among other factors, people are bound to move. The COVID-19 pandemic caused massive internal movement of people in China and India. This had a major impact on these two largest nations in the world. What could the church have done? At the time of writing (April 2024), due to the recent conflict in Western Asia, between Israel and Palestine, it is estimated that nearly 85 percent of the total population of Gaza which is nearly two million people are internally displaced.[3] Nearly six million Palestinians are displaced.[4] Internal migration will continue to increase not only due to conflict but also due to climate change, as more people will be forced to migrate, especially those living in South-East Asia. These migrants will be people who have never heard the gospel and a few who have. It is certainly clear that this will not be the last incident of internally displaced people in the world. Some of the internal displacement is going to be prolonged just like in the case of Syria also in Western Asia since 2013 with over 6.5 million people displaced; Afghanistan in Southern Asia with 6.1 million displaced for over twenty years; and Myanmar in South-East Asia with over 1.2 million displaced since 2017.[5] What makes these cases of particular concern for Christians is that Asia is the region with the most unreached people groups in the world. How can and should the church prepare for this? How can the church reach the unreached and partner with those who are Christians? Chapter 16 in this volume suggested some ways.

This volume discussed the nagging issue of global human trafficking. With the expected growth of human migration, this menace is likely going to continue to increase. The global church needs to have this issue central in its missionary engagements. Combating this issue requires raising awareness and the participation of the church from countries of departure, transit, and destination. The abuse happens at all of these three points.

---

3. United Nations Security Council, "Israel's Aerial Bombardments Intensify."
4. Davis Jr., "Plight of Palestinian Refugees."
5. See Concern USA, "The 10 Largest Refugee Crises."

Asian diaspora workers are indispensable globally, especially in the Middle East. In the United States, they are the fastest-growing racial population and thus the labor market.[6] Some of these workers are Christians. How can they be effective witnesses of Christ in their workplaces? A few groups have succeeded at this. Asian diaspora Christians are a significant force in Christian missions today. South Korea ranks only second to the United States in the number of missionaries sent around the world. The Filipinos are also another global mission force through Overseas Filipino workers. Many Filipino Christians who work in construction, in the medical field, as domestic workers, especially in the Middle East, and on ships have contributed immensely to global missions. Asian diaspora Christians are also in the leadership of many major Christian organizations like Lausanne Movement, InterVarsity, National Association of Evangelicals (USA), Gospel Coalition, Westminster Theological Seminary (California), Claremont School of Theology, Bread for the World, etc. The GDN since its inception has been led by Asians like T. V. Thomas as its chairman, Sadiri Joy Tira, Sam George as a current catalyst to mention a few. These Asian contributions could be further studied.

There are still many areas of Asian diaspora contributions awaiting further studies and research. There is a need for diaspora studies to expand, grow, and indeed to become a key paradigm of reading Scriptures and doing theology because diaspora and migration have always been the way God has worked and expanded the church throughout history. He is a God on the move and when people move, he moves with them and speaks to them and through those who are his. There are thousands of churches in diaspora which need to be closely examined, although many of the new diaspora churches cater primarily to their own immigrant groups. This study did not explore the challenge of reaching the host nations with the gospel.

Though this book discussed the implications of policy development for the Asian Christian diaspora, it did not directly address politics and governance, economics, entertainment, religion, etc. What are their implications for missions among Asians on the move? Asian influence is felt strongly in the technology, software, and automobile manufacturing sectors, affecting every facet of life globally. For example, Taiwan is the global leader in the manufacturing of semiconductor chips, making more than half of the chips used in the world.[7] At the Jeju consultation, we had a presentation on the contributions of Asians

---

6. Hester, Geron, Lai, and Ong, "Asian American Workers and Unions," 78.
7. Wingfield-Hayes, "Secret Sauce for Taiwan's Chip Superstardom."

in technology by a Silicon Valley entrepreneur cum pastor that unfortunately could not be included in this book.

Asians in diaspora have integrated into many countries of the world where they migrated to. Asians in East Africa have been integrated into the Kenyan Society and given an official status. Indians whose ancestors came to South Africa as indentured servants have integrated into South African society. The descendants of Christians among them have formed vibrant Christian communities in South Africa, especially in the Durban area. These chapters have described the challenges facing the church. The leaders of many Caribbean countries, Malaysia, Singapore, Ireland, Portugal, the UK, and the Vice President of the United States are or have been people of Indian or of Chinese descent. Some of them claim to be Christians. How can the Asian church disciple its members to provide godly leadership that will create just communities and societies?

Asia is without question a major player in the global economy. Of the five top world economies, three are in Asia (China, Japan, and India). Major economies of the world wield a lot of power and influence global conversations and determine the general direction of major decisions. However, Asia is also home to some of the poorest people in the world. These major world economies have pockets of abject poverty embedded in them. What are the implications of this for the Asian diaspora? How can the church contribute to ensure a more even distribution of wealth in these countries?

Asia is a global force in entertainment through movies and music. Asia has four of the top ten movie industries in the world in India, China, South Korea, and Japan. Asian music of Bollywood, K-Pop, and other genres and Japanese Anime are having a global impact. As we have observed earlier, Asia is the home of most of the largest world religions, like Islam, Hinduism, and Buddhism. They comprise some of the largest traditional most unreached people groups of the world. These people are a significant population of Asian migrants. Many of the Western destinations of these immigrants have sent missionaries to reach them and now they live next door. This has significant implications for the church in these host nations. Another important issue that this study did not address is the plight of persecuted Christians in Asia, like in North Korea, Pakistan, Afghanistan, Yemen, Iran, India, and China. What are the implications of these issues for global missions? I hope that you have learned about the state of Asians in diasporas and diasporas in Asia and are prayerfully considering how God wants you to respond to the enormous population of the unreached Asians in diaspora around you and how you can collaborate with Asian Christians in the work of missions locally and globally.

The field of Asian theological education is another area to explore further as many world-class institutions that train pastors and leaders for the global church now exist in Asia. Asian Christian leaders and theologians are writing and contributing to theological literature for the global church, in addition to funding many global mission efforts. There are numerous Asian theologians and scholars whose theologies are contributing to and shaping global theological discourse. What is happening among Asian Diasporas indeed carries portend lessons for global Christianity.

Jesus said, "Open your eyes and look at the fields! They are ripe for harvest" (John 4:35). We hope that this volume will open the eyes of all Christians and especially those interested in the Asian diaspora Christianity and encourage prayerful discussion and more studies among students, mission leaders, church leaders, and the laity.

References

Concern USA. "The 10 Largest Refugee Crises to Know in 2024." Concern Worldwide US, 15 December 2023, https://concernusa.org/news/largest-refugee-crises/.

Davis Jr., Elliott. "The Plight of Palestinian Refugees, Explained. Palestinians are the world's largest stateless community." *US News & World Report*, 5 January 2024. https://www.usnews.com/news/best-countries/articles/2024-01-05/explainer-the-complicated-plight-of-palestinian-refugees.

Hester, Johanna, Kim Geron, Tracy Lai, and Paul M. Ong. "Asian American Workers and Unions: Current and Future Opportunities for Organizing Asian American and Pacific Islander Workers." *AAPI Nexus* 14, no. 1 (Spring 2016): 78–96.

United Nations Security Council. "As Israel's Aerial Bombardments Intensify, 'There Is No Safe Place in Gaza,' Humanitarian Affairs Chief Warns Security Council." 12 January 2024, https://press.un.org/en/2024/sc15564.doc.htm.

Wingfield-Hayes, Rupert. "The Secret Sauce for Taiwan's Chip Superstardom." *BBC News*, 16 December 2023. https://www.bbc.com/news/world-asia-67213293.

Author Profiles

Sam George, PhD, is the director of the Global Diaspora Institute at Wheaton College Billy Graham Center and serves as a global catalyst of the Lausanne Movement. He teaches global migration, diaspora missions, and world Christianity in several countries. He holds degrees in mechanical engineering, business management, and theology. Originally from India, he has lived in five countries and currently makes his home in the northern suburbs of Chicago. Before that, he worked for a leading software technology company based in Asia. He is the author or editor of a dozen books, including his recent three-volume series *Asian Diaspora Christianity*.

Bulus Galadima, PhD, serves as a global catalyst for diasporas of the Lausanne Movement. He was dean of the Cook School of Intercultural Studies at Biola University, California, and Provost/President of Jos ECWA Theological Seminary (JETS) in Nigeria. He has studied at JETS, Wheaton, University of Edinburgh, and Trinity Deerfield. Originally from Nigeria, he now lives in Camp Hill, Pennsylvania. His research interests are in diaspora studies, theology, and philosophy in Africa.

Jeanne Wu, PhD, was born and raised in Taiwan. She serves on the board of Gospel Operation International and is involved in ministries and research related to the Chinese diaspora. Jeanne and her husband were involved in refugee ministries in the USA and then the Middle East with an international organization, and currently co-lead equipping, training programs, and research in the Middle East region.

Kirsteen Kim, PhD, is Paul Pierson chair in world Christianity and associate dean for the Center for Missiological Research at Fuller Theological Seminary in Pasadena, California. A native of the UK, she taught as a professor in South Korea, India, the UK, and the US. She is widely involved across mission and church bodies including the Lausanne Theology Group, the World Council of Churches, and the Catholic Church. She is editor of the journal *Mission Studies* and the book series *Theology and Mission in World Christianity* and co-editor of *The Oxford Handbook of Mission Studies*.

Rev. Dr. Francis Tam, serves as executive director for the Chinese Coordination Centre of World Evangelism, Canada, and also as the interim principal of the Canadian Chinese School of Theology, Calgary. He previously served as a church planter, senior pastor, executive director for the Canadian Chinese Alliance Churches Association, general secretary for the Association of Canadian Chinese Theological Education, and coordinator for the Chinese Alliance World Fellowship. He earned a Doctor of Ministry degree from Trinity International University and taught as a sessional instructor at Tyndale University and Seminary, Ambrose University, and Canadian Chinese School of Theology. He and his wife reside in Ontario and are blessed with two children and six grandchildren.

Prof. Prabhu Guptara was a distinguished professor of global business, management and public policy at William Carey University, Shillong, India. For fifteen years, he was in Switzerland working for the then largest bank in the world and now lives in Cambridge, UK. He has several business publications and has written for *The Times*, *Guardian*, and others on issues related to culture, society, politics, technology and economics. Amid the COVID-19 pandemic, Prabhu entered the world of publishing for the first time in 2020 at the age of seventy-one – with an imprint that focuses on India and Indians, Pippa Rann Books in memory of his wife. He launched a second imprint in 2022, Resilience Publishing that focuses on global challenges like climate change, international financial system, global governance, ethics of technology, etc.

Tereso C. Casiño, ThD, PhD, is a professor of missiology at the school of divinity of Gardner-Webb University in North Carolina, USA. He is the author of numerous journal articles and editor of the *Asia-Pacific Journal of Intercultural Studies*. Earlier, he served as professor of systematic theology and intercultural studies at Torch Trinity Graduate School of Theology in Seoul, South Korea. A native of the Philippines, he has resided in South Korea and the USA while traveling widely across the world. He is married to Dr. Cecilia J. Casiño, who teaches in the area of pastoral care, and they have two adult children.

Yoon Jong Yoo, PhD, serves as dean and professor of the Old Testament at Pierson School of Theology, Pyeongtaek University, South Korea. He studied BTh at Yonsei University, MDiv at Yale Divinity School and completed his PhD at Cornell University in Hebrew Bible.

Hanna Hyun, PhD, is an assistant professor at Presbyterian University and Theological Seminary. Her dissertation focuses on comparative religious studies and migrant Ahmadiyyat Muslims in the US. She served as the director of the Centre for Islamic Studies in Sydney since 2016, working with believers from Muslim backgrounds and Messianic Jews in Sydney, in addition serving an Arabic church. She taught at Kosin University (2013–2015), Sydney College of Divinity (2016–2019), and Juan International University (2020–2021). Research interests are Islamic studies, migration, refugee and home theology, multicultural church planting, and platform churches.

Prof. Datuk Dr. Denison Jayasooria is head of the secretariat for the All Party Parliamentary Group Malaysia on Sustainable Development Goals since October 2019 and a fellow of the Institute of International Harmony and Sustainable Development, Hong Kong, China. He holds a PhD in sociology from Oxford Brookes University, United Kingdom, while his first degree is a Bachelor of Divinity from Union Biblical Seminary, Yeotmal, India. Previously he was a principal research fellow at the Institute of Ethnic Studies, National University of Malaysia (UKM) and is now an honorary professor. He served as a member of the Human Rights Commission of Malaysia and the Royal Police Commission. He and his wife Rose Cheng Jayasooria worship at the DUMC Methodist Church in Petaling Jaya, Malaysia and they have three children and two grandchildren.

Kangmuk Ghil, PhD, is the senior deputy director of the Presidential Committee of National Cohesion and the chief of Immigration Detention Agency of the Ministry of Justice of South Korea. Earlier he served as director of general affairs of the Incheon Airport Immigration Agency and as councillor (Chief Consul) of the Korean Embassy to Mongolia, the Ministry of Foreign Affairs, Korea (2017–2020) as well as director of immigration policy of the Ministry of Justice, South Korea (2016–2017). He serves as an adjunct professor at Sungkyui University and chairman of the Vision Committee of Namboo Presbyterian Church.

Dr. Ng Oi Leng, is the present executive and education director of ElShaddai Centre Berhad, a registered NGO with a vision to disciple nations at our doorsteps, committed to catalyze disciple-making movements and build sustainable holistic care systems among the marginalized diaspora communities in Malaysia. She is also the founding core committee member of the Malaysia Diaspora Network and the steering committee member of 2015, 2017, 2019 and 2023 National Diaspora Symposium, Malaysia. Former associate pastor of Mustard Seed Company and a Dental Surgeon by profession.

Bishop Noel A. Pantoja is the national director of the Philippine Council of Evangelical Churches (PCEC), the umbrella organization of seventy-eight evangelical denominations, more than 40,000 evangelical local churches, and 268 missions and para church organizations in the Philippines. He is concurrently serving as the president of Philippine Relief and Development Services (Philrads), the Relief and Development arm of PCEC. He also serves as the president of the Philippines Bible Society.

Dr. Jacob Bloemberg, moved with his family to Hanoi, Vietnam in 1997 and became the lead pastor of Hanoi International Fellowship in 2005. HIF launched the Love Hanoi campaign in 2012, which has become a citywide movement, inspiring Christian leaders across the world to start their own Love [Your City] campaign. Jacob published his book *Love Your City: 5 Steps to Citywide Movements* (Westbow Press, 2020). He holds a doctorate in transformational leadership from Bakke Graduate University, and an MA in organizational leadership from Regent University.

Leiton and Lisa Espineli Chinn have collectively pioneered and established International Student Ministry (ISM) in local churches and campuses and mobilized the global church for ISM for more than forty years. Leiton served as the president of the Association of Christian Ministries to Internationals (ACMI) and Lausanne Catalyst for ISM (2007–2017). Lisa served as the national director for ISM of InterVarsity USA (2000–2014). She was previously an InterVarsity Philippines campus minister, after which she went on to complete her graduate studies as an international student in the USA and returned to develop new departments of InterVarsity-Philippines before being called to be a missionary to American campuses. The couple have pioneered the field of International Student "Reentry" and contributed chapters on ISM in several diaspora missiology books.

Tessa Tubbs (MAR, Gordon Conwell Theological Seminary) works for TeachBeyond, a nonprofit specializing in using education transformationally to help build God's kingdom. Tessa taught at the Black Forest Academy, a school specializing in the needs of children of missionaries in Germany. In 2021 she joined TeachBeyond's member care team, and now supports other teachers at international boarding schools around the world. Her passion is for the global community to understand the ways God uses the hybridity and movement of children of missionaries to contribute to God's kingdom.

Grace Eun-Sun Lee, MDiv, serves as the ministry coordinator for Discipleship, Group Life, and Women's Groups at Grace Chapel, a nondenominational, multicultural church with five campuses in the Greater Boston Area. Grace has contributed an article on worship and spirituality for the North America volume of the Edinburgh Companions published in June 2023. Grace's passions are in ethnodoxology, cross-cultural communications, wholistic and integrative approach toward health and spirituality under the umbrella of world Christianity.

Rev. Dr. J. N. Manokaran, is a Civil Engineer, called to serve as a cross-cultural missionary in North India for eleven years. Since 1997 he has been involved in teaching, training and writing. He has authored over twenty books and traveled widely to many nations. Currently, he serves as regional director for South Asia of Community Bible Study International. He is married to Rosia Selvi, their daughter Hosanna who was a student missionary in Belarus went to be with the Lord in 2011. Their son Thambos and his wife Sayali are pioneering churches among elite urban youth in major cities in India.

Christa Foster Crawford, JD, is an international expert in human trafficking and sexual exploitation with more than 25 years of grassroots and policy experience in Thailand and around the globe. As founder of Freedom Resource International, she spends her time teaching, training, writing and speaking about ending all forms of exploitation more ethically and effectively. She is editor of the *Stopping the Traffick* book series, including the most recent volume *Stepping Out of the Traffick: Pausing for Theological Reflection on Christian Response to Sexual Exploitation and Trafficking* (Regnum, 2024), along with other publications. She has also founded and led international and local anti-trafficking organizations and taught graduate courses for Fuller Seminary and other institutions. An ordained minister, Christa holds a Juris Doctorate from Harvard Law School and a BA in Philosophy & Public Affairs from Claremont McKenna College.

Jasmine Kwong serves as a Lausanne catalyst for Creation Care. She is a creation care advocate with OMF International and based in the Philippines. With a background in conservation biology and community development, she often works in the intersections between people and the natural world. Her interests are in food security and marine conservation. She also serves on the board of Christians in Conservation in the Philippines, which is an affiliated project of A Rocha International.

Bible Expositors

Elizabeth Mburu, PhD, is the first woman to gain a PhD from Southeastern Baptist Theological Seminary, North Carolina, USA. She is an associate professor of New Testament and Greek at International Leadership University, Africa International University, and Pan-Africa Christian University in Nairobi, Kenya. Dr. Mburu is on the board of the Africa Bible Commentary and is the editorial coordinator and New Testament editor for its revision, as well as the Anglophone Africa regional coordinator for Langham Literature. She is author of *Qumran and the Origins of Johannine Language and Symbolism* (T&T Clark, 2010) and African Hermeneutics (HippoBooks, 2019).

Narry F. Santos, PhD, is associate professor of Christian ministry and intercultural leadership at the seminary of Tyndale University in Toronto, part-time senior pastor of Greenhills Christian Fellowship (GCF) Peel and GCF York in Canada, and vice president of the Evangelical Missiological Society Canada. He holds two PhDs, one in New Testament (Dallas Theological Seminary, 1994) and another in Philippine studies (University of the Philippines, 2006). He wrote several books, including *Family Relations in the Gospel of Mark* (Peter Lang, 2021) and *Slave of All* (Sheffield Academic Press, 2003). He also edited mission compendiums and contributed chapters in diaspora books and biblical articles in academic journals.

Yoon Hee Kim, PhD, is the president of Torch Trinity Graduate University (TTGU) and president of Faith and Work Institute Asia. She also serves as the vice president of Korea Evangelical Fellowship and vice president of Asia Theological Association Korea. She is also an adjunct faculty of Trinity Evangelical Divinity School (TEDS) Korea DMin program. She completed her PhD in Old Testament at TEDS. Earlier she served as professor of Old Testament Studies and dean of student affairs at East Asia School of Theology in Singapore.

Samson L. Uytanlet, PhD, has been involved in pastoral and teaching ministry in the Philippines for more than twenty-five years. His works include *Luke-Acts and Jewish Historiography* (Mohr Siebeck, 2014); *Matthew: A Pastoral and Contextual Commentary* (Langham Global Library, 2017); *Multidimensional Pastor* (Resource, 2020); and *Manual for Sojourners: A Study on Peter's Use of Scripture and Its Relevance Today* (Wipf & Stock, 2023). His essays have appeared in AMA, EMQ, and CT.

Index

A
Abraham 15–16, 70, 83–84, 90–92, 94, 262, 284
adapt, adaption 27–28, 30, 32, 35, 37–39, 105, 121, 148, 180, 222, 250, 260
advocacy 36–37, 59, 127–29, 133–34, 136, 156, 292
Africa 57–58, 63, 98, 100–101, 105, 113, 244–45, 291, 295
aging 56, 149, 151, 153
assimilation 79, 151

B
biblical theology 174
birth rate 149, 151, 153, 267
Buddhism 291, 295

C
Canada 27, 48, 58, 74, 164
caste, caste system 45, 215–17
China 17, 27, 29–30, 36, 49, 56–58, 62, 98–103, 105–6, 108, 111, 141, 144, 185, 187, 189–92, 194–96, 203, 292–93, 295
Chinese 30–31, 74, 97–101, 104–7, 187, 189, 191, 291, 295
Chinese Educational Mission (CEM) 185, 187
chosen people 95, 257, 269, 271
Christian Community Development 177
Christians, Christianity 14–15, 17, 19–22, 29, 47, 56, 59–61, 72, 84, 94, 98, 100, 103, 108, 111–12, 126, 133–34, 155, 157–58, 168, 172, 175, 182, 187, 194–96, 203–5, 209, 223, 228, 232–33, 235, 239–40, 243, 247–51, 256, 260–62, 265–68, 275, 278–81

American 103
Chinese 30, 98, 187
culture 207
diaspora 175
Filipino 167–68
global 14, 271
Jewish 260
Korean 17
Syrian 45, 47
Western 209
world 14, 17, 22–23
church(es) 14, 16–17, 19, 31–32, 34, 36–37, 39, 47, 56, 60–61, 65, 78–79, 102, 112, 114, 117, 153–54, 156–57, 159–61, 172–73, 175, 181–82, 195–96, 208, 221–22, 227, 229–30, 232–41, 250–51, 256–58, 269, 272, 279–80, 292–94
Chinese 27–29, 32–39, 97–98, 101–4
diaspora 60, 167–69, 174–76, 179, 181, 183, 294
evangelical 20
Filipino 164, 167–68
gathered 22
global 115, 224, 243–44, 247–50, 293
Hong Kong 32
immigrant 60, 168
international 172
Korean 18, 112, 151–52, 154, 181, 194, 204, 275
local 118–19, 122, 151, 153, 163, 167, 223, 232
Malaysian 155, 159, 161–62
scattered 22
church growth 22, 29, 34, 152
citizen, citizenship, flexible citizenship 20, 22, 69–70, 72, 74, 76, 78–79, 102, 128, 136, 139, 141, 147, 149, 151, 178, 267, 276–77, 293

305

citywide movements 172, 178, 180–82
civil society organizations (CSO) 132–34
climate change 14, 62, 71, 122, 221, 231, 243–47, 249–51, 293
colony 31, 107
community 22, 34, 37, 45, 51, 59–60, 65, 77, 94, 114, 134, 152–53, 156–59, 167–68, 172, 174–75, 178, 181, 228–29, 231, 235, 261, 269, 283, 285, 288–89
  Canadian 36
  Chinese 97
  Christian 14, 23, 31, 168, 279, 289
  church 152–53, 178
  diaspora 64, 73, 208
  faith 29, 39
  global 228
  host 73, 218
  Jewish 15
  Latino 18–19
  local 135, 177
  migratory 74
  online 63
  Syrian Christian 45–47
compassion 77, 136, 247
creation care 62, 244, 249, 251
cultural 60, 72–73, 76, 78–79, 104, 111–12, 114, 122, 126, 131, 150, 153, 161, 165, 167–68, 174, 176, 205–7, 209–10, 213, 218, 230–32, 260, 267
culture 29–30, 58–60, 64, 70, 73, 75, 78, 83, 114, 145, 147, 173, 175, 178, 204, 208–9, 211, 213, 235, 261, 268, 270
  alien 60
  church 60
  dominant 60
  Filipino 166
  home 204
  host 114, 222
  Korean 111, 114, 208, 210
  local 105, 205, 210
  native 19, 73
  school 204

D
deglobalization 49, 51–52
demography 147
development 39, 52, 63, 102–3, 115, 129, 148–49, 152, 154, 156, 158, 161, 166, 193, 206, 210
  church 31–32
  community 176–77
  economic 111, 220–21, 236
  industrial 216
  policy 294
Development Assistance 50
diaspora 14–19, 22, 27, 32, 55–56, 58–64, 77, 100–101, 106–7, 112, 114–15, 117–19, 122, 156, 158, 160, 162, 185, 203, 227, 229, 241, 257, 259–62, 265–68, 270–72, 275, 283, 285
  academic 58
  Asian 204, 206, 292–96
  children 206
  Chinese 27, 29–32, 39, 98–103, 105–8
  Christian 14, 17–18
  communities 271
  Filipino 163–64
  global 121–22, 246
  Hong Kong 32
  Indian 41
  involuntary 228
  Jewish 15, 72, 232, 259–60
  Korean 13, 17, 112
  Middle Eastern 98
  Muslim 157
  students 186, 192, 197
disciple 15, 20–79, 113, 116, 152–53, 156, 160, 162, 174, 256, 287, 295
discipleship 59–60, 65, 78, 104–5, 114–16, 156, 158, 160, 167, 234–35, 238, 249, 251
discrimination 14, 20, 30, 61, 73, 112, 126–27, 131, 133, 145, 151, 218, 267–68
diversity 28–30, 34, 37–38, 69, 72, 78, 121, 140, 142, 145, 150, 161, 206, 270

domestic servitude 62

E
economy 17, 147, 158–59, 173
  global 30, 222, 295
  God's, of salvation 22
  local 149
  Philippine 164
  South Korean 18
education 158, 161, 165, 173, 186–87, 190, 194, 197, 204, 216, 291
  cultural 153
  theological 13, 38, 78, 296
ekklesia 16–17
emigration 18, 46
environment, environmental 159, 173, 214, 243–44, 251
Esther 229–32, 235, 240
Europe 15, 18, 101–2, 104, 113, 164, 166, 185, 246, 266
  Eastern 244
evangelical 19–20
evangelism 19, 22, 34, 59, 102, 104, 112, 114–15, 152–53, 158, 167, 223, 277
evangelist 22, 182, 191

F
faith-based organization (FBO) 126–28, 132–35, 228
family 16, 20, 22, 30, 44–46, 60, 73, 75, 77–78, 144, 148, 152, 157–58, 166–69, 182, 188, 204, 218–20, 228, 230–31, 240, 292
  of God 64, 269–72
Filipinos 74, 107, 113, 133, 163–64, 166–69, 189, 294

G
gender 60, 75, 126, 166, 227, 230, 235, 239
generation 151–52, 166, 168, 229, 234, 249, 279, 292
globalization 16, 47, 49, 71, 106, 128, 148–49

H
hermeneutic
  missional 76
  political 75
  socio-economic-anthropological 75
  theological 75
Hindu 44–45, 47
holiness 275–76, 284
Holy Spirit 115, 156, 161, 211, 257–58, 262
Homi Bhabha 204, 206
Hong Kong 27, 29, 31–32, 35–37, 99, 101, 103, 107, 191, 193–94, 196–97
  out-migration 27–29, 31–32, 37–39
hospitality 14–17, 22, 78, 83–84, 90–92, 94, 135, 204, 207–9, 211, 248, 293
human rights 29, 37, 125–26, 128–32, 134–35, 141, 144, 231
humility 289
hybrid, hybridity 70, 204–10

I
identity 15–16, 28, 30, 36–37, 39, 45–47, 62, 64, 69–75, 78, 116, 151, 206, 209, 232, 235, 257–58, 261, 265–66, 269–71, 284, 288
image of God 5, 64, 86, 223
imago Dei 5, 75, 83–85, 92–94
immigrant(s) 28, 31, 35, 51, 59–60, 74–75, 99–100, 106, 113, 139–40, 144–45, 148–49, 151, 153, 265–66, 294–95
  anti- 148
  Chinese 30
  Hong Kong 32, 37
  illegal 266
immigration 18, 20, 29, 31–32, 135, 141–42, 144, 147–49, 151, 265, 267
incarnation 20–21, 64, 173
India, Indians 21–22, 42–45, 47, 49, 51, 56–58, 62, 113, 185, 189–90, 192,

194–95, 197, 203, 213–15, 219, 221–23, 232, 291, 293, 295
South 50, 221–22
integration 28, 35–37, 47, 50, 61, 79, 112, 114–15, 141–42, 144–45, 147–48, 151, 153, 250
internally displaced persons 103, 122
International Labour Organization (ILO) 127–28, 135
International Organization for Migration (IOM) 244
international student ministries (ISM) 58–59, 185, 193–97
international students 56, 58, 61, 100, 116–17, 140, 148–50, 152, 155, 185–86, 188–97, 209, 244, 266
investment 30, 46
Islam 291, 295

J
Japan(ese) 2, 17, 56, 164, 185, 187–89, 192, 194–95, 197, 292, 295
Joseph 70, 72, 229–32, 235, 240

K
Kerala 45–47, 50, 220, 223
kingdom of God 16, 20, 65, 69, 76–77, 79, 107, 156, 236
Korea(ns), South Korea 13, 17–18, 56, 59, 111–12, 114–15, 139

L
labor 125–26, 128, 134–35, 141–42, 144, 146–47, 150, 165–66, 215–16, 228, 230, 233, 246, 292, 294
  bonded 62
  forced 227
  migrant 127, 132
language 29–31, 38, 51, 60, 62–63, 73, 104–5, 107, 112, 114, 117, 142, 145, 167, 206, 213, 215, 218, 223–24
  covenantal 262
  Korean 18, 114, 150

of honour 269
  royal 88
  sociological 267
  third culture 204
Lausanne 55, 61–63, 115, 193, 247–48, 294
Lausanne Covenant 63
Lausanne Occasional Papers (LOP) 63
leadership 34, 103, 114–15, 122, 160–61, 179–80, 187, 190, 287–88, 294–95
  church(es) 35, 60, 172, 285, 287

M
majority world 98, 118, 233
Malaysia 97, 125, 128, 132, 135, 155–58, 162, 191, 193–95, 197, 295
Middle East 18, 45, 98, 100–103, 105, 107–8, 164, 166, 294
migrant (s) 15–18, 20, 22, 41–42, 44–45, 47, 50–51, 55–57, 59, 63–64, 69–74, 76–79, 95, 99–100, 106–7, 112, 114–19, 122, 125–35, 139–42, 144–52, 154–55, 158, 216–24, 267, 292–93, 295
  children 219
  Chinese 30
  Christian 14, 74, 117
  climate 244–45, 250
  domestic 119, 122
  economic 61, 244
  Filipinos 164–66
  forced 228–29
  global 119, 265–66
  Hong Kong 28–29, 34–39
  illegal 59, 141, 266
  internal 213–26
  international 57, 62
  labor 125, 219
  marriage 140–42, 152
  voluntary 227, 229
  women 219
  workers 97, 101, 112–14, 116, 126–28, 132–36, 220, 292

migration 14–22, 27–29, 32, 34, 37, 45,
47, 49, 51, 55–56, 59–61, 64, 69,
72, 75–77, 83, 99, 117, 120, 125,
129–31, 139–41, 148–49, 153,
163–64, 168–69, 213–22, 224,
236, 293–94
  Christian 14
  climate 62, 244–45, 247–48, 250–51
  forced 227–30, 235, 239
  global 55, 64, 112, 122, 169, 213,
244, 265–66, 272
  illegal 266
  internal 62, 214–15, 293
  international 142, 144, 146
  involuntary 228
  labor 125, 127, 132, 164, 214
  marriage 142
  of the people of God 15
  population 147
  voluntary 228, 259
ministries 31, 35, 52, 98, 102–3, 107,
117, 120, 151, 193, 196
  diaspora 64, 161
  family 153, 168
  labor 127
  migrant 112, 152, 154, 159
  parachurch 233
missio Dei 21. *See* also mission of God
missiological 7, 14, 55, 63–65, 100,
112, 163, 168–69, 203
missiology 117
  diaspora 27–29, 39, 99–100, 112,
115, 152, 159
mission
  Christian 27, 77, 260
  diaspora 122, 159–60, 243
  integral 20
  of God 14, 20–22, 65, 115, 250. *See*
also *missio Dei*
  world 22
missional 6, 21, 56, 77–78, 113, 119,
123, 152, 161, 168–69, 172, 204,
210–11, 233, 278
MK(s) (missionary kids) 203–9
  American 206

  Korean 203–6, 208, 210
  North American 204
  Western 206
mobility 21–22, 76, 78
  international student 186
  spatial 76
  upward 45, 164
mobilization 35, 159, 181
move, movement 14, 16, 18, 21–22, 29,
62, 64–65, 70–71, 73, 75, 77–79,
101, 147, 205, 213, 215–16, 219,
234, 240, 244, 246, 266, 269, 272,
293–94
multiculturalism 117, 142, 150, 152
Muslim 45, 47, 97, 102, 105, 157

N

natural disaster 3, 14, 62, 216, 245–46
nomad, nomadic 15, 70
North America 29, 47, 74, 99, 101–2,
106, 113, 164, 185, 204, 246

O

One Belt, One Road Initiative (BRI)
100, 105–6
overseas 112–13, 133, 141, 145,
163–64, 166–69, 232–33

P

Pakistan 57, 194, 295
partner, partnership 37, 62, 132, 134,
149, 153, 156, 159, 161, 178–80,
193, 235, 237, 293
Pentecostal 19–20
people on the move 16–17, 64–65,
75–76, 79, 115, 159, 161, 240,
292
persecution 28, 71, 103, 256–57, 260,
263, 275
Philippines 57, 125, 127–28, 158,
163–64, 168, 189, 191, 195–97,
203
policy 141, 145–46, 149, 151, 235, 292
  family 142
  immigration 144, 147–48, 151, 266

no-visa 292
one-child 292
welfare-oriented 142
population 28–30, 35, 39, 48, 56–57, 71, 97, 99–100, 114, 139–41, 146–47, 149, 151, 162–64, 167, 190, 203, 215, 218, 243, 246, 261, 291–95
  vulnerable 60, 233, 248
postcolonial 204–6
poverty 14, 19, 127, 159, 173, 215, 220, 295
prejudice 60, 112, 122, 145, 160

R
refugee(s) 20, 55–57, 59, 61, 75, 77, 98–99, 101, 103–4, 112, 116–17, 119, 121–22, 146, 157–59, 228, 231–32, 244–45, 266
religion 18, 291, 294–95
religious 19, 27–29, 31–32, 34, 36–37, 45–46, 64, 76, 100, 102, 106, 135, 153, 157, 172, 205, 230, 259–60, 263, 292
remittances 30, 41–42, 57, 71, 127, 164–65, 220, 246
  half-life of 51

S
scattered 271
settlement 14–17, 74–75, 147, 149, 246
sexual exploitation 125, 228, 231–32
short-term mission (STM) 98, 101, 103–6, 233
Singapore 44, 56, 58, 107, 191, 193–94, 196–97, 203, 292, 295
slavery 62, 230, 234
  modern 134, 227
social justice 29, 37, 127, 221
sojourn, sojourner(s) 266–70, 272, 283, 285, 289
spiritual 31, 34–35, 37, 76–78, 86, 101, 104, 107, 114, 128, 154, 158, 167–69, 209, 224, 233–34, 238, 248, 250, 262, 269, 271, 285, 287

stereotype 151, 211
Sustainable Development Goals (SDG) 132–33, 135, 155–56

T
Taiwan 30–31, 97, 99, 139, 185, 192, 194, 196–97, 294
Thailand 63, 111, 125, 128, 191, 195–97, 203, 209
theology 14, 20–21, 55, 69, 86, 103, 173, 175, 227, 234, 250, 258, 278, 294
  diaspora 122
  migration 83
Third Culture Kids (TCKs) 204, 206
trade 70, 147
trafficking 125, 133, 229–30, 232–33, 236
  anti- 232
  human 62, 71, 134, 227–28, 233, 235, 239, 293
transnational 15, 22, 69–73, 97, 106–8, 119, 122, 163, 166–69
Trinity 20–22, 258, 262

V
Vietnam 111, 141, 171–72, 182, 185
vulnerable 126, 134, 166, 228–30, 246–48, 250, 272. *See* also population, vulnerable

W
war, conflicts 14, 17, 57, 71, 74, 98, 122, 172, 190, 214, 228, 231, 243, 246, 263, 266, 293
WiThee Mission International (WMI) 112–17, 119–20, 122, 292

Global Diaspora Network Publications

Scattered and Gathered: A Global Compendium of Diaspora Missiology
Sadiri Joy Tira and Tetsunao Yamamori | 9781783687640

Africans in Diaspora and Diasporas in Africa
Bulus Galadima and Sam George | 9781839739842

Asians in Diaspora and Diasporas in Asia
Sam George, Bulus Galadima, and Jeanne Wu | 9781786410382

GLOBAL DIASPORA NETWORK

www.GlobalDiasporaNetwork.org

"Fulfilling God's Redemptive Mission for the People on the Move"

GDN's Vision
To empower the global church and respond effectively to the missional opportunities arising out of global migration and diaspora communities worldwide.

GDN's Mandate
1. To catalyze the global Church to demonstrate and proclaim the whole gospel to, through, and beyond diasporas everywhere.
2. To foster theological thinking on diaspora through dialogues and consultations with reflective practitioners and scholars for the development of relevant resources.
3. To network with local churches, denominations, mission agencies, NGOs, theological institutions, and other mission networks.
4. To accelerate the development and adoption of diaspora missiology in leading seminaries, universities, and institutions worldwide.

Global Diaspora Network
4th Floor, Back to the Bible Bldg., 135 West Ave
Bungad, Quezon City, Philippines 1104.

Global Diaspora Institute
Wheaton College Billy Graham Center
500 College Ave, Wheaton, IL 60187.

https://lausanne.org/network/diasporas

Langham Literature and its imprints are a ministry of Langham Partnership.

Langham Partnership is a global fellowship working in pursuit of the vision God entrusted to its founder John Stott –

> *to facilitate the growth of the church in maturity and Christ-likeness through raising the standards of biblical preaching and teaching.*

Our vision is to see churches in the Majority World equipped for mission and growing to maturity in Christ through the ministry of pastors and leaders who believe, teach and live by the word of God.

Our mission is to strengthen the ministry of the word of God through:
- nurturing national movements for biblical preaching
- fostering the creation and distribution of evangelical literature
- enhancing evangelical theological education

especially in countries where churches are under-resourced.

Our ministry

Langham Preaching partners with national leaders to nurture indigenous biblical preaching movements for pastors and lay preachers all around the world. With the support of a team of trainers from many countries, a multi-level programme of seminars provides practical training, and is followed by a programme for training local facilitators. Local preachers' groups and national and regional networks ensure continuity and ongoing development, seeking to build vigorous movements committed to Bible exposition.

Langham Literature provides Majority World preachers, scholars and seminary libraries with evangelical books and electronic resources through publishing and distribution, grants and discounts. The programme also fosters the creation of indigenous evangelical books in many languages, through writer's grants, strengthening local evangelical publishing houses, and investment in major regional literature projects, such as one volume Bible commentaries like *The Africa Bible Commentary* and *The South Asia Bible Commentary*.

Langham Scholars provides financial support for evangelical doctoral students from the Majority World so that, when they return home, they may train pastors and other Christian leaders with sound, biblical and theological teaching. This programme equips those who equip others. Langham Scholars also works in partnership with Majority World seminaries in strengthening evangelical theological education. A growing number of Langham Scholars study in high quality doctoral programmes in the Majority World itself. As well as teaching the next generation of pastors, graduated Langham Scholars exercise significant influence through their writing and leadership.

To learn more about Langham Partnership and the work we do visit **langham.org**

www.ingramcontent.com/pod-product-compliance
Lightning Source LLC
Chambersburg PA
CBHW051628230426
43669CB00013B/2224